FAIRY ENCOUNTERS IN
MEDIEVAL ENGLAND

Exeter New Approaches to Legend, Folklore and Popular Belief

Series Editors:
Simon Young, University of Virginia (CET, Siena) and
Davide Ermacora, University of Turin

Exeter New Approaches to Legend, Folklore and Popular Belief provides a venue for growing scholarly interest in folklore narratives, supernatural belief systems and the communities that sustain them. Global in scope, the series encompasses milieus ranging from ancient to contemporary times and encourages empirically grounded, source-rich studies. The editors favour the broad multidisciplinary approach that has characterized the study of folklore and the supernatural, and which brings together insights from historians, folklorists, anthropologists and many other branches of the humanities and social sciences.

FAIRY ENCOUNTERS IN MEDIEVAL ENGLAND

LANDSCAPE, FOLKLORE AND THE SUPERNATURAL

JEREMY HARTE

UNIVERSITY
of
EXETER
PRESS

First published in 2024 by
University of Exeter Press
Reed Hall, Streatham Drive
Exeter EX4 4QR
UK

www.exeterpress.co.uk

Exeter New Approaches to Legend, Folklore and Popular Belief

ISSN 3049-7329 Print
ISSN 3049-7337 Digital

British Library Cataloguing in Publication Data
A catalogue record for this book is available from the British Library.

ISBN 978-1-80413-095-7 Hardback
ISBN 978-1-80413-240-1 Paperback
ISBN 978-1-80413-096-4 ePub
ISBN 978-1-80413-097-1 PDF

https://doi.org/10.47788/YNHI9747

EU Authorised Representative: Easy Access System Europe –
Mustamäe tee 50, 10621 Tallinn, Estonia, gpsr.requests@easproject.com

Typeset in the UK by BBR Design, Sheffield

Cover image: A man encounters a demon in the woods. From the St William
window in York Minster, *c.*1415, drawing on a lost miracle text.

Contents

Preface   vii

PART I: PEOPLE

1.   Strange Meetings   3

2.   Tales of Wonder, Tales of Sorrow   19

3.   Inconstant Shapes   51

PART II: PLACES

4.   Haunted Landscapes   73

Afterword   125

Elfin Place-Names: A Corpus   127

Notes   150

Sources   180

Index   204

Preface

Many people nowadays hope to see a fairy; many in the Middle Ages wished they never had. To encounter a spirit was to step out of the warm world of human solidarity and turn, for hours or maybe a lifetime, onto a path that could lead through madness and pain. The long medieval debate over the nature of otherworlders was also a conflict between popular narrative and clerical interpretation—not about the actuality of these strange beings, which few disputed, but their moral status. The wisdom of the folk differed from orthodoxy not through claiming that these undefined spirits were real, but because it proposed that they could, sometimes, be trusted.

This book is an enquiry into encounters with—well, the beings who broke into human life were never very forward in identifying themselves. I have used 'fairy' as a catch-all for these outsiders, representatives of a world that is both like and unlike our own. Historically this was the word that, at the very end of our period, would come to prevail over the mixed and contested descriptors previously used in both Latin and the vernacular. To call them 'spirits', in medieval terminology as well as our own, allows for a certain ambivalence in these beings, who might be good, bad, or amoral. The older generation of scholars spoke of 'creatures of the lesser mythology'; more recently, of 'small gods'.

Who met these beings of another world? When and where? What happened, and what did the percipients made of it afterwards? This enquiry is founded on two premises. The first is that encounters did happen, and were only afterwards worked up into a story. The second is that we can still recover those stories, even though we do not have them as they were told but mediated through clerical renditions. Students of medieval writing can be jittery with claims that an oral narrative has been uncovered behind the surface of Latin prose. *Il n'y a pas de hors-texte*: disciplinary honour demands that we commit to the autonomy of the written work and are not led astray by its hypothetical origins. I think this is wrong; it fails to do justice to the writings themselves, and throughout the second section of the book, I have hammered home, genre by genre, the evidence that where the otherworld is concerned, medieval texts do not function as they were supposed to—they do not make the theological points that they should, they do not enforce the morality that they profess, they do not teach the historical lessons that they propose—because their literary integrity was continually subverted by pressure from the talk going on around them. Things happened, including supernatural things; stories were told, mostly in the languages of the laity; some writers wrestled to harmonize these with what they thought to be true, but most simply went with the flow, so that we read is not very far from what they were told, even though this might contradict their views on how things should be, as reality so often does.

The theology, pastoral strategies and contemporary significance of Latin authors have been mined to the exclusion of those who gave them their material. In studying fairies—unlike, say, agriculture or war—the rule has been to foreground writing as writing, so that a report of someone's experience is not treated at all differently from a romance or fable. The proper focus of discussion, one gathers, is what the preacher or historian thought as they sat describing these things in their study, not the voice of the people to whom they actually happened. Would it be so naïve to turn from the art or artlessness of these texts and look instead at the original narratives from which they derive?

To make things simple, I have followed two ground rules for presenting stories of supernatural encounter. Firstly, I have written as if things actually happened as they are said to have happened. This is not an ontological claim, but a position forced on us by the evidence. It all took place a long time ago and the witnesses are not available for interview. If a man says he met a fire-breathing raven which turned into a black dog, we are not in a position to contradict his report, and reports are what we want.

That underlies my second rule, to describe events in a running paraphrase. Whilst always keeping my eye on the text, I have been wary of the translationese which comes when you adhere closely to a Latin original; this is a book about tales and I wanted them told in something like a normal vernacular voice. When a spectral hound says *Da mihi gladium tuum!* I have rendered it as 'Give us that sword, mate' because—well, how else would a talking dog talk?

Reaching for the narratives that people actually told, rather than their afterlives in clerical discourse, brings us to the native interpretation of these experiences. Calling them 'fairies' or even 'spirits' barely covers the cognitive gap between the vernacular, which draws on many terms found in place-names but not the word *demon*, and Latin, which hardly ever uses anything else. There were lay people in the Middle Ages who took a quite different view on these matters from that taught in church, but the records are so few, and the temptation to romance the seers and herb-wives so strong, that I have only indicated here and there what they may have thought about dealing with spirits. Otherworldly experience had a quality of its own that transcended people's own models of what it should have been: cruel saints, helpful fiends, honest goblins.

This is a book of two halves: one is based on the hundred or so encounters reported in the literature, the other on the thousand English place-names referencing supernatural beings. Both corpora of evidence deal with the same subject, and in the ordinary line of research we might expect to understand each through the lens of the other. If we could walk into the Middle Ages as an ethnologist arrives in a village—if we could sit down, listen and converse without restraints—that might be the case. But the surviving evidence is so fragmented that I can only offer suggestions from experience and tradition about how place-names should be read. These names were not fanciful embellishments to the landscape but described what had happened at a particular place, or what might go on there. Elves, like crows and caves and bogs and barley, were part of the known workaday world.

In both sections, the documentary and the onomastic, I have focussed on primary sources, on the experiences people had at the time rather than our reflections on that experience. For its narrative, this book draws on what the epistemologists call first-order knowledge. It is in the endnotes—below the water-line, as it were—that you will find the higher-order knowledge of textual issues, historical setting, cultural expectations, parallels, and some gentle engagement with secondary sources. This is an arrangement that comes naturally to me though it is not the general rule, and may seem ungrateful to my predecessors and contemporaries. Of course I owe everything to them. Presenting the evidence as it comes from primary material would be impossible without the cumulative labours of scholars from Thomas Wright to Francis Young and I am in their debt.

It has been said that some historians hunt by gaze, and some by scent. I admire, and owe much to, colleagues who scan the big picture, the overview of fairy tradition, but by temperament I'm much closer to the ground; there is more detail than scope in this book, more juxtaposition than synthesis. The one distinct tool of folkloristics, its wide comparison of motifs and tale-types, was ruled out by the focus of the project on medieval England—with the occasional foray into other Angevin lands, as my source authors crossed to and fro. The more I knew about twelfth-century England, the more I was reminded of parallels in France, Ireland and Scandinavia: but also aware of the pitfalls of pick-and-mix comparativism. If each region had its own informed collation of onomastic, medieval and contemporary narrative evidence, we would know … a great deal more than we do now.

PART I

People

CHAPTER ONE

Strange Meetings

'Many will not believe they can be seen; and, if any man shall say, swear, and stiffly maintain, (though he be discreet and wise, judicious and learned) that he hath seen them, they account him a timorous fool, a melancholy dizzard, a weak fellow, a dreamer, a sick or a mad man; they contemn him, laugh him to scorn; and yet ... Leo Suavius ... will have the ayre to be as full of them as snow falling in the skies.'

Burton, Anatomy of Melancholy

It is high summer in Cumberland, 1343.[1] William Wynfeld is riding through the fields, young, active and carefree, the light wind brushing his face. He is pleased to see the wind shake the barley, which ripples like waves in a green sea.[2] Suddenly the head of a little red man appears between the stalks. William cannot keep his eyes off this strange small head. It gets bigger and bigger, the red man steps out of the corn, he walks up and grips the bridle, pulling horse and rider deeper into the field. As they pass over the ridges, they come to a place where a lovely lady sits among a ring of young girls. She gives orders: at once William is pulled off his mount and stripped of his clothes. The girls slice through his skin, flay it off and tug it away, and then the lady bisects his head, pulls the two halves apart and takes out his brain. Patched together, he is lifted back onto his horse and sent to wander where he will: the young man is now quite, quite mad.

Only one person bothers with mad William—a girl who used to work alongside him in their master's household, and who had always been sweet on him. She looks after her young man although he is now so fierce and wild that she has to tie chains round him before he can be taken in search of a cure. All this time the red man is at his side, fidgeting with the chains as if attempting to set him free. So for six years they trail from shrine to shrine, each as useless as the last, until at last they land in Yorkshire. The young couple disembark and trudge along the road to Beverley, then step into the cool air of the Minster where they ask permission to pray beside the holy tomb of John. There William sinks into a deep sleep in which he sees the lovely lady once more; again she grips and splits his head apart, and this time she puts the brain back in place. When he wakes up he is sane: he hears the story of what he was and where he has been and what the girl had done for him, he asks her if she will marry him and of course she says yes.

They lived together for many years until in time his wife died and William, finding himself again at a turning-point in his life, took holy orders and was ordained priest. Eventually he became rector of the nearby church at Thorpe Bassett, where once, just once, he was confronted with something from his suffering long ago: at the moment of the Elevation, as the people in the nave knelt before the Host, he saw the red man who turned to him and said 'I am no longer your keeper: he whom you hold in your hands knows better than me how to protect you.'

Another look into the mirror of the past: it is the 1240s now, and we are at Dunfermline in Fife.[3] Christina and her mother Helen have been out walking in the home park of their mansion; evening comes on, most of the household have retired, and before turning in they sit down to watch the sunset. From a hollow dell nearby, mother and daughter both hear a child's voice, calling pitifully for someone to help. 'It's got to be a poor family that's lost', says Helen. 'We should take them in before nightfall. Jump to it, girl, go and see what's up.' 'But I'm scared', says Christina, 'there's something spooky about that voice.' 'Don't talk back' says her mother, 'you never do a thing I say—now *up*', and Christina doesn't dare disobey. She runs down into the hollow and in the gathering darkness her mother sees her cradling a little child. Christina looks at the boy: it is her brother, who died a month ago. 'Kiss me, Chris', says the child. 'I daren't', she says, holding him away from her. 'Little brother, there is no warmth between the dead and the living.' And at that, the child-shape wriggles and grabs her throat with his left hand and punches her hard between the shoulders, knocking her down, and after that she knows nothing.

Looking down the slope, Helen sees her daughter fall insensible; she runs to her, and then howls so loud that all the servants are roused. Everything is in a rush, lights are brought out of the big house; one of the menservants carries Christina back indoors and lays her down on a day-bed. Meanwhile her father has come out of the inner chamber, guessing that something is not quite right. Someone fetches the family Psalter and he reads aloud. It is midnight when Christina stretches, looks up with sightless eyes and says 'This is the house of company. The men are here, the women, the boys and the girls', and after a short while 'This is the lovely queen, the gracious, the beautiful. The singers are leading the chorus.' 'No more of this', says her father 'say the Lord's Prayer, Christina, say the Creed.' But she talks more and more about a bright hall and a lovely lady until he, frightened and furious, snatches up a whip and says it will be the worse for her if she does not repeat God's words instead. She flinches and recites the Lord's Prayer obediently, then the Creed, her father joining in until just after they reach *vitam eternam* she says in an ordinary voice: 'The company have gone, all but my brother, who clutched me, and he's at the foot of the bed.' Her father picks up the Psalter and stands at the far end of the bed, reciting. In a little while Christina says 'The company have gone, all gone, and brother's gone too. Oh, Dad, you should have heard them singing!'

Meanwhile the servant who had carried her in was lying senseless in an outhouse, and did not come to until cockcrow. By then the house was full of priests and neighbours whispering about what had happened, while the family sat around Christina's bed, holding her hand so that she could not be carried away from them. All Sunday morning they talked it over, and then at vespers they carried their daughter to Dunfermline Abbey and laid her down before the altar of holy Margaret the queen. Her parents sat up through the night praying for her until late the next day she got up, stumbled to the tomb when Margaret was first buried, and curled up on the flat stone before going to sleep again. A little later she stretched out her neck, then returned to sleep and finally woke up, stepped off the stone slab and greeted her parents, healthy and sane.

What happened? She had three dreams, she said. In the first, the saint had told her to arise and go to her appointed place of healing at the tomb. In the second, holy Margaret cradled her head, reaching inside her mouth and touching her throat, which restored her senses and the proper power of speech. Then the third time, when she could speak, she asked humbly, 'Queen, if you could touch the place where the demon struck me, I would be as well as ever I was', and Margaret said 'It is Christ's mercy that heals. I will touch you and care for you if you will agree to enter his service day and night.' So now that she was well, they dedicated her as a nun and she received the habit at Elcho.

One last glance into the past: this time it is 1171 and Richard, Roger's son, is walking through the great gate of Sarum—not Salisbury, which won't be built for another thirty years yet, but the hilltop city of Old Sarum.[4] It is early morning; Richard has a long journey ahead, and a heavy message, to tell his uncles at Marlborough that mother is dead.[5] Outside the city gate an old woman sits begging and Richard, who has been brought up to be kind to the less well-off, pulls a bun out of his pocket and gives her half.

So he sets off with the steady pace of a teenager, and has covered about five miles over Salisbury Plain when he sees, standing in front of him and blocking the track, three men of noble bearing. They are dressed in white like hermits, the middle of the three a little taller than the rest, white-headed, and bearing in his hands a brass bowl full of blood. Richard is terrified, especially when he sees the blood. They've knocked a man down, he thinks, and bled him to death; we're miles from any village and there's no-one else in sight, so maybe I'll be next. And yet they don't seem like robbers, more like men of God: and politeness is always best. So when the tall man asks Richard where he's from and what way he's going, the boy bows the knee as you would to a knight or a canon and gives a civil answer. 'Tell me', says the tallest of the three, 'are you carrying any bread?' 'Yes, sir', says Richard, and pulls out one of the buns to show him. 'Not that one', says the tallest. 'I want to see the half loaf that was left after you remembered the old lady this morning.' And then: 'Do you remember your dream?' For the night before he set out, Richard had dreamt of a young man with the face of an angel who led him up onto a high wall from which they could see all heaven and hell. It comes back to him now, and he is amazed that his actions and even his dreams are known to these strangers. Plucking up courage, Richard asks the tall one what's with the blood. 'It is the blood of Thomas the Archbishop: and you, boy, must abandon your journey and return to the dean of Sarum, telling him to go in procession round the city. If he will not, then he must know that the greatest storm that ever blew will fell his town. Now go quickly, and take care that you do not look back until you are a furlong away from us.' And when, having covered the distance, Richard looks back, there is no-one to be seen on the endless, level, lonely Plain.

Back he came, forgetting his uncles and kinsfolk, to carry a new message: when he told his story to the dean and canons, they believed him. And this was the first Sunday after the martyrdom of the blessed Thomas of Canterbury, who died cut down in his own cathedral, where the monks wept to see his blood shed in defence of God's Church, and gathered it … in a bowl.

Reader, are you edified? You ought to be. Thomas Walsingham, the miraculist of Dunfermline and Benedict of Peterborough weren't writing for amusement. They set these stories down to make us wiser in the path of faith: how else could you see the world then, if you were an educated cleric writing in Latin? And yet the content of the stories continually threatens to subvert their frame. Richard encounters three strangers with a strong hint that one of them is an angel, but he takes them for thugs who will slit his throat as soon as look at him, which doesn't sound very angelic, and their leader says that if his wishes are not performed he will bring on a great storm; raising storms was usually the province of demons. There is also something fairy-like in their command 'take care that you do not look back'—not to be spied on is one of the first concerns of the hidden people. So what might seem at first to be a didactic vision is laced with threads of contradictory imagery.

Christina's story, too, is full of contradictions. She loves her dead brother but is afraid of him—or 'him'; at first he is the lost child, when mentioned later he is definitely a demon. She wavers between one identification and the other, just as she moves from a vision that frightens her family because she sees a lovely lady to another in which she reassures them by seeing a beautiful queen. They hold her hand all night so that she cannot be carried off and yet at the end they are glad that she has been taken away to a nunnery. Her narrative flips between two incompatible rules for judging events. As for William, what makes his story so uncanny is the absence of judgement: terrible things happen to him, but he does not demonize the agents of his suffering. The lady who shatters is the lady who heals, and the little red man not only leads him into danger but also looks after him afterwards and, at the very end, when we feel that the capricious sphere of magic is giving way to the power of faith, up pops the red man again but this time advancing a quite orthodox religious viewpoint.

These stories have been mediated, of course; they are not first-hand memorates of supernatural encounter, but they are as close to it as we can get, and their incoherence is itself evidence that something original has passed undigested through the clerical process. Even as texts they open windows onto the otherwise silenced world of the laity—though in a crisis this idiom might be rejected by laypeople themselves. Christina's father threatens her into saying Latin prayers rather than eerie words about the elf-queen, not because he wishes to enforce the hegemony of clerical discourse but because he loves his daughter and is terrified of losing her. Frightened people will seek protection wherever they can, never mind its ideological underpinnings. Between the twelfth and the fifteenth centuries Western Christians came more and more to see the uncanny as devilish, in line with the aggressive doctrines being pushed by theologians, but this was not just a triumphant imposition of Church views.[6]

But who constituted the folk groups that shared these stories? If they were layfolk, they were certainly not working class. Christina's family have a landed estate with an *amenitas* to sit down in, servants (so many that the collapse of one is hardly remarked on), religious books at hand and the ability to read them, and the social cachet to put their daughter in a nunnery, which didn't come cheap. A hundred years later, when her Norfolk namesake Christiana the daughter of Nicholas Nevenon of Inglethorpe fell into a swoon after losing her demon lover, it is clear that this family too were literate, for Christiana's fingers were contracted until her little brother brought the family Book of Hours to the bedside and inserted it in her twisted grip, which at once recovered some of its strength.[7]

William Paternoster, who saw strange lights in the woods at Bielby when running in search of a playmate, was struck dumb for six months until his parents brought him to John's shrine twelve miles away at Beverley Minster: once he had language again, he spoke both French and English, which suggests a high-ranking background.[8] Paternoster is a byname—we are in the 1160s, too early for surnames—which could have been used because a family held land by the notional service of prayers for their patron's soul. William's father put him to school at the Minster and he afterwards became almoner at the hospital there, the sort of job likely to be given to someone from the knightly class.

Tradition-bearers in later times often modelled their ideas of supernatural intervention on the careless, unchallengeable way that gentry interfere in the lives of the poor. But this is not so obvious in the medieval apparitions, which are just as capricious whether they descend on hard-scrabble lives or those of the comfortably well-off.[9] William was in the household of the Barons Greystoke of Cumberland, one of the major families of the North. Walter Barker was the household servant of a celebrated figure, not named, but living near Luton in 1485: he was out walking in the dusk when three strange men rushed on him, knocked him down and vanished, taking his wits with them.[10] A teenager in the Dunfermline area had entered the service of a knight, but obtained permission for a visit to his parents' house. Everyone was glad to see the young master back home but one evening when he was out walking he heard a sound of galloping hooves, and then saw hideous riders. He ran, but did not run fast enough: one of them gained on him, the horse reared up its hooves to strike him down, and he fell to the ground like a dead man.[11]

For this elite *adolescens*, the supernatural took its shape from the conflicts for which he was being trained, as it did for Ranulf, although for him the imagery of war came in the healing, not the illness. Riding carelessly in the woods he lost his way, then lost his mind; his people found him and confined him to bed where he dreamt, as a soldier might dream, of Edmund galloping after him in full armour, spitting him with a lance in the back, unhorsing him and at last when he was down, sitting on him to deliver the deathblow.[12] This was a strange way for a saint to behave but it evidently spoke to something in Ranulf, who was cured and became a monk.

Status did not always match circumstances, however. Reinburgis of Cirencester came of a noble line but after her father's death the family moved to Wallingford where her mother married the worthy Ranulf le Gros. Worthy he may have been, but apparently he kept a smaller household than the first husband, because when Reinburgis began her strange visions of women warriors, there is no mention of servants and she appears to be sharing a bedroom with her little brother. The visions, with their demands for a visit to the shrine of Æthelthryth, might not have gone on so long had the family finances been sounder: there is a hint that Reinburgis was responding to a refusal from her mother—'Dear, we can't afford to go to Ely and that's that'—although she got her own way in the end.[13]

It sounds as if Reinburgis' mother had made the best of a bad deal socially, and that Ranulf was a townsman of Wallingford rather than another knight. The urban elite do not feature much in these stories although one of the earliest miraculous cures involves a wealthy citizen of Winchester struck down with paralysis after encountering three terrible women in the water meadows of the Itchin.[14] Richard of Sarum seems like a typical son of a burgess, sent to run errands but treating old beggar women with polite condescension, respectful but confident in his dealings with the nobility (once he has established they are not armed hoodlums, a mistake more easily made in the twelfth century than today). By the end, he is giving confidential messages to the dean of Sarum Cathedral: like Reinburgis, he benefitted in social standing from an encounter with the supernatural.

Richard was running, not riding; this was to be expected of servants and the young, although otherwise even ordinary townsfolk or country dwellers would go about their business mounted. A man who meets a ghost while he is on horseback and carrying a sword might be thought to have gentry connections, but Snowball of Ampleforth did both and he was just a tailor.[15] If you did travel on foot, it exposed you to extra dangers, supernatural or otherwise. In 1294 a kelpie-like creature attacked a young wife who had been riding pillion behind her husband on the way back from Haddington fair. They were on the last uphill stretch, the horse was getting tired, and she offered to walk so that he could be home sooner. She regretted it when a pale thing resembling a seven-year-old girl came out of the stream and ripped into her with a hand like a horse's hoof.[16] A young priest's clerk was walking through the woods south of Taunton, trying to keep up with his master who had ridden ahead. He heard noises from the undergrowth, picked up his heels and ran, but whatever it was kept pace with him. Then as he paused for breath in a clearing, three women caught him and threw him to the ground, paralysed.[17]

So often we hear of illness following an encounter with beings of another world. People used visible suffering to validate stories which might otherwise have been dismissed as fantasy: the disability which followed a fairy encounter was proof of a claim with no supporting witnesses, for people always saw spirits when they were alone. And our sources are biased, for the most vivid narratives of encounter come from the compilations of cures in *miracula*. People who met a fairy and survived unscathed to tell the tale would not need to visit to a shrine or come to the attention of its literate guardians.

Nonetheless, *miracula* have enough overlap with other reports to show that illness was a real risk for anyone encountering a fairy. In both bodies of evidence the strange people cause blindness.[18] In both, they twist around the heads of those who arouse their displeasure.[19] In both, they reduce women to a dull stupor by their persistent aggravation.[20] Fairies were dangerous. Most of what we know about Anglo-Saxon *ælfs* derives from charms intended to counteract the illnesses that they caused.

The association of spirits with illness cannot have been a malicious invention of the clergy, for it was just as firmly held among their opposite numbers, the cunning folk and village healers. When brought in front of the bishop of Bath and Wells in 1438, Agnes Hancock skipped over reports that she'd boasted of friends among the *feyry*, who she could contact at any time to ask questions and receive advice. No, my lord, she was just an honest poor woman who helped poor innocent children when they were *tactos vel lesos* by creatures that only she could see. The two words are evidently synonyms, not alternatives: to be touched by the spirits of the air was to be harmed by them, and Agnes cured the invisible wound with a few pious charms: though the charms, when recited in court, turned out to contain some magical or garbled wording that she couldn't translate into honest Somerset, so the bishop told her to abjure and be more careful next time.[21]

He seems to have been sceptical, but holy orders were no prophylactic against popular belief: whatever bishops and Masters of Arts might preach against superstition, the lower clergy were just as afraid as their parishioners of the spirits that haunted wood and stream. Though there were separate learned and vernacular discourses about the demonic, these did not always map reliably onto the lay and clerical populations. A boy was training for a clerical career at the Thornton Abbey school in Lincolnshire, but that didn't protect him from the two cruel women who carried him out of his room and squeezed the speech out of his throat.[22] Like William Paternoster and William Wynfeld he was cured at the shrine of John of Beverley, but neither the intervention of a saint nor a subsequent career in the church was enough to make any of them abandon their original memories in favour of stereotyped devils.

The same ambivalence was found in clerical families. Until the twelfth century, marriage had been the norm for most secular clergy. Under Lanfranc and Anselm, celibacy was enforced gradually from the top down, which still left a large conservative contingent of priests in relationships; just as the reformers feared, their domestic relationships put them on a line with the laity, socially and culturally. So we find a priest and his partner anxious in the 1170s about whether their baby might be a changeling.[23] Alice of Reading was a clerk's daughter but her parents were as helpless as their neighbours to safeguard her when she saw a pale body standing in a winding sheet among the sheepfolds in the early morning light. She screamed, lost her reason, and ran home, where she had to be prevented from picking up the burning fire and throwing it in her face.[24] Wymond, the rector of St Martin Ludgate, had one daughter and made a lot of her, teaching her to read and write and providing her with a governess. As she grew to womanhood she had several suitors including, much to the alarm of the family, a phantasm; the girl told him where to get off, but he was persistent, and got rough when she persisted in saying no. Even when she was crippled with pain and being carried on a stretcher towards the shrine of Bartholomew the Apostle, he kept pace with her, whispering that everything would be alright if only they could make a fresh start together. But she held firm, and was healed.[25]

Demon lovers flourished in a pious milieu. Nicholas Nevenon had a family Book of Hours, as we saw earlier, and the maiden of Dunwich who turned down the offers of a *faunus* was able to call on several priests in witness to her plight.[26] This kind of story is always stereotyped, even more than the narratives of illness and recovery; but even the most edifying reports suggest a certain ambivalence. Christiana had an on-off relationship with her incubus for five years, so there must have been something in it for both of them.[27] Perhaps the refusal of the demon lover stood for the refusal of *all* lovers; the virgin saints—including Margaret, who gave her persuasive diabolical suitor a very hard time—provided a template for assertiveness not usually open to young females.[28] And perhaps the tale-type had another kind of appeal for those who had grown up in a clerical household, but found themselves first excluded by gender from the family business, and then prevented by canon law from marrying into it. A demon was a passport to the spiritual life, after all, even if he was working for the rival firm.

In a sermon story, not too far removed from fact, a household servant is introduced as a forceful character when she cracks open the head of a fellow-servant with a beer jug after he tries to get fresh with her in the cellar. This counts as abhorring the sin of lust, and gets good marks from the preacher, but soon the moral tone changes. Someone, or something, gets in touch with the woman and teaches her to say the *Ave Maria* and *Veni creator Spiritus*. That would fit a pastor better than a demon; true, he sometimes appeared as a young man, but sometimes he could be a beautiful woman—or maybe she was making contact with a whole realm of spirits. They gave her advice: not to work too hard, to eat properly, to flirt with young men and to take regular baths. Again, that sounds like words from a spiritual adviser telling a young convert to look after herself and not overdo the austerities, apart from the flirtation, and even that could have been advice to be friendly and professional rather than shunning the other sex. Reading against the grain, you wonder if the woman was building up a bricolage of spiritual practice from wherever she could, while still living in the world, like the beguines of a later century. She took an oath not to reveal the secrets of her soul-friend, and he also began to reveal occult matters to her. Some hints of this came to her master, who brought in two friars, at which point the story takes a sharp downhill turn, for next she saw the demon in loathsome fiery form threatening to kill her, so the following day she confessed everything ... and there the story leaves her, hard-working, unwashed and orthodox once more.[29]

But what was it actually like to meet a spirit? These encounters are not timeless, universal experiences; they depend very much on the cognitive framework of their day. When people see a ghost nowadays, it is as if we were watching a performance: the apparition passes before us like a film being shown. But medieval people lived in a more face-to-face world. They met spirits on the road and at the marketplace—strangers who unexpectedly helped you or attacked you or asked you to do something for them. There was no doubting their physicality: the kelpie of Haddington threw the young wife into the stream and as she struggled out it ripped a gash down her shoulders, tearing off flesh while she crawled away from the water.

Other encounters took place in some kind of altered state. William, whose awareness of spirits began as he watched the barley rippling in the wind, sounds very much as if he were falling into trance, and everything that happens to him afterwards is inner experience. That doesn't tell us what the experience looked like from the outside: somehow it seems crass to ask this about inward suffering and redemption, but people did, even at the time. Reinburgis had a half-brother who sat up with her when she experienced visions, and he testified to her part of the dialogue, though he couldn't hear or see the imperious *virago* who commanded her. Evidently this lady occupied physical space, because when she returned for the third time Reinbergis had to move to a quiet place and find somewhere for her to sit down.[30] In the same way, Christina's dead brother was actually present at her feet, not just in her imagination; when their father walked round reading the Psalter, the brother was moved on. When Wymond's daughter was interrupted in conversation with her impalpable lover by the family nurse, the old lady could only hear one of them—the demon; his voice was clear as anything, though there was nothing she could see.[31]

Through sound the otherworld found an entry into our own. A Huntingdonshire girl was out in the woods, gathering nuts with her brother, when suddenly she heard music, as if a consort of instruments was playing around her. It struck her into such a trance that she could neither speak nor see, although her brother, who had gone ahead, heard nothing. It was not until he ran back to see what held his sister up that he found her standing witless in the woods. At last, brought in desperation to the shrine of Ive, she was taken around the last bend in the road that leads to the priory, said 'Look, there's the church', and was healed.[32]

Sometimes we hear of visions, sometimes of dreams, but although learned writers are very strict about discriminating *visio* from *somnium*, it is never clear how they were to be judged by sensory criteria. Often in the stories of healing, someone falls asleep and in their dreams they are harassed by a phantom that takes away their sight or strength or sense; awake, they begin the long journey to the saint's shrine, where they fall asleep once more, but this time to see the kindly vision of the saint who heals. Apparitions drive out apparitions.

Adelais the daughter of Sewald was sleeping at her father's manor house in Curridge, north of Newbury, when she felt a fierce black dog savaging her leg. She woke up screaming: there was the proof, a dark bruise on her leg, and soon afterwards she lost her hearing and the strength of her body. Later, unconscious in a fever after being washed with holy water from the martyrdom of Thomas, she sees two saints coming to her side—the archbishop, and Laurence. When she wakes, she is healed. 'Are you sure it wasn't a dream?' asks her father. 'It was no fancy', says Adelais. 'Look, I'm up and well, and that's the work of a vision, not a dream.'[33] But when a midnight traveller was bitten by a black dog that suddenly vanished, it was neither a dream nor a vision, but the attack of an evil spirit, and it would have gone ill with him if he had not invoked the glorious confessor King Henry.[34]

To understand such encounters, we must train ourselves away from a modern mindset in which everything depends on the vehicle of experience—dreams, fantasies, stories Not Real, physical encounters in waking consciousness Real. Instead what mattered was the content of experience, not its vehicle. There were spirits of truth, there were others who had a quite different allegiance, and establishing which was which mattered much more than whether you met them in your sleep or on the highway.

John of Powderham first saw a spirit in his dreams, and afterwards while he was out walking they met, as one man meets another. 'Remember me?' said the other. 'Whenever you saw me in sleep, I promised you good things, and they always happened, didn't they? Am I trustworthy, or what?' John, like the victim of a confidence trick, can't help agreeing with that opening line. Next comes the bait—'Do you sincerely want to be rich?' John would very much like that, and to rise as high as he can imagine. Then comes the hook: 'Do homage to me and I shall make you king.' No! Don't do it … for homage is always, unambiguously, the demand of a devil lusting for a soul. John fell for it, and his pathetic attempt at a coup ended on the gallows.[35]

At least, that was the official story. But John had a large following in Oxford which he can hardly have gained by turning up, as stated by the historians, with a dog, a cock and a tomcat to announce that he was the devil's servant. What was his version? Did he arrive bringing testimony from an angel who had come to him in the fields saying 'Go, right England's wrongs, and I will be with thee'? Reading between the lines is always hazardous but if we are going to identify a popular strain in descriptions of spirits, then we must allow that there was also a popular understanding of why they came, and that this could run quite contrary to orthodox interpretation.

Ieuan ap Gwilym ap Rhys the curate of Kilpeck was not firm in the faith, according to his parishioners in 1397, because he was always out at nights with a troop of delusive spirits.[36] They weren't too happy either about him knocking off Maiot Leduart and Margaret, Robyn Noke's daughter, so keeping company with fairies may have been just one more stick to beat an unpopular minister: but assuming that Ieuan really was doing something arcane in the evenings, it must have made sense in ways that the archdeacon did not understand, or want to understand. Did he learn who was going to live, and who to die? Did he join the troop of good spirits in battle against the bad ones? There are good anthropological parallels for this, but not on English soil.[37]

We have one reasonably sympathetic account of the inner life of a seer. Passing through Caerleon in 1188, Gerald of Wales heard many stories of the wise man Meilyr, who had died fourteen years earlier. He was just like everyone else until one Sunday evening when, out on a walk, he saw a girl that he'd fancied for a long time. The place was sheltered, they were alone together and she didn't seem to have any objections so things went just as he had hoped until, at the critical moment, he found himself clasping—not the girl, but a hideous, hairy *something*. And as Meilyr looked down, his wits left him and he ran mad. In time he came to the shrines of the saints at St Davids where he recovered his reason, but retained the ability to see and talk with spirits. As reported by Gerald, he was a guest of honour at South Welsh monasteries, due to his ability to detect deceit (a little demon danced up and down on the

liar's tongue), unchastity and lack of monastic vocation. He must have been a
rather formidable visitor. Meilyr couldn't read, but could spot false doctrine
if someone opened a book, where his unholy companions would point out the
doubtful passage. News from other foundations was reported immediately via
the demons, days before it arrived by normal channels. In predicting the future,
he was not infallible but mostly got it right. If you wanted to know the name
of an incubus, or the costume of evil spirits—they liked to dress as hunters,
with horns round their necks—then Meilyr was your man.[38] He spent much
of his career in one monastic house after another. This would have involved
lodging along the way in lay Welsh-speaking households and it may be that,
out of sight of the brethren, his predictions and divinations were credited to
other, less diabolical agents.

Meilyr the wise man was no fool, tailoring a life-narrative of healing and
transformation to let him exercise his gift of prophecy with the blessing of the
Church. John of Powderham was less shrewd, though he also had a demonic
friend who could tell what was going to happen: going public with the wrong
kind of story, he suffered for it. Most spirits proffered advice, regardless of
their ontological status. Snowball the sword-wielding tailor of Ampleforth
had a long and demanding series of encounters with a dead man, in which
events kept drifting away from and then returning to the conventional purgatorial narrative in which a soul seeks absolution *post mortem*. Finally, when
to the relief of both parties the ghost was about to stop messing around and
enter eternal rest, he gave Snowball some spiritual advice, but then changed
character completely and told him that if he stayed in one place he would be
rich, while in another place he'd be poor; also he had certain enemies, whose
names could perhaps have been shared if Snowball had asked. But Heaven called
and the conversation broke off.[39]

John Bromyard, the learned Dominican, wrote in some detail against the
superstition of those who consort with fairies, although a lot of what he has
to say is lifted from standard legal texts such as the *Canon episcopi*. But he had
evidently met with—and been rather rattled by—women who dismissed his
fancy Continental demonology.[40] 'No', they said, 'we have no faith in the devil
or his works, our mentors are the fair folk.' This is the *pulcher populus*—are the
women making a folk-etymology out of the word 'fairy', or translating Welsh
tylwyth teg, or is the Welsh phrase itself an imitation of the English *fairefolkis?*[41]
These fair ones sometimes spoke to them, or flew with them, or took them
away to places strange and lovely; this sounds like a summary of the different
modes of interaction with the fairies. It was not all smooth going: they said that
in these encounters the folk sometimes beat them and left them ill. We have

had ample evidence for illness caused by an encounter with spirits, but here is a hint that it might be part of a larger story. Agnes Clerk of Great Ashfield in Suffolk met with elves who wrenched her head and neck right round. At this point we might expect to hear that she suffered for many years before being delivered by a saint, but not a bit: she was sitting in her parents' house when a good old man came in, blessed her to take away her deformity, and told her what was in store. Though Agnes was still only a girl, the old man said, she would marry, and have a daughter, who would be wise and holy and do wonderful things. Which came to pass, for little Marion grew up a favourite of the elves and saints, who taught her prophecy and healing. This is not a story that we usually hear, and we wouldn't have heard this one if Agnes and Marion hadn't over-reached themselves in 1499, inviting the curate of Great Ashfield into a syndicate for blessing an elfin holly branch so that it could detect hidden treasures. It was the curate, seemingly, who shopped them to the church authorities.[42]

If the strange people flayed bodies and split heads, perhaps it was to replace the brain with a new one, capable of seeing and understanding secret things. This could turn out well or ill: there is no reducing stories of visionary initiation and stories of desolation and madness into a single master narrative, even if we allow for a clerical transmission that emphasized bad trips over good ones. One evening in Co. Durham, around 1135, Walter of Kelloe was setting off home from a party when a great pack of dogs ran down the road towards him: all jet black, with rough shaggy coats. They barked furiously, rushing at him, then gripped onto his clothes as if trying to tug him in amongst them. But he got home safely and shut the door on them. What a relief! And it was puzzling, they hadn't behaved like an ordinary pack of dogs at all, so he went to look out at them outside the window. (Remember this is a medieval window, just an opening in the wall with wooden bars.) Suddenly one huge dog, blackest of them all, sprang up with its paws on the sill, broke through the bars, and threw itself down Walter's throat. He could feel it going down, its claws scrabbling inside him; could feel its back, as far as the tail, scraping down his throat.

And from this point Walter is the standard madman, raving and foaming at the mouth, trussed with chains to stop him doing further harm. His brother hurries to Durham and consults Aldred the sacristan. Aldred realizes this calls for something strong and sends a clerk with an ampulla of the water of Cuthbert. It's in his hood, but the demon knows it's there, because demons are pretty smart, and makes Walter jam his mouth shut; his friends have to lever his jaws open with a bit of stick but at last they get the water down his throat. His jaw drops open like a dying man's, his eyes bulge, and all at once he shouts, 'He's gone, he's out!' There's the black dog, shaggy with malice, running through the house, bounding out over the threshold; looking back just the once, panting with laughter and threat. Quickly Walter warns everyone to sprinkle the water of Cuthbert on the threshold and all round the house. But three nights later they hear a sound outside and it's the demon. He says he misses their time together and would like to keep up the relationship. Who was this Cuthbert that he'd taken up with? Nobody outside liked *him*, and isn't it better to stay with old friends? Walter says that he rejects forever the demon and his company, and away he goes with growling and gnashing of teeth.[43]

When an infesting demon is driven out, there is often a closing scene where they appear for the last time. The red man came to say farewell, in a more conciliatory spirit than Walter's dog; the godly servant with the beer-jug had one last encounter with her demon guru, when he stood a long way off and spoke to her like someone afraid. Stephen of Hoyland was infested for thirty years by a nightmare; every night it came to suffocate him, every night he would wake screaming and the servants struggled to bring him back to full consciousness. Doctors claimed this was the disease *ephialtes* but Stephen insisted it was a demon, which proved to be the case, for as soon as he invoked the blessed Thomas the thing was banished. For one last time it appeared, running around him in the shape of a dwarf but keeping its distance, while he just laughed at its presumption.[44]

Yes, these episodes provide each tale with a satisfying coda that proves the occupying power is well and truly banished, but note how often the storytellers put conciliatory words in the mouth of the demon. Like the phantasmal abuser of Wymond's daughter, they show more regret than anger: we could have been so good together, they seem to say.[45] Demons are sociable. The company that Walter of Kelloe rejects at the end of his story is *pompa*, the same word used for the troop in which Ieuan of Kilpeck was glad to take part. 'Be amongst us, be one of us', say the mysterious green riders to Richard of Sunderland, one of the few supernatural encounters to model itself on the fairy narrative tradition.[46] What stands out in this story is not just the machinery of elfland—the valley which opens of its own accord, its lofty mansion and endless pleasures and otherworldly king—but the determination of these strange people to bring him into their world. One of the oddest things in Walter's odd story comes when the pack, which had been threatening him as stray dogs would, start tugging at the hem of his clothes instead, pulling him in amongst them. What is this pack? Just as he, after possession, is a man with a dog inside, are these dogs with men inside?

In his demoniac phase Walter had remarkable powers. Once, when a tired young man nodded off in the house, mad Walter announced that he was having a wet dream, which the young man on waking sheepishly confessed to be true.[47] Apparently a demon inside the mind of one human can recognize a succubus getting into the sleeping consciousness of another. There is a theme of insight running through all these stories, from Walter's involuntary perceptiveness, through the judicious prophecies offered by Meilyr, to the mixed pains and delights of the women who went with the fair folk.

Being out of your mind evidently had its consolations. Its negative and positive connections are both present in the Old English word *ylfig*, used to gloss a Latin text where a madman, like Walter, has been possessed by a demon and is bound in chains. It explains *comitialis* 'epileptic', which carried more than a hint of demonic attack, and is coupled with another word *garritor* 'utterer'. Uttering what? In a second gloss, *ylfig* explains *fanaticus*, 'pagan priest', and is coupled with 'one foretelling the future'. Suffering and strange powers again: but, etymologically, *ylfig* is 'of an elf'.[48]

The spirits who took away the wits of William Wynfeld and Walter Barker, who left Alice of Reading crazily throwing firebrands in her face, are never named in the sources: that is part of their sinister unknowability. In Latin such misfortunes were blamed on demons but when people discussed them in the vernacular, they talked of madness brought by elves. Attributing mental illness to fairies could be a cure as well as diagnosis, offering the path by which a split mind could negotiate with its fragmenting forces. Once a troubled person had remembered themselves as someone taken by fairies, they could imagine their way back to human society, returning to it with the gifts of those who had been lost on the other side: prophecy and healing. If there were such beings as fairies, of course, and that was controversial.

CHAPTER TWO

Tales of Wonder, Tales of Sorrow

Who Are They?

There are no fairies. John Bromyard is quite clear about this.[1] There are angels in glory, and former angels that have fallen and roam the lower air as devils. There are men and women, living and dead: of the dead, some are in Heaven beyond our reach, some in Hell beyond our help, and a third class in Purgatory where they may benefit from our prayers and the sacrifice of the Mass. That's it. Since the good angels are incapable of deceit, and the purgatorial dead have no motive for it, any supernatural apparitions that don't fit must be demons, and you can be sure that they are up to no good.

Angels rarely appear in medieval tales of the unexpected, though a similar rank is occupied by saints who (as Bromyard would have conceded) have their place in Heaven but help us in this world. So the official supernatural consisted, in practice, of saints, fallen angels, and dead people briefly released from Purgatory. What the modern world calls a ghost (as the classical once did) is a dead person stuck in this world rather than the next; but there was no room for these in the medieval afterlife, and by and large they did not appear, although there were persistent stories of men who physically walked after death, and could be laid by traditional rituals.

And yet, as we have seen, people were continually being assailed or seduced by supernatural agents who did not fit the templates of scholastic thought.[2] Theologians had no difficulty in dismissing these as devils but even they had to admit, when confronted by particular cases, that they didn't behave in a very diabolical way. Authors with a well-stocked library might think of them as the *longaevi*, a term originally applied to the fauns and nymphs of classical poetry who were ageless but not immortal. Poets writing in the vernacular might say that they were of Faerie, meaning that they came from a mysterious magical realm governed by rules other than those which apply in our world. But both of these terms came from the sphere of fiction, not from those of religion and real life.

Meanwhile people who'd never handled a book in their lives continued to talk about a range of beings, from the *ælf* to the *wælcyrige*, who didn't fit anywhere into the theological template. There were dozens of these words but it does not follow that there were twenty or thirty kinds of being, each as different from the next as an oak is from an ash. Grendel in *Beowulf* (426, 939) is at once a *scucca*, a *scinna* and a *þyrs*. The Green Knight in *Gawain* (681) is *half etayn* but also an *aluish mon*. The semantic field of supernatural names is one of overlapping contexts, suggestive equivalences, hints and whispers.

These uncertainties are precisely what the preachers condemned. Salvation required clear border control between otherworld realms and was threatened when saints, demons and the returning dead did not, as experienced, fit so neatly into a *Summa Theologica* and might indeed turn out to have something in common with each other. A poltergeist threw Thomas of Ely out of bed in 1389 before summoning him into a strange and lovely place to attend on its lady, who introduced herself as the saint Æthelthryth and threatened to send a summer so hot the lead would melt on the church roofs. Then she crippled both his legs, just to show that she meant business.[3] Thomas obeyed and recovered, but could be forgiven some uncertainty as what exactly he had been dealing with. When the supernatural broke into people's lives, it did not march under a clear blazon of fiend, angel, or phantom—nor under that of elf and goblin either.[4]

Of course this assumes we have reliable testimony for what was happening supernaturally. Given that there is no document in any of the medieval languages written by someone directly reporting their anomalous encounter, you might wonder whether a project looking at personal experience is doomed to failure. In fact the texts often present us with testimony which, although mediated, has been transmitted more or less as heard—certainly without enough distortion to destroy its value as evidence. But to establish this we need to place our sources under scrutiny, genre by genre.

Hagiography

Lives of the saints do not make for easy reading, not least because of the difficult writing that went into them: a mesh of biblical quotation, wordplay, and the elaborate style of those who wrote Latin as an acquired language and wanted you to know just how much of it they had acquired. When it came to encounters with the demonic, the Lives are repetitive because they all trace back to Gospel originals: the Christ who cast out unclean spirits, and the Christ who was tempted in the wilderness.

The longest biblical encounter with a demoniac is in Mark 5, followed by the other two synoptic Gospels.[5] Jesus crosses the Sea of Galilee and meets a man possessed by a demon, who has fled to solitary places, living naked amongst the tombs. People have tied him up with chains, but he always breaks the chains and runs away. When he sees Jesus, he—that is, the demon inside him, who is both one and many—screams out, saying that he does not want to be tortured. The demons ask instead to go into a herd of pigs which are grazing nearby, and as soon as this is done the pigs throw themselves into the water and are drowned. Meanwhile, the man has got dressed and is waiting quietly for Jesus.

The shadow of the spirit whose name was Legion hangs over the medieval mad. Compared to mental illness as we know it now, it displayed a very limited range of behaviour. People had a clear idea of what it was to run mad, and conformed to it until the sacred drama of contact with the saint let them snap back into their previous selves.[6] Whatever it might be, a demon was physically present. It could be seen wriggling about under the skin of the possessed man like a puppy.[7] Spirits are rarely said to trouble or afflict people, but seize them—*arreptus* is the word used, regardless of whether the sufferer is visibly whisked up into the air by the demon, or goes mad on seeing one, or has one inside them.[8]

As for the other class of demons in saints' Lives, those derived from the Temptation in the Wilderness, they occupy an ambiguous state between soliloquy and dialogue. The Desert Fathers who retreated to silence and isolation in third-century Egypt found that when they had left the chatter of the world behind them, they heard other voices, their own but not their own. The Life of Antony the Hermit was translated into Latin in the 370s, about a hundred years after he went into the Western Desert. His demons begin by tempting the fallen will, but as he grows in constancy, they become more active. Psychological or physical, they are always noisy, distracting, intimidating, trying to shake his mind by a sudden raw appeal to the emotions. The Antonine template was repeated in native English hagiographies such as the Life of Guthlac. After a brief military career in the seventh century, he turned hermit; deserts being scarce in East Anglia, he retreated to the Fens instead. Though described vividly and with relish, the demons that assail Guthlac are very much a fantasia on their classical prototype, ugly degraded human figures assimilated to a despised group: sub-Saharan Africans for Antony, Welsh for the Anglo-Saxon author.

There is no doubt that hermits saw demons, but hermit literature conforms to stereotype and it is hard to get a handle on what was really being experienced. The exception is the Life of Godric of Finchale, a unique collaboration between a solitary living in some woods on the banks of the Wear and Reginald of Durham, who wrote down his memories in later life when the old man had become the monastery's prize recluse. It was a long collaboration, for despite—or because of—his austerities Godric was tough as oak and outlived several of his would-be shrine guardians. He had a grasp of conversational Latin and French but spoke English and was no scholar, so that his spiritual life came from popular culture rather than books. As presented by Reginald in his convoluted but vivid style, it included some thirty encounters with demons.

About half of them follow standard lines, which is not surprising when you remember the many years that Godric had been preparing for the eremitic life. Wild beasts menace him and mocking voices and sneer at his ambition to be a holy man, just as in the Lives of his precursors. Sometimes they were the standard devils he'd seen in wall paintings—huge-eyed, fire-breathing monsters with clawed feet—but more often they look just like ordinary villagers peering over the garden fence or helping him dig his smallholding. In the first years of his solitude Godric had been obsessive about shunning human contact and in his early visions hell is still other people. But with time he settled into the give-and-take role of a village holy man, accepting food and help and giving out spiritual counsel and little miracles. The demons too change character. In the later chapters of the Life they take on curious forms, far more vividly realized than in the standard literature. A headless, limbless bag of straw; a jingling goldsmith, sitting making trinkets on the floor; a horse with a man's head; a man with skin like holly bark, all hollow behind.[9] As time passed and Godric became more reconciled to who he was—a man of God, but still a peasant's son, a *rusticus*—so his otherworld began to draw more on homegrown imagery.

Miracles

Miracles were part of medieval life, but books of miracles were not. Not every shrine produced a *miracula* witnessing the wonders done by its patron saint, and when they did the manuscripts had a limited circulation, often coming down to us as unique copies.[10] Pilgrims travelled dozens or hundreds of miles to the shrine, the blind shuffling with hands stretched out to their guides, the crippled stumping along with wooden stools to protect their scarred hands; but they were drawn by common fame and oral testimony, not by the written word.

A miracle story was a joint construction of the facts that the shrine guardians would accept, and those the cure seekers and their friends would present; where causes of disease were controversial, both parties usually left them out.

So back-stories are rare in *miracula*, and frustratingly for us, stories about super-natural encounters rarer still. They appear in about 1% of miracles overall. Many miraculists ignored them completely, though in a few counterbalancing collections the proportion rises to something like 4%. The two related miracle collections of Æbbe and Margaret have the highest proportion of supernatural stories, although the hinterlands of Coldingham and Dunfermline cannot have been uniquely fairy-haunted; these are simply texts which reject the self-censorship of other *miracula* to reveal what people actually believed.[11]

The twelfth century was the golden age of miracle collections: they grew longer and took shape as a distinct genre, instead of just providing a coda of contemporary interest at the end of a saint's Life. By 1171, a year after the death of Thomas Becket, a project was already under way to record the explosion of miracles at the martyred archbishop's tomb.[12] But in all these collections, great or small, it is not the number of miracles which sticks in our throats but their sheer impossibility. Faced with one walking paralytic or a blind beggar shouting 'I can see!', we can invent some sort of plausible medical explanation; but they keep on coming, in their hundreds, the symptoms more bizarre than anything one has ever seen and the cures implausibly dramatic and instant.[13] Even so, miracle stories keep within the parameters of reality. People come round after being drowned, but they do not get up from the ashes of burnt buildings; broken bones are restored, not amputations. Every now and then the descriptions in *miracula* surprise us with a medically plausible narrative. In four of our miracles—from the collections of Swithun, Wulfstan, Æbbe and Godric—the touch of a spirit brings on a hemiplegic loss of motor skills and speech, with the patient gradually recovering over days or weeks.[14] The obvious diagnosis is that these people had a stroke.

We cannot always rely on miracles for this sort of medical reportage, just as we cannot always expect them to project the right kind of pious fiction: first and foremost, they are narratives. Some miracle stories were assembled from multiple sources, but others preserve the individual voice.[15] Behind the eerie tale reported from Richard of Sarum in Benedict's collection, we can hear the frustration of a Wiltshire visitor trying to explain Salisbury Plain to a Man of Kent. 'They vanished—I mean *vanished*. There was nowhere for them to go. It's a bare plain, you could spot a midget six miles off.'[16] Personality counted for much in these encounters. Three weeks and many visions after her first traumatic encounter with the supernatural, Reinburgis of Wallingford arrived at Ely with her extended family tagging behind in the evening light.[17] With the confidence of a born lady, she explained she was here for a vigil beside Æthelthryth's shrine, lay down briefly on the sacred flagstones and then arose with blood streaming from her right eyelid. Deftly catching the flow in her folded sleeve, she swung the other hand in front of her injured eye to confirm it could now see, and moved to the altar where she stood, lovely, penitent and radiating charisma, to tell her tale to all who would hear.[18]

The process of negotiation can already be seen in the earliest English *miracula*, written for the shrine of Swithun in around the year 975. Eadsige the sacrist loved his patron saint so much that he rang a bell every time a miracle was performed, including those which happened in the middle of the night. Deprived of the already minimal sleep enjoined by the Rule, his fellow monks told him to put a sock in it, which led to one of those simmering disputes that thrive in small communities until Swithun appeared in a dream to a noblewoman and told the brethren to let Eadsige ring as often as he wanted to. Not long after, the Frankish hagiographer Lantfred of Fleury arrived at Winchester to set down scattered traditions of the saint in good Latin prose. As a native speaker of Old English with a bit of a grudge and a fund of good stories, Eadsige was a difficult but prolific informant, and probably acted as a go-between for Winchester people who had experienced the healing power of Swithun but might not have spoken directly to a foreigner.[19]

The man who had been challenged by three wild women in the meadows of the Itchen did not keep his story to himself; Lantfred wrote it down some ten years after it happened and the experience was still being talked about twenty years later, when Wulfstan the Cantor rewrote the prose text in hexameters.[20] But when we are told that he met women like Tisiphone who were as Aethiopians, we can take it that a Winchester townsman, however well-travelled, would have been surprised to hear such bookish terms replacing his original words.[21] Lantfred had read Virgil very closely, so he knew his Furies; he remembered the morality battles of Prudentius and would have been familiar with the *Dialogues* of Gregory the Great, in which demons regularly feature as Aethiopians.[22] True, Gregory was the owner of large estates in a late Antique Mediterranean society, so he actually knew what Black people looked like, while to Lantfred they were probably as mythical as Gorgons, but it is not necessary to have clear ideas to write dignified prose, especially for someone trained in the ornate hermeneutic vocabulary which he brought to his hagiographical labours. Wulfstan improves the narrative with two references to Furies and three to Eumenides, and some cold snakes' venom.

But was this just the use of a classical register, or did Lantfred edit the events of the story? His text is rich in Virgilian echoes but none of them rises higher than verbal influence of the sort to be expected when writing high-class Latin.[23] In any case, the Winchester story is so similar to the other meetings with otherworldly females reported in local *miracula* that it cannot have been adjusted much from the original. It is the subtleties that have been lost—hints about the supernatural which would have coloured the vernacular but were bleached out in a more artificial language.

The miraculists added Latinity to their narratives as a cook might throw stock cubes into a lacklustre stew. The original ingredients can still be seen. Though the admonitions Reinburgis receives from her visitants in *Liber Eliensis* are couched in a very high style—'There is no emperor's daughter in the world, no child of a ruling consul, who does not readily take heed of an utterance of mine!'—the upgrade remains purely verbal; the actual story is left as incoherent as it ever was, and we never find out exactly who these *viragos* are.[24] A hundred years later, the Miracles of Margaret follow a different strategy in telling the story of Christina. Instead of high-flown language, we are offered biblical quotations by the handful—Genesis, Job, Lamentations, Genesis again.[25] These citations give a rich effect but don't relate to the main text, as a genuinely literary allusion would: none of them are relevant to the situation of a girl plucked out of her mind by the grip of a dead brother. And again, the author is not contributing anything but style. Just as at Ely, Christina's story fails to cohere: has she seen her dead brother or a fiend in his likeness? Who is the lovely lady surrounded by boys and girls and why is the brother—or demon—in attendance on her? The episodes do not make theological sense, because Christina told them in a way that did not make sense: not superficially, and not in the cultural framework of the monks who recorded them. But they wrote them down episode by episode, because that was how you recorded miracles. The rest was simply window-dressing.

If miraculists paid so little attention to the plotting of these narratives, we should think twice before reading exegetical significance into their smaller details. In the story of Mutinus there is a curious episode where two of the fey ladies want him killed but the third says no, 'It will be enough if we throw an apple into his mouth and condemn him to perpetual silence.' And there it remains for 35 years until at the feast of Margaret, the gracious saint plucks the apple from his mouth and he can speak once more.[26] Of course it is tempting to see this symbolically, as if Mutinus had gorged on the fruit of sin whose mortal taste brought all his woe.[27] But why should the influence of Genesis be confined to such narrow bounds?—one miracle from a small northern shrine, and a copycat reference some years later where Margaret heals a Clackmannan girl by removing an apple from her mouth, though this time no-one seems responsible for putting it in.[28] Both times it is *pomum*, not *malum*, the word that would come more naturally to anyone alluding to the wicked fruit. It may just be that the storytellers had a thing about apples. After all, cheeses appear in several of the Canterbury miracles, and nobody has suggested deep scriptural significance for cheese.[29]

If miracle collections were revised for a clerical context, this was done through leaving out mistrusted episodes rather than by inserting symbolism. It was not just that Benedict, William or their colleagues could strike a line through any story that did not seem to project the right image of their saintly patron.[30] Cure-seekers themselves were complicit in this process. They were a long way from home, struggling perhaps with another language or dialect, and dependent on the shrine for charity or casual labour.[31] Politely, they reported the sort of experiences they ought to have had according to the people who wanted to hear them. Visions, for instance, were much more likely to be reported by elite male *miraculés* than by those at the bottom of the social scale. Peasant women stuck to saying that they had been ill, and had prayed at the shrine, and were now very much better, thank you: all public facts, which nobody could deny.[32] To talk about your inner experiences, like the girl from Pointon who had a strange story of battling figures on a hill, invited an immediate rejoinder: who are *you* to see visions and dream dreams?[33] Whereas a monk could wake up from a theologically plausible nightmare knowing that he would be believed, if he skipped the bits that didn't fit, and relied on the miraculist for a final edit. Stories reported from the cloister are close to their literary prototypes in Gregory's *Dialogues*, which made them sound more dependable at the time and renders them less convincing now.

People whose experiences called for validation, but who lacked the status or the learning to couch them in patristic terms, could resort instead to folk models to justify their right to be heard. An old man of Bemerton went on pilgrimage to Jerusalem and when all his prayers and circuits were at an end, booked a passage home from Jaffa. He sat on the waterfront, dozing off with his shirt undone in the Mediterranean sun, when into his dreams there steps a lady, more beautiful than you can imagine, and asks who he might be. The sleeping pilgrim replies, with a touch of pride, that he is an Englishman—Wiltshireman, actually—he's from Sarum. 'You wouldn't happen to know Bishop Osmund, would you?' 'Yes, seen him dozens of times.' 'Well, I have here a letter with my own seal, and I'd like you to give it to him. He'll know it's from me because'... and here she leans forward and touches him with her hand: five finger-marks on his bare chest, and he bore them for the rest of his life. And all at once he was not in Jaffa any longer, but back at home, sitting on the ground just outside St John's Hospital.

This *mulier valde speciosa*—another of those mysterious masterful females without portfolio—leaves her imprint in the traditional way.[34] The pilgrim's story was handed down for generations, from the time of Osmund in the 1090s until the commissioners into his sanctity interviewed witnesses from the new city of Salisbury, more than three centuries later. We can easily believe that a pilgrim came home after the First Crusade, a conflict from which many returned with more than scars on their chest; perhaps he showed off the marks to close friends on his return, and answered their questions in growing detail. But for most of us, instant transvection from the Levant to the banks of the Avon is a miracle too far. The story has grown in the telling.

When the town and priory of Christchurch were burnt to the ground by a five-headed dragon—incredibly long, and breathing sulphurous flames—the sight left an indelible impression on Hermann of Laon. Or rather it would have done had Hermann been there, instead of just saying he was, forty years after the event. Guibert of Nogent, who wasn't there either but had access to the original witnesses and a more sceptical turn of mind, says the town was struck by lightning.[35] The passage of time could work wonders on a miracle; a process which need not take centuries, or even decades. A woman who was troubled by a demon went around England for two years, out of her mind.[36] At some point in those vagrant years, the wild-haired dogs that followed her and were invisible to everyone else must have become more real than her dwindling memories of family and home. At last she came to Dunfermline and a cure. Faster than human judgement could imagine, the weathered darkness disappeared from her face, which had been as ugly as the demons themselves. No doubt the monks' willingness to listen to her story played its part in this, along with a wash and brush-up, and the healing powers of grace.

Tales of saintly or demonic encounters were the stock-in-trade of shrine guardians, but they did not necessarily originate with them. Lay people could assemble a narrative just as easily. It did not matter whether they had come to the shrine only a few days after illness struck, or whether they were spiritual old lags who had been waiting years for a cure and knew all the dodges. If they were to identify an otherworldly cause for their troubles—though most people didn't, at least not in the hearing of the miraculists—it would have to be one which made sense in both the vernacular and Latinate worlds.

A woman in Devon was much troubled by a demon in the shape of a young lad. News came to Bartholomew Bishop of Exeter, who gave her good counsel, and he consulted Hugh Bishop of Lincoln, who added his own twopennyworth on contrition and confession, but none of this left her any better than she had been, and though she kept her virtue, the demon carried on harassing her with his raging lust, till she was quite worn out. Then one day, sitting with only her tears for company, she looked up and saw a stranger. He seemed pleasant enough, though with her quickened senses she could see that he, too, was a spirit: still, he was sympathetic and seemed to know all about her troubles. 'Oh', she says, 'what wouldn't I give to get rid of the thing that harasses me.' 'Listen', says the stranger, 'you're a nice girl—I'm not putting it on or anything, I just want you to be happy again—and I can show you a way out of your troubles, come with me.' She follows him, and he points to a clump of St John's-wort. All she needs is to tuck a sprig down her dress, and cut some slips and lay them round about the house: try it! She does: and when the stalker spirit returns to vex her, he cannot get past this barrier of the powerful herb, storm and swear as he likes. All is peaceful for a while until she hears her new friend whispering at the window. 'Well done—I told you it would work! There's so much more I could share with you, the two of us together. Just lift up a corner of that herb so I can slip in....' But she'd had enough of spirits by then, and left the St John's-wort where it was.[37]

The story is told—and very well told—by Adam of Eynsham, on the authority of Bishop Bartholomew, whose account made a great impression on Bishop Hugh, so it reaches us through impeccable clerical channels. But this cannot disguise its popular origins. Like most of the supernatural lore we have met so far, it is not edifying: quite the reverse. Although Adam rather lamely ends 'Trusting in faith and devotion matched with a good lifestyle—far better armament than a sprig of herbs—she lived on in the fear of God', he's just told a story in which *timor Dei* comes a poor second to occult advice from a fiend on the pull. Adam has not recognized what the woman from Devon must surely have known, that the alternation of nasty demon and nice was not original to her, but a tale-type already well-known and with many years of circulation yet to come. Like many medieval short stories, it was a cante-fable, with key points in the dialogue memorized as rhyming couplets: just before the end, Mr. Nice should say

> If thou hope to be Lemman mine
> Lay aside the St John's grass, and the Vervine.[38]

The last we hear of her, the woman from Devon was on a pilgrimage to Canterbury Cathedral, some *Hypericum* still stuffed down her cleavage, just in case. She pulled it out to show the herbalist at St Augustine's monastery and he was very impressed by her story, so much so that when, a year or so later, he heard about people in Essex who were similarly afflicted with diabolical apparitions, he was able to recommend use of this plant. It worked like a charm, and so the lore passed on, from demon to laywoman to monk: not the most orthodox channel of transmission for spiritual teachings. No doubt she told the story to other people too, people who weren't monks, to explain … what? her knowledge of herbs, gifted from an uncanny source? Admittedly she was a pilgrim to Canterbury, but then so was the Wife of Bath, who had her own views on the omnipresence of spirits, the inadequacy of clergy, and women's problems managing awkward males. In a world where official knowledge was closed to women, both institutionally and by its anti-feminist content, how tempting to be promised *all the wyssedom off the world* by a devil, like the girl in the old ballad.[39]

Medieval working layfolk appear so fleetingly in our records that it is hard to put together the story of their lives. But saints attract biographers, so we know a little more about the handful of working-class recluses like Godric who rose to saintliness. Bartholomew of Northumberland had seen a lot before he settled down as a hermit on Farne Island. He was a footloose youngster with the North Sea wind in his sails, until his thoughts turned in a spiritual direction and he was ordained as a priest; but he had other interests as well. One day he was on the road in Norway with a friend who was reputed to be something of a seer. 'He's here, right here', says the friend suddenly. 'Who?' 'Kamban, the Crooked.' 'I can't see him', says Bartholomew, 'but I'd like to.' 'Nothing easier', explains the friend—'Just place your feet on my feet, and you'll see everything, now and forever afterwards.' That made Bartholomew very uncomfortable: perhaps foot on foot seemed too much like hand in hand, the sign of homage made by Theophilus in the story when he gives himself to the devil. So he laughed it off, and soon lost contact with the friend: but this seems to have been a turning point, for many years later, when he was a holy man and people came to him for wisdom and advice, this was the story he told about how the wandering years ended and let him come home to silence and to God.[40]

Bartholomew had rejected the magician's path, but he knew where it went and what kind of things walked there. When he saw demons, as most hermits did in the long hours of soul-struggle, they were not the typical literary figures of the Antonine tradition, but indigenous spirits: little bearded men on goats that shook lances at him, sent forth their screaming spears. Bartholomew knew that the sign of the cross was his surest protection, but he knew other traditions too, how nothing of that kind can get past a straw: so he made a little fence of straw crosses in the sand, and the goat-riders left him in peace.[41]

Bartholomew was not the first hermit to dwell on Farne; he trod in the footsteps of Cuthbert, the great patron of Durham and its satellite communities. Although the saint's body rested at the cathedral city, the island to which he had retreated for contemplation remained a holy place, and Bartholomew was one amongst a succession of hermits. A small collection of Farne miracles survives, appended to Reginald's much longer and more elaborate book of the wonders worked around Durham. The smaller *miracula* dates from around 1200, and seems to have been written from conversations with Bartholomew about the help he gave to those seeking healing on the island. And it contains one of the most detailed stories from the miracle literature of an encounter with another world: how Richard of Sunderland fell in with three green riders on green horses who took him to a place that opened up to let them in, how he was made welcome amongst the people of endless holiday, and how he was tempted to drink from a horn and refused, so they drove him out with the curse of a dumb mouth. It is the earliest telling of a tale-type that has been repeated again and again down to our own times, but it is not the original of the tale—Richard himself, when he had miraculously recovered from his dumbness, said that even while he was being tempted by the fairy feast he remembered the stories he had heard while he was among men about things of this kind.[42] Wisely, he put down the untasted drink.

But who midwifed those memories? Who brought Richard from his suffering state, a mute blowing out noises and bowing up and down at the sight of Farne Island, to become a persuasive *miraculé* with a story of other worlds? It seems likely that Bartholomew, who was blessing holy water when the boy first rushed into his hermitage trying to say 'Cuthbert, Cuthbert', restored him to speech and then worked with him until between them they had a narrative which explained what had happened. Like the pilgrim of Bemerton and the woman from Devon, Richard gained a sense of who he was by making himself the hero of a familiar old story. Is this so different from the work of a hypnotist who sits nowadays with someone presenting troubled memories, and guides them step by step until they remember the beam of light, the hovering spaceship, the levitation and operating table under the dark watchful gaze of the Greys?

We cannot tell what happened—'really' happened—to these people: even if they were sitting here with us now, we could have no knowledge of such inward experience. But it is clear from parallels in later folklore that texts like the Farne *miracula* keep close, despite the transition to Latin, and despite every temptation to stylistic excess, to the stories told by those struggling to express what they had gone through. Even secondary and tertiary sources can retain something of the original. Lantfred's story from Winchester was versified by Wulfstan for the *Narratio Metrica*, which was afterwards abbreviated for the *Miracula S. Swithuni*, which was in turn summarized for John of Tynemouth's *Sanctilogium*.[43] That's five centuries of copying and boiling down, and yet the story retains its uncanny elements: three terrifying women, a towering figure, the breath that makes a man collapse into illness. Miracles were memorable.

Exempla

In the thirteenth century, *miracula* split into two subgenres: proceedings of inquiries into canonization, which were severely formal in character, and the looser narrative collections produced by particular shrines. The more anecdotal style found in the Miracles of Æbbe and Margaret owes much to another class of writing, the collections of *exempla* or short tales picked out for use in sermons. These were first put together in the 1240s and rapidly increased in number, if not in originality.

It was the Fourth Lateran Council which made collections of *exempla* into must-have handbooks by imposing two duties: the outline of the faith was to be preached to the laity in the vernacular, and they were to make regular confession. Not every parish priest could or would stir up his neighbours to the required pitch of penitence and contrition, and the work increasingly fell on the mendicant orders of friars, Franciscan and Dominican, who fanned out over Europe on preaching tours.

So *exempla* in the friars' sermons stressed the one theme that miracle collections had largely ignored: sinfulness. When the supernatural appears in these tales, it is not a capricious interruption of daily life, but something imposed by eternal agents with a clear didactic purpose, dragging the impenitent hellwards, showering infinite mercy onto those who make full profession of their sins. A miracle story had been so intent on the saint's wonderful intervention in granting a cure that other details, such as a mysterious background story, might be added without bothering whether they were orthodox or not: but an *exemplum* was all story, and the friars who preached them were there to root out unorthodoxy.

In the end it was not doctrinal laxness but sheer avidity for material which weakened authorial control over *exempla*. Collectors trawled with a net so wide that it sometimes caught firsthand reports from friends, family or common gossip: stories which, infrequent as they are in the literature, have the rawness of personal experience. John the clerk is heading through the Staffordshire countryside one night to see a girl. He carries a sword hung round his neck—it says a lot about medieval disorder that, when walking between two villages a mile apart, it was best to go tooled up—and is surprised to see a strange dog walking in front of him, and still more astonished when the dog turns round and says 'Give us that sword, mate.' 'Christ! No!', says hot-tempered John, and hearing the sacred name, the dog vanishes.[44] This was told to the narrator by John himself; another story, attested at one remove by the parson at Edenham, comes from Sir Robert who one Sunday, instead of going to hear said parson preach, galloped off to hunt the Lincolnshire countryside. Soon he saw a hare, which was no earthly hare, as events proved: for it led him further and further from church until, when he shot at it, the illusive thing vanished, while the arrow rebounded through the air and … ripped a nasty hole in Robert's Sunday clothes. The bathetic ending confirms this story has not been worked up much from the initial report.[45]

Very few *exempla* were as close to experience as this, but several betray signs of popular origin. Like the odd tales preserved in *miracula*, they stand out from the more standardized narratives by their failure to toe the clerical line, and the presence of elements found in other accounts of the supernatural. A girl walks out of the house one drowsy summer afternoon, and sees a beautiful woman at the door. With the imperiousness that has characterized her fellows in other stories, the woman commands the girl to eat. She does: now she must obey, and soon the strangers are trying to pull her away. A crowd of people gather; two of them hold the girl's head and two hold her feet and two stretch out on her body to restrain her, but even so she is carried up into the air in full view of them all.[46]

Many another supernatural account must have passed from mouth to mouth before the preachers pinned it down with a Latin moral. The field of story was wide, and friars were not alone in it: jongleurs, *mimi*, *histriones* and gleemen also depended for their living on an extensive repertoire. Sacred or secular, if a folktale seemed memorable, in it went, interrupting the roll-call of godliness with such old friends as the Emperor's New Clothes, the Wise Men of Gotham, the Three Foolish Wishes and Godfather Death.[47] If a preacher had the gift, he could turn the Latin prompt-text into a vividly realized narration; although *exempla* are literary, they show the repetition with variation that characterizes all folklore.

As repetitive as modern joke cycles, *exempla* follow the same rule of painting human nature with a broad brush and clear outlines. Wives: frisky, quick-witted. Peasants: smelly, slow on the uptake. Lawyers: cunning evil bastards. You know where you are with an *exemplum*, but genre expectations like these only work when they are shared between the performer and the crowd. Thirteenth-century audiences clearly had a good idea of what was going to come next; they might even anticipate it in their own stories. The bailiff of Turvey, Co. Dublin, was on the road when he saw a wild creature heading towards him: hideous, indescribable, not of this world. There was no time to run, so he pulled out his axe and cut a circle around himself, notching it with crosses. Closer and closer came the beast. Now his sins weighed heavy on him until one by one he began to confess them to the Lord, and as he did so, the circle grew into a wall, rising up course by course as he acknowledged each sin, until he stood within a little tower, hearing each motion of the fiend-beast as it scrabbled and tore at his fortress. It had just reached the top and was leering down at him when daylight came.[48] That afternoon he came to the friars and told them everything, with full permission to use the story in their preaching. Even after passing through clerical hands, the bailiff's tale still bears signs of its peasant origin, with a magical protective circle cut by a weapon and a very unorthodox method of confession; but these are details in a story which otherwise shares the imaginative world of the preachers.

All the supernatural machinery of *exempla*—visions, curses, instant crushing destinies—went unquestioned within the (perhaps temporary) suspension of belief among people who might have travelled a long way to hear the good man preach. More disquietingly, there is no sign of resistance to the bleak moral vision of these tales. A priest lived with a woman, and she bore him sixteen sons: then died, impenitent to the last. Like good children they all sat up around her bier until at midnight a devil came into the church, stood by the coffin and whistled. She stumbled out and he flung a leg over her, turned her into a mare, and galloped off down the nave to Hell. 'This story a friar told me, who was that whore's son.'[49] You might feel that a man who would tell a story like this about his mother shouldn't be trusted on any subject, in this world or the next: but the audience evidently went along with it. It is true that damnation, if there is to be damnation at all, inflicts infinite penalties for a mundane offence; true, also, that fairytale and fable can be just as unforgiving in the way they hand out justice. But every third or fourth *exemplum* seems to end in a chorus of Serve Them Right. Black dogs appear out of nowhere and carry off a new-born baby, spring up at an old lady and rip out her throat, run down a young man in the woods: as long as these people have been clearly labelled as sinners, the listeners are expected to cheer.[50] If the imaginative world of the late thirteenth and early fourteenth century is truly reflected in *exempla*, then that world was becoming more hostile to those who didn't fit.

The division between saved and damned is paper-thin but knife-sharp, and to make it more vivid the preachers often had recourse to demons, who appear in about 16% of *exempla*. Unlike heretics, who never feature in a story unless they are doomed to endless pain, demons get a grudging respect. They are, as it were, fellow religious professionals and have a legitimate claim to lost souls, even if the Virgin Mary occasionally pulls a fast one in favour of her devotees.

Not less than angel dimmed, these demons often speak of the heaven they have lost, and wonder that humans should pay so little thought to getting there.

Sometimes the unclean spirits speak in their own person, but more often through the mouth of a demoniac. This trope may have some foundation in reality: perhaps clergy, after a lifetime spent studying immaterial spirits, couldn't resist the chance to converse with one in a human vehicle. Once communication was established, with the demoniac functioning as a kind of walking ouija board, lay people were keen to pose questions as well, though the answers could be unexpected. A man speaks (through his human envelope) to the fiend Guinehochet:

> Hey, demon, how many kids have I got?
> Just the one.
> Sucker! There's two waiting for me at home.
> Yes, but you've got just the one. Isn't the priest a regular visitor at your place?
> (Nasty silence.)
> OK, but which one's mine?
> Oh, I'm not telling you *that*. If you don't know which is which, you'll be a good dad to them both.[51]

Promoting family harmony seems rather off-script for a spirit of Hell.[52] With their magpie eye for memorable anecdotes, the friars have thoughtlessly incorporated one where a spirit speaks through the mouth of a possessed (*ylfig?*) person with answers more appropriate to a sardonic oracle than a victim of diabolical attack. *Exempla* are usually more conventional than that. Vivid testimony from the likes of Staffordshire John or the bailiff of Turvey is rare: clichés are the rule. Still these stories, even if understood on both sides of the pulpit as conventional, claim to report real encounters with spirits of another world, and not fictions. Stereotyped though they are, they bear witness to experiences that people thought they could have, one unlucky day.

Charms

The genres we have encountered so far are official, though they can incorporate irregular details. But charms were subversive right from the start, regarded with disfavour even when they were written by clergy—probably because they were written by clergy. They testify to a clerical underground which made its own accommodations with folk learning.

Portable charms against spirits have not survived in large numbers from the Middle Ages, but then children's books from the early modern period are few as well: in both cases they may simply been worn out by rough use. A fourteen-year-old called John was walking near his father's house when he met two women, one in green and one in white. They ran quickly to the boy and snatched away a charm he carried around his neck and hid it in a nearby bramble patch.[53] This sounds like two big kids roughing up a little one, and John reacts in kind, running away and throwing stones at them; but now that he has lost his *breve*, things take a more sinister turn, for these were no ordinary women and as soon as he steps over the threshold of his home, he falls paralysed and dumb, to be cured three days later at Margaret's shrine in Dunfermline. The charm is introduced without remark and you wonder whether *brevia* were as routine in thirteenth-century Scotland as *omamori* are in contemporary Japan.

The word was used for all sorts for small written slips: in this case, pieces with some sacred text or special invocation written on them. Snowball the tailor of Ampleforth must have had a set of these, for when news got about that he was to keep an appointment with a ghost, and his neighbour offered to accompany him, the tailor says: 'If you wish to come with me, let us set off, and I will give you a part of the writings that I carry on me because of night fears.' The neighbour backs out and he has to go alone: by this time there's quite a rapport between him and the ghost, which offers some helpful warnings about the other, worse things that haunt the moor, ending with the advice to keep all his best writings by his head until he goes to sleep.[54]

About fifteen miles away in Ingleby Arncliffe, a parchment strip was found rolled up inside a hollow crucifix; had it not been hidden two hundred years before Snowball's encounter, it could have provided one of his best writings. Secreted like a time capsule in an enamelled crucifix, this has survived where other examples have worn away in clutching hands. *Coniuro uos elphes & demones & omnia genera fantasmatis*, the charm begins, mastering the elves and demons by invoking all the company of heaven, and punctuated by a great many crosses.[55] The formula is common, found in manuscripts of the fourteenth and fifteenth century and reported abroad from Uppsala, Gotland and Heidelberg.[56] This must be a piece of learned lore being passed from one study to another, not translated from the lips of the folk, even though the words were written out each time to serve a popular need.

At its simplest level, a charm was something so holy—or magical—that by its own virtue it kept evil at bay. The sprig of St John's-wort worked like this; so did a pouch containing scraps of Becket's clothing, tucked into the bedclothes of a seven-year-old with night fears. As soon as it fell off, he stared around him screaming 'They're coming to get me', but when it was tied more firmly round his neck the nameless they receded.[57]

Pre-Conquest England had a tradition of narrative charming which relied on powerful stories. Two of these involve the incursions of spirits: the charmer imagined what the *miraculé* experienced, a terrifying outside force breaking into everyday life and causing illness. In *Wið dweorh*, 'Against a Dwarf', the spirit comes creeping in, a bridle in his hand, and rides his victim through the sky: this may be poetic imagery for a fever, but it also suggests that the trope of demons riding souls in the shape of horses, so popular among preachers, did not originate with them but was adapted from earlier stories of spirit possession.[58]

The longest and most enigmatic text is headed in the manuscript *Wið færstice*, usually but not very helpfully translated 'Against a Sudden Stitch'; whatever it is supposed to cure, it was much more serious than what we call a stitch nowadays.[59] You are to begin by simmering herbs in butter. While the feverfew and plantain crackle in the pan, you are to recite (read? or chant from memory?) a long poem. Modern folk charmers usually know verses of from 8 to 12 lines: *Wið færstice* is 26 lines long, suggesting that two or more texts were combined because they had a common theme of shooting and projectiles. The first and longest section concerns mighty women who ride over the hill, sending forth shrieking spears. With a refrain of 'Out little spear, if it be in!' the charmer imagines smiths working on knives or slaughter-spears which will seemingly act as counter-weapons against these riders. Two more lines, perhaps originally an independent couplet, sum up the situation: 'If there is a fragment of iron inside/The work of a *hægtesse*, it shall melt.' Then comes a conventional charming formula which imagines all the things that could be wrong—shot in the fell or skin, shot in the flesh, shot in the blood (at this point an alliterative 'shot in the bone' seems to be missing): in every case, the patient will recover. And next comes another formula of inclusion: whether it were shot of the *esa*, or shot of the *ylfa*, or shot of the *hægtesse*, nevertheless help is on its way. The *ylfa* are elves, in West Saxon spelling; the *esa* were once gods, the *Æsir* of Norse mythology, whatever they are thought to be in this text. The *hægtesse* (pronounced, and in later Old English spelled, *hætse*) are something to do with witches, like German *Hexen*, although that does not in itself tell us whether they are women, or female spirits, or the emanations of sleeping witch-women riding through the land as spirits. In the middle couplet they were definitely the cause of the illness but if the charm is spliced from multiple origins then there is no knowing which of these supernatural forces, if any, is to be identified with the mighty women of the first section. *Wið færstice* is a difficult text; the charmer did not meant it to be easy. It is a song of shrieking, hammering, galloping forces from a paganism already receding beyond the horizon of time.

Fragments survived in later tradition. John Bromyard, condemning superstitions in the early fourteenth century, has hard words for the mothers who chant 'Holy Mary sang over her son, against the sting of elves, and against the sting of men; and she joined bone to bone, and blood to blood, and joint to joint; and so her child grew well'.[60] Here the elves (*alphorum*) have survived, alone of all supernatural terrors, in an inclusion formula which has been coupled with another century-old charm about healing by joining part to part.

Chronicles

Magic and allusion are all very well, but if we want to know what really happened, we should turn to the pages of history. Or so one might hope, and certainly medieval histories describe encounters that come date-stamped with locations and the occasional witness, so that their best tales—Malekin, the stolen cup, the Green Children—have become paradigmatic of medieval fairies, leaving the more prolific *miracula* and *exempla* in the shade.[61]

A compelling story gave the historian a chance to show off his narrative prose and since in chronicles, as in the annals which preceded them, stuff simply happens year after year, it was easy to throw in the occasional supernatural episode. History was a porous genre. It could accommodate shrine miracles, like that of William and the little red man from Thomas Walsingham. It could present tales which belong in spirit to the literature of marvels, as William of Newburgh does. And it could preserve stories which originated as *exempla*, the presumed origin of many anecdotes in the Lanercost Chronicle.

The canons of Lanercost Priory adopted a manuscript originally written by friars, which would explain its popular character. This would also account for their bias against the regular clergy, as in the entry for 1266 telling how Markby Priory went to law against some peasants claiming rights of pasture at Strubby, on the Lincolnshire coast.[62] Judges were bribed and the jurors leaned on heavily until they gave an unjust verdict. The usual indignant voice of a monastic chronicle, you might think, except that in this case the bribers and instigators of perjury were the monks themselves, who ploughed up the land so that their neighbours could no longer graze it. But there is a Judge who takes no bribes, and vengeance is his. Soon one of the jurymen died. Not long after, men saw something like a plough at work on that stolen land; but it was of brass, red hot and glowing. There was the man, tied in the traces and dragging it along the furrow, and every time he slackened, the fiend at the plough handles lashed him on. One by one the false jurors died, and every time a man was carried off, his likeness would join the team, until all twelve were yoked to the burning plough and the whip played on their backs as they staggered and dropped.[63]

I wouldn't have believed it, says the author, until I heard particulars from a certain nobleman, who lived not more than three miles from the place in question. This was how chroniclers got their news, from stories swapped among the landowning elite. Some monastic houses were better networkers than others. Situated on the north road out of London, St Albans heard most of the news of the kingdom, so that Thomas Walsingham had easy access to memories from the parson of far-away Thorpe Bassett. Coggeshall, a small house outside Colchester, was more parochial and most of its stories came from Suffolk and Essex. The more people who saw a prodigy, the better its chances of appearing in the record: hence the historians' fondness for eclipses, sundogs and freak weather. Thousands could have testified to the storm that devastated Yorkshire in 1165, and many of them also apparently witnessed the shape like a giant black horse that raced across the land, with lightning lashing his flanks, to leap into the sea at Scarborough after leaving huge footprints in the castle ditch.[64]

Dating storms was easy but other events resisted straightforward chronology. Walsingham placed William Wynfeld's misadventures under the year when they began, in 1343. By contrast the Lanercost Chronicle waited twenty-three years after the original trial before inserting the story of the perjured jurors, presumably to make sure that the full damned ploughteam had been despatched by divine vengeance (or average life expectancy). Though chronicles were compiled year by year, like a glacially slow newspaper, it was not always wise to insert a portent as soon as it happened. What if it turned out not to portend anything? The Peterborough recension of the *Anglo-Saxon Chronicle* vividly records the dark goat-riders, great and loathsome, with their glaring-eyed black dogs, who rampaged through parkland and woodland at the beginning of February 1127 when Henry of Poitou was made abbot.[65] What could it mean? As events were to prove, not a lot: far from being slung over a black saddle and carried off to the darkness appointed for Norman prelates, the domineering Henry remained in office for another five years.

Portentousness was still a problem three centuries later, when a chronicler segues from the *gret hot somere* of 1473, when wheat withered in the grain and harvesters dropped dead among the stooks, to the gush of Womere water, always a sign of dearth and pestilence. This Womere can be seen at Markyate in Hertfordshire, the author tells us, and is a predictive stream like those at Lewisham, Croydon, Dudley Castle, Langley Park and the Kentish Nailbourne.

He'd certainly done his homework. Further enquiries produced the apparition of a headless man on Dunsmore Heath who, as forty witnesses could testify, overcame his disability to shout 'Bowes, bowes, bowes!'.[66] This terrifying climax leaves us in no doubt that, after twenty years of insurrection and fratricidal war, forces in this world and the next are massing for some final horror.

Except that 1474 was in fact followed by a decade of tranquillity, which is why the chronicler prudently broke off writing at that year. We never even find out what the apparition meant by 'Bowes, bowes, bowes'.[67] Maybe he's been misquoted; after all, the chronicler gets the name of the heath wrong, and can only locate the spot vaguely between Leicester and Banbury, towns which are fifty miles apart. Forebodings of doom were more important than accurate transcription or an exact match between prophecy and politics.[68]

So did chroniclers set down rumours and memorates more or less as they heard them? Or were they artfully selecting, composing and adapting them to create overall significance for their work? Trained in exegesis, the monks of Peterborough desperately wanted the black riders to be a divine judgement rather than what they really were, a random inscrutable marvel; and, at a literary rather than a literal level, we hope for the same from the headless man of Dunsmore and the wild man of Orford and the apparitions who fought so horribly beside the road from Bedford to Biggleswade. We are so accustomed to books with a unified structure and meaning that, faced with the formlessness of medieval narrative, we read their histories as a conspiracy theorist reads events, taking the absence of overt purpose as proof that there must be some subtle concealed plan. But maybe there isn't.

The chroniclers treated history casually, sometimes even telling the same story twice. In 1337 Joan from Kingsley in the deanery of Alton, diocese of Winchester, had a lovely dream about meeting her boyfriend William in the woods. Next day she found an excuse to go wandering in the glades of Woolmer Forest. There he was, and everything went just as she'd dreamed. Tired but happy, Joan drifts back to the village that evening, and sees William just outside his house—that's a bit odd—and he asks where she's been because he's been looking for her all day—that's very, very strange. Joan turns pale when she realizes what she met in the woods and what she was doing with … it. She screams, confesses everything, and after three days of suffering which fill the house with an indescribable stench and swell up her body in black putrefaction, she dies. And eight strong men could hardly support the weight of her coffin as they took it to the graveyard.[69]

That sounds like useful historical testimony to supplement the more impressionistic accounts of demon lovers in miracles and *exempla*; Walsingham certainly thought so, since he included the story in his *Historia*, following the capture of a two-headed fawn in the same Forest of Woolmer. But he uncritically repeats what is obviously the same story—well, it's about a Joan in the deanery of Alton, diocese of Winchester, village of Headley, which is just a mile down the road from Kingsley, and it doesn't seem likely that there were two. Joan II does not have a misadventure in the woods. Instead, she stands up at the end of a revivalist sermon and makes a clean break of her sins before all her neighbours, confessing that from childhood onwards she's devoted her body to lust and unspeakable vice. She does penance, pours out her soul in prayers, and dies just as the Host is being elevated. Either story would pass muster as a miracle, but the two of them cancel each other out as evidence.

Strange phenomena cluster together; William of Newburgh has two sections devoted to them, and Ralph of Coggeshall has one. Each story suggested the next, so that William, having described the cult of the pseudo-martyr William fitz Osbert, moves on to the walking dead because they are another kind of body being treated wrongly by the living, while Ralph follows the wild man of Orford and the girl-spirit Malekin with the mysteries of the Publicani, who being heretics are also a sort of monster.[70]

Ralph tells us that Malekin was witnessed—heard, to be precise—by everyone in the household of Osbern at the manor of Dagworth, just outside Stowmarket.[71] She spoke English to the family but Latin to the chaplain, although as she is also said to have had the language skills of a one-year-old, presumably they had to fill in a lot of the sense. Though only ten years and twenty-five miles intervene between event and chronicler, there have been breaks in communication, as apparently the knight's name was Osbert, not Osbern.[72] Malekin was only a voice except to one favoured servant girl, who saw her as a child in white. Her story fuses two traditions: that of the sharp-witted household spirit, which has analogues in other medieval sources, and that of the girl abducted by the fairies, for which parallels can be found only in later material. Her captivity for seven years, her need to eat human rather than fairy food, the punishments that await her for consorting with mortals—these are all attested in more recent tradition. She was taken by the others, *alii*, when her mother took her out into the fields and left her unprotected during the dinner hour; this is the traditional opening to a changeling tale, but Malekin does not otherwise resemble the classic changeling.

Her identity is ambiguous. At one point she is a human child taken from her mother in the fields at Lavenham; at another, a spirit living with her spirit mother and brother in a neighbouring manor. Maybe the various tale types had not yet become set traditions, perhaps Ralph failed to understand what was obvious to the household at Dagworth, or maybe we should be careful of taking such creatures at their word. In the spring of 1397 a spirit arrived at a widow's house near Bedford, invisible but conversational. She—they? it?—introduced herself as the woman's stillborn daughter, who had been buried under a tree in the garden many years ago, and now came to bring her mother news of eternal damnation.[73] 'Get lost', said the widow, 'I've confessed and done penance for all that business': she had a good grasp of theology, says the annalist, for a laywoman and a country girl. Having failed to induce existential despair, the spirit settled down and joined the household. She was particularly fond of her presumed brother, a priest but a rather irregular one who spent most of his time hunting. 'You really shouldn't waste your time like that', said the disembodied voice, quite forgetting that she was supposed to be advancing the cause of evil: 'it's shocking, the careless way you say Mass.' She gave advice, repeated prayers on request, and shifted beer-barrels in the cellar like a regular poltergeist.[74] This went on for three years, so there was every opportunity to put her existence to the test.

Oral testimony from a person of knightly rank who was in a good position to know what was going on: that was the gold standard for medieval historians.[75] Malekin qualifies, and so do the Green Children, who uniquely appear in two separate histories, giving us a chance to see how knowledge was circulated.[76] First, Ralph of Coggeshall. He was told about the children by Richard de Calne, who held the manor of Wykes in Bardwell; Richard died in 1187, so conversations with him and his family must date before then. Ralph began work on the chronicle late in his time at Coggeshall Abbey, writing the section which includes the supernatural appearances in about 1205.[77] His account is therefore written from conversations twenty years ago, themselves remembering events thirty or forty years before. It was high summer in the village of Woolpit which (like Dagworth) is a few miles outside Stowmarket. The harvesters were surprised to find two children near the pits, a boy and a girl. Their skin was green, a rich dark green; they were crying inconsolably; when they tried to talk, no-one could understand them. The villagers led them off to Wykes, about eight miles away, and presented them to Sir Richard. Though the children were obviously famished, they refused all food, until someone brought in some freshly mown beanstalks. They gestured for these, and broke open the stalks, looking for food; when they could find nothing they burst out crying again; at last someone showed them how to open the pods and they glutted themselves on the beans, not eating anything else for a long time. Soon after, the boy died, but the girl recovered her health, was weaned onto an ordinary diet, and gradually lost her green colour. She learnt English and would talk about the place she and the boy had come from. Everything there was green, and there was no sun, only a kind of twilight. They had been looking after the animals when they found a cave and started to explore it, following the sound of bells, until they came out at the far end. The light was so bright and the air so hard that it knocked them into a swoon and they knew nothing until they saw the harvest people coming towards them.

The account in William of Newburgh is close to this, so close that there must be a shared text: no two oral deliveries would present the curious detail about the beans and stalks in exactly the same way. William began work on the *Historia Rerum Anglicarum* in 1196 and died some three years later.[78] That leaves time for draft notes from Essex to make their way to Yorkshire. Coggeshall was a Cistercian house—so was Byland near Newburgh, a foundation where William had friends and patrons—and the Cistercians had meetings for joint management of their individual foundations, as well as being interested in strange stories. William keeps close to the primary narrative; he leaves out information of purely local interest such as Richard and his house, provides background for what is not obvious to outsiders like the location of Woolpit, and adds details such as the name of the country from which the children came—St Martin's Land. The two accounts vary most when it comes to the information given by the girl, and since William speaks of evidence from many reliable witnesses, it seems that he had access to other accounts of what she had said, a remarkable level of interest for what might have been thought a local story.

Medieval channels of communication were evidently capable of transmitting a story 150 miles without its accuracy being much compromised—'accuracy' of course giving us not what happened but what Richard de Calne and the Green Girl *said* had happened. Much effort has been put into countering the facile assumption that this is a fairy story. Green is not always and everywhere a signifier for the otherworld and the children were certainly flesh and blood; the girl was remembered as a housemaid who was inclined to talk back and flirt with the menservants, and ended up marrying a man from Kings Lynn and leaving the neighbourhood.

And yet there is a curious air of enchantment hanging over the whole story, with its forever twilight and coloured land, its underground realms and distant melody of bells. If it belongs with stories of supernatural encounter, it does so in a strange, looking-glass way.[79] Here are two children; in our stories, encounters are often remembered as experiences in childhood. The Green Children were taking care of their parents' livestock; in our stories, children who go to sleep while pasturing sheep or cattle are most at risk. The Children were struck senseless by the sunshine (Ralph) or the sound of bells (William);

in our stories, supernatural encounter leads to swooning and paralysis. They tried to get away from the harvesters; our victims attempt to run from their attackers but are chased or ridden down. They were brought, like it or not, to the nearest elite household; our captives are taken to the palace of some strange king. They refuse to eat our food; we have traditions forbidding us to eat fairy food. It all adds up to a story of abduction but told from the perspective of spirits in the world of mortals, and not vice versa. How the story should come to be told like that is one of the mysteries of this perpetually mysterious case.

Wonder Stories

Complementary in so many ways, Ralph of Coggeshall and William of Newburgh take sharply different approaches when presenting the Green Children. For Ralph, their story is simply an entertaining curiosity, following unusual experiences with a wild man caught off Orford Ness and preceding by a few years the mysterious Knights Templar who arrived at Coggeshall Abbey and vanished from a room with no other exit while dinner was getting ready.[80] But William worried over it, a lot.[81] *Hesitavi*, he says, but 'finally I was so overwhelmed by the weighty testimony of so many reliable people that I was compelled to believe what I cannot grasp or investigate by any powers of the mind'.[82]

William's doubts, though not all his anxieties, were shared by a small group of scholars writing about *mirabilia* in the decades on either side of 1200. None of the others were historians. The versatile pen of Gerald of Wales was mostly directed to topography, Gervase of Tilbury adapted encyclopaedic tradition to the (presumably low) boredom threshold of emperor Otto IV, while Walter Map was writing largely for himself, though if *De Nugis Curialium* had been edited for general circulation it would have followed the genre of courtly literature. All three were something like professional writers, or raconteurs. Gerald's delivery of the *Topographia Hibernica* at Oxford culminated in a three-day reading, the like of which was not remembered in any age—at least according to Gerald, who may be less reliable on this subject than he is with prophets and poltergeists.[83]

William, an Augustinian canon who never got out much, is the odd man in this company. But he shares their interest in marvels, not just as stories, but as events. All four broke new ground by asking themselves and their readers whether these things were true—and by truth they meant not theological congruity, edifying significance, or value as portents: they wanted to know whether they had actually happened. And if so, how?

Against the grain of previous thought, these writers turned from subjective experience to think about objective reality. *Mira*, the sensation of wonder—as Gervase is careful to explain—can be elicited by two classes of event. *Miracula* are the direct operation of God, but *mirabilia* happen in the course of nature; their marvellousness is not intrinsic but comes from novelty, or rarity, or our ignorance of how they came to happen.[84] But the path of understanding was set with man-traps. Augustine, the prime source for these distinctions, is adamant that when things arouse *mira*, and look like *miracula*, and yet are produced from outside the faith, then they are the deceptions of demons.

Hence the anxieties which beset William of Newburgh. He was writing to record events, including marvellous ones; he knew, as well as we do, that they stood outside the regular course of nature; but he did not intend to be the dupe of evil spirits. He tells the story of the countryman who rode past an ancient burial mound, heard singing and revelry and saw a bright spacious house in the barrow.[85] How the revellers offered him a cup, how he spilled out the contents and put his horse to the gallop, and how escaping pursuit he kept the cup, of unknown material and strange form: these were all matters of record, but William is still uneasy about those revellers in the hill, who sound to him very much like illusion and magic. At any rate the cup was real, and even then it might not have found a place in the *Historia* had it not provided analogical support for the Green Children, who were clearly no phantoms, however anomalous their arrival in Suffolk.[86] So it is by the closest of shaves that we possess the earliest record of an international migratory legend.[87]

'Let us return to the regular thread of history' says William with some relief, after devoting ten chapters to the antics of ambulatory corpses in the North of England.[88] Stories pulled him one way, doctrine another. It was different with Gerald of Wales, who was a writer first and foremost, and would gladly have gossiped with a devil if there was copy to be made out of the interview. The closest he came to this was the house of Stephen Wiriet in Pembrokeshire, haunted by poltergeists who threw things around, ripped clothes, and addressed visitors to reveal the secrets they would have preferred not to go public. Gerald was mystified. They were unclean spirits, he'd guessed that; what was puzzling him was the nature of their game.

Meilyr the prophet was another conundrum. No doubt a man who spends most of his leisure time with demons is risking a bad end, and Gerald says as much: having been assured by them that he would survive the siege of Usk, the soothsayer died of wounds, and that's how the common enemy of man rewards his friends. But after this perfunctory tag Gerald gets down to what really interests him: how did Meilyr, a man, see spirits? If it was because they had assumed corporeal form, how come he saw them but no one else in the room did? If they were invisible, then was he aware of them 'by some supernatural sort of physical vision'? Meilyr's story is rounded off by these physical or paraphysical questions which evidently mattered much more to him, and his prospective audience, than the spiritual issues raised by a man who socialized on equal terms with fiends and monks.[89]

In another story, Gerald presents an elusive Otherworld with no moral condemnation at all. When he was twelve years old, Elidyr ran away from school and while looking for somewhere to hide he met two small men, no bigger than pygmies. They offered to take him to a land where it was always playtime, which he accepted with delight: after going down a long dark tunnel they came to a beautiful country, where there was neither sun nor moon but an overcast light. Elidyr was taken to the king, who was amazed to see him and appointed him companion to his son. There were many pathways from that secret world back to this, and Elidyr came and went, but revealed himself only to his mother. He told her everything about the country, how fine the people were, how they valued truth above everything else and despised the lies of the human world, how gold was as common there as pebbles here. His mother listened attentively and asked if he could bring her a souvenir. When he was next at play with the prince, Elidyr scooped up the golden ball and ran away with it, followed by the little people in hot pursuit. As he came home he fell panting over the doorstep and the ball slipped out of his hand. Two little men took it back from him, showing every sign of scorn and derision: he was left to think over what he'd done, and when he went back there was no sign of the secret tunnel, though Elidyr searched again and again.[90]

It is a wonderfully child-like story. The land of play, the little friends even smaller than yourself, the innocent egotism (*of course* their king would be amazed by you and make you special), the easy elision from scenes of wonder to mam in her parlour, the stern moral admonition and the hot shame when it is broken: all these suggest a nursery tale.[91] But that is not the version we hear: like Richard of Sunderland's abduction or the attempted seduction of the woman from Devon, the folktale comes to us within the story of a life. This land of gold and dim light is a wonderful picture, but what sticks in memory is the young boy running down to the bank, battering at the rock for weeks and weeks in search of the tunnel that will take him back to where everything was kind. Eventually Elidyr returned to school, knuckled down to work, got a living as a priest, and grew old; but he could never tell this story without bursting into tears.

And this account itself is nested, like a set of Chinese boxes, within Gerald's efforts to make rational sense of it. He never heard Elidyr directly, getting his account from an uncle who was bishop of St David's, so the fragments of speech that he had learned from the little people have a rather suspect transmission: but their term for 'salt' was cognate with those in with the other seven languages that he knew, which suggested it was a real word. And geography could be brought to the aid of philology. When he retells the story, Gerald has Elidyr coming and going 'from our hemisphere', implying that the little people lived in the other hemisphere, the Antipodes.[92] Gervase makes the same assumption when he tells of a swineherd getting lost in the passages that lead from the Peak Cavern, and coming out amongst wide cultivated fields; it was July in that land, though it had been winter when he set out from Derbyshire.[93] The facts about the inversion of seasons on the far side of the world were known to medieval scholars, although 6000 miles seems a long way to go in search of a lost pig. But then these stories were never meant to stand up to critical scrutiny—Gerald places Elidyr's account 'among those which cannot be rejected out of hand and yet which I cannot accept with any real conviction'. What mattered was the freedom to pass on a narrative without being accused of complicity with demons.

Fairies gave space to think about things being different. Elidyr's little people were lovers of truth who 'had no wish for public worship'—a challenging concept for 1191. Imagine no religion! But they came from a realm where much could be supposed and nothing had to be accepted, which made it alright.[94] Gerald, like Walter Map, was of mixed Welsh and English blood and both of them liked to locate their marvels just over the edge of the Anglo-Norman state, where rules were relaxed.

Gervase was an Englishman abroad, amusing a Holy Roman Emperor for whom his father's homeland had a touch of the exotic. Neither man spoke English and much was lost in translation, but the charm of distance has preserved some peasant lore which nobody bothered to record in its country of origin.[95] According to Gervase, the spirits called *neptuni* in France are *portuni* in England. The French name is a standard Latinization of *nuiton*, the modern *lutin*, but no-one knows what original is represented by the dictionary-word *portunus*: the nearest guess is Middle English *pouke*, reflex of *pūca*.[96] Whatever they were called, the *portuni* were tiny old men, wrinkled and clothed in rags, appearing at night beside the embers of the fire on which they delighted to roast frogs. Inside the house, they carried out useful tasks in the manner of a brownie; outdoors they could be more of a nuisance, though they never hurt anyone. They would wait at night by the roadside until a traveller rode past and then invisibly seize the reins and lead the horse into the mud, which sent them into fits of laughter.[97]

The same behaviour was witnessed by a Yorkshireman called Ketell, from Farnham near Knaresborough. After his horse had stumbled and thrown him, he looked closely at the road and noticed two little spirits laughing their heads off. From that day onwards he had the gift of seeing their kind, and built up quite a local reputation; with time he took on some of the trappings of a hermit—single, vegetarian, devout—but unlike Godric or Bartholomew he kept the day job, working for an unbeneficed clergyman in the village. Like Meilyr he maintained a running dialogue with these spirits, which took the form of Aethiopians, some large and hurtful, some little and none too bright; Ketell reported them all as demons, but he may have tailored what he saw for a clerical audience.[98] Gervase takes a kindlier view of the *portuni*. After describing them as demons, who in the usual way have cloaked themselves in bodies of condensed air, he changes tack and says 'though I admit I do not know whether I should call them demons, or mysterious apparitions of unknown origin'.[99] This interpretation—with a prudent *nescio*, in case the theologians come sniffing—is as close as any of our writers come to admitting a separate class of supernatural beings, neither angelic nor demonic.

This was, as far as we can tell, the popular notion: the terminology of *ælf* and *dweorg*, *pūca* and *þyrs*, would have been pointless if there had not been a race or races corresponding to these words. This folk taxonomy was neither simple nor naïve. It was and remains the standard Islamic explanation for *djinn* and down to the seventeenth century maverick clerics hoped to smuggle it into Christian thought.[100] But when medieval thinkers felt unhappy with a hard binary of angels and devils, most claimed that the spirits of popular belief really were demons, as the Church taught, only demons who weren't too bad. In a later passage Gervase, belatedly realizing that a book stuffed full of fauns, follets, duses, strigas and dracs called for some kind of pneumatology, repeats the orthodox Augustinian position that they are all spirits of damnation but then in the last paragraph concedes that fairy mistresses may be spirits 'whose pride was less grievous'.[101]

Walter Map explored the theme further with two short stories in romance style. One retells the magical career of Gerbert (Pope Sylvester II) as an affair with the spirit Meridiana, who is not as innocent as she seems; the other is the story of young Eudo, apparently a fiction of Map's.[102] Eudo has wasted his patrimony and is mooching around in a wood when a demon accosts him. He's much relieved to hear that Olga (so his new friend is called) isn't a bad demon, just one of the playful ones who love tricks and illusions: like the *portuni* 'we can do anything that makes for laughter, but nothing that makes for tears'. To prove his point, Olga tells an anecdote about his friend Morpheus who got a painter out of trouble, even though the artist had depicted him horribly. Eudo cheers up, does homage, and is promised three signs of his approaching end.

Given limitless resources, he goes rapidly to the bad, killing and burning with a company of ne'er-do-wells. Olga reappears as an angel of light and advises Eudo to think of his end, which is announced by the promised signs; he throws himself at the feet of the local bishop, who says that his crimes deserve no penance less than throwing himself into a raging fire, which he does without question.

In short, a very moral story: or is it? While making all the proper doctrinal noises, Map presents us with a plot and actors very much at variance with them. Eudo is not the victim of temptation but a mean little thug who starts killing and plundering as soon as he is able to do so. The bishop is not a healing influence but a bigot who refuses to engage with a desperate penitent. The only character to come out well is Olga the demon, who delivers everything he promised without equivocation, including the three signs, and comes to warn Eudo that he's gone too far and should think of his soul before he falls into despair.

So the story's content subverts its frame, and not accidentally.[103] Walter is guying up the traditional sermon-demon: his tale of Morpheus deliberately scrambles two *exempla* so that the fiend ends up in a role normally reserved for the Virgin Mary. There wasn't much that Walter did take seriously. He was a funny, catty retailer of gossip, the sort of person who gets everyone laughing with waspish anecdotes about your friends and who you know will tell one about you as soon as you're out of the room. An assiduous follower of the royal court (he said he hated it, of course) Walter was in a position to hear all sorts of *mirabilia* when the aristocracy exchanged reminiscences. He describes the elfin brides of Edric Wilde, Gwestin Gwestiniog and Henno *cum dentibus*, he tells of women returned to life from fairy abduction in England and Brittany, he thrills you with the walking dead of Herefordshire and Worcestershire, but there is no moral, it is all table talk rounded off with 'and aren't the works of the Lord marvellous' before he retails some royal gossip or a dirty joke about monks.

If there is one common denominator for the stories in Gervase, Gerald and Walter, it is class; they feature kings, earls, emperors, bishops and the occasional knight. These sources moved in circles far removed from the tale-spinning of the village soothsayer or the cures of pauper cripples. And yet there are continuities. Osbert Fitz Hugh rode into Cambridge one winter night. This was in the 1130s so there was no university then, but the town had a castle, and it would have been within its keep, or in some other wealthy and noble setting, that he sat beside a blazing fire while the cup went round and stories were told. Tales like that of Wandlebury, the ruined fort where, if a man was brave enough to ride by night in silence, and pass through the gap alone in the moonlight, and cry 'Knight to knight, come forth!'—why, then he sees another knight come mounted and armed for fight, heading to him at full charge. And they fight, and one of them falls, or the other.

'Enough!', shouted Osbert, determined to do, not hear. He called for a squire who knew the country, ordered the servants to bring his mail coat and great horse, and set off. They rode to the hill and Osbert left his squire waiting, passed through the rampart, and shouted the words. From the shadows came the other knight at a gallop, lance against lance. But their horses slipped on frosty ground, and the lethal points passed harmlessly by; as he passed shoulder to shoulder with his adversary, Osbert saw his chance and struck a blow, so that the other fell down from the saddle. And when Osbert took the reins of the strange horse, as victors do, his enemy reached for the lance, and hurled it at him, where it pierced his thigh. But Osbert called his squire and rode back to the castle, the two of them and the horses; he made light of the wound, though his leggings were stiff with blood. Everyone in town was woken by the commotion and crowded round the strange horse, with its proud high neck, fierce eye and shining black coat. They stood wondering until the first break of day, when the cocks crow, and at that the strange horse broke out of the groom's hold and vanished from amongst them. Then Osbert rode away and never returned; but every year, on the same night that he had fought his fight, the wound that was healed would open again, and he would bleed as much as he did before.[104]

This is a knight's story, as surely as that of Elidyr was a child's. The feasting in hall, the tales as wonderful as any Christmastide *aventure* at the court of King Arthur, and the hero's readiness to ride against his uncanny adversary: this is in the spirit of romance, and also of rivalry. Osbert was a stranger in town, perhaps keen to prove he wasn't the sort to be spooked by a fireside tale. But although the action is couched in chivalric language, it fits the wider template of supernatural encounters. Osbert is attacked by something galloping down on him, like the Dunfermline teenager; pierced by the spear of a black rider, like the cautionary figures in *exempla*; wounded by a supernatural missile, like the man with a sudden stitch.[105] Out little spear, if it be in! If this were a charm, its drumming chant would have sung the missile free from Osbert's leg; if it were a miracle story, he would have suffered terribly from his recurring wound at shrine after shrine till healing came. Instead he gritted his teeth and set off for the Second Crusade, a pilgrimage of another kind, from which he did not return.

Some four decades had passed since that winter night when Gervase, who seems to have originally heard the tale from Osbert's family, had it confirmed by people in Cambridge.[106] That is plenty of time for the narrative impulse to work on the original events: nevertheless, they were events, not a legend, and that is how they were presented. Gervase is at pains to point out that the squire, who was a local, could see the combat from outside the earthworks, and that the fierce black horse was viewed by most of the town. Modern writers routinely exaggerate the time-depth of these stories.[107] When William of Newburgh says that he has known about the theft of the fairy cup 'from my childhood', it is easy to imagine the tale being passed down generation after generation in the valley of the Gypsey Race, with little William listening spellbound to the old lore. But that's not what he is saying. The story goes with the cup; they need each other, and both must have been presented at the same time to Henry I, who then gave the mysterious vessel to David I of Scotland, which means it came on the royal exchange market between 1124 and 1135. William was born in 1136, so he is not telling ancient tradition but recording, as he says 'an extraordinary event' which was still recent gossip while he was growing up. In the late 1180s—while Henry II was still alive, and a few years before work began on the *Historia* in 1196—William I of Scotland gave the cup back, prompting new interest in the story.[108] Of course the tale-type was earlier, but we can't expect William to have known that. What we do know is that prior to 1124, nobody was walking past Duggleby or Willy Howe and saying 'That's the barrow where they stole the fairy cup', and then a few years afterwards everyone was doing just that because of something that had happened—or, to follow William's wise caution in dealing with the anomalous, because somebody had described something that they said had happened to them.

These descriptions have been our quarry in the long chase through courtly tradition and histories, sermon stories, saints' lives and miracle collections: each genre with its own bias of presentation and selection, but all of them willing, under proper conditions, to report what people actually said. The irregular supernatural found its way into the written record by many routes. Sometimes it came through respect, born of legal training, for witness testimony; sometimes deference to the favoured anecdotes of high-ranking laymen; and sometimes, surely, there were writers who just gave up. The local scribe, faced with fading light and congealed ink, trying to translate from an unfamiliar dialect to an imperfectly mastered language, can be forgiven for not tailoring his production to the best theological standards. And he was curious. Something strange had happened and he wants us to know what it was.

The voice of experience, when we can make it out over the static of literary convention, betrays an unexpected fluidity not just across genres but between separate supernatural taxonomies. As encountered, spirits turn out to have much in common with each other, and it is to these cross-genre themes that we now turn.

CHAPTER THREE

Inconstant Shapes

Company

Whatever context framed them, there are common themes in the accounts of those who met fairies—using 'fairy' less as a definition than as shorthand for experiences that resisted shoehorning into any other category. They were, for instance, liable to appear in threes. Richard of Sarum encountered three men in white on the road over the Wiltshire Downs. Walter Barker of Luton was thrown into terror by the three men who rushed angrily at him, so much so that he lost his mind. The young priest's clerk at Taunton was also terrified, enough to run panicking through a wood, but three women caught up with him and threw him down in paralysis. The citizen of Winchester was accosted by three women in the water meadows and though spared the worst of their attack, he too was left paralysed by the encounter.[1]

The group of three usually breaks down into two plus one. The centre figure of the Richard's trio was the tallest, and the only one to speak to him. Character is much more sharply demarcated in the Winchester story, where the first two women are foul black creatures, naked and aggressive, while the third is taller (again), pale, and wearing freshly laundered white clothes. She turns away the dark Furies, bent on destroying him herself.[2] Likewise there was a dissenter among the trio of supernatural women remembered by Mutinus. As he lay asleep in the fields, they approached him, ready to carry him off: two agreed that he should be killed, but the third proposed instead to throw into his mouth the apple which would condemn him to perpetual silence.[3] Mutinus was only 5, so that the three women are in effect forecasting the rest of his life. They are performing the work of the Norns or Fates, who in France would become *fatas* and ultimately *fées*, the dispensers of destiny in fairytale.

These stories are full of alternations between kindness and cruelty. The apparitions to Reinburgis begin with a splendid *virago* who strikes her so the blood flows from her nose, then goes away without speaking. A week later the noble lady returns, clad in white garments, to tell Reinburgis that she has not fully recovered and needs more treatment. The lady then touches and opens up her side, pushes her arm in up to the elbow and touches her heart, three times. Then she closes up the point of entry with an ointment, and orders her patient to go immediately and give thanks at Ely. When the girl points out that it's not as easy as that, the lady falls into a rage and says that as Reinburgis has refused to go, she must suffer further: her right eye shall be twisted awry, which she does by pulling the eyelashes. Another week goes by and the lady appears once more—'I have returned again to you in person, being worried about you'— when along comes another mannish woman, short and bad-tempered, who demands that Reinburgis be punished for her failure to carry out orders. The short angry woman plunges a nail into Reinburgis' head, between eye and brain and disappears, when immediately the lady lets a drop of healing liquid fall on the iron nail and pulls it out. 'Now', she says, 'you *must* go and give thanks at Ely, the destined place for your final healing.'[4]

This *virago* oscillates between angry violence and loving concern, like the bad mother of the psychologists, until two weeks into the vision-sequence she splits altogether into two characters, a tall caring woman and a short grumpy one. The kindly supernatural can furnish humans with the lore that enables them to withstand frightening attacks, as with the harsh and pleasant demons who met the woman of Devon and led her to the protective powers of St John's-wort.[5] One inflicts, the other takes away—the same duality that we find in the charms. *Wið dweorh* opens with the spirit preparing to ride its victim, in a kind of possession equivalent to fever; but before this can take effect, the sister of this creature walks in and swears oaths that bind the *dweorg* from doing further mischief.[6]

Females

Often a charm assures us that a supernatural figure, usually a female one, has been bound or coerced not to hurt human beings who use it. In a medieval charm for *the nygthe-mare*, George goes searching for *þat fowle wygth* and beats and binds her until she promises not to approach any who invoke his name.[7] Here the nightmare is female; the distorted reference in Shakespeare to 'the night-mare, and her nine-fold' implies that she has a family, or at any rate companions.[8] So did the *theomacha*, the foe of God who pursued a deacon through a vast forest somewhere in South Wales. The deacon's story is close to that of the clerk at Taunton: he hears a noise, runs in terror through the woods, and is then brought down by a supernatural woman who leaves him almost dead on the ground, only to make a gradual recovery. When Samson—for this story comes from his *Life*—commands the woman to halt and tell her story, she turns out to come from a family with eight sisters, a nine-fold who live in this forest and in another yet more remote. Mysteriously, she says 'I was made over to this wilderness by my husband, and my husband is dead, and because of that I cannot withdraw from this wood.' In some sense she is an exile in the wasteland, a living person—at least until Samson commands her, if she does not repent, to meet her end and she drops down dead.[9] But you wouldn't expect an elderly lady, even one reduced to refugee status, to sprint after clergymen stabbing them with a blood-dripping trident; this text—the earliest supernatural encounter that we know—is already uncertain about the status of such a being, for her behaviour is that of a spirit of waste places, as malignant a foe of the human race as Grendel's mother: who, it should be remembered, was also a physical, mortal being with family connections.

Grendel's mother was a *mihtig wīf,* in a phrase which appears only once more in Old English to describe the company of *Wið fǣrstice,* apparently the same as the unnamed 'they' who ride loudly over the mound, over the land.[10] Like these riders, the woman in the *Life of Samson* carries a threatening stabbing weapon: she is old and ugly with shaggy grey hair. The two black women who threatened the Winchester townsman—'naked to their foul skin and terrifying with their swarthy hair'—may have been worked up for a clerical sensibility but their hideousness is unlikely to have been invented by Lantfred, since he says nothing pejorative about the looks of the other tall woman in shining white.

Just as ugly are the women seen in dreams. Reginald of Durham has a long story about a young man from Norway who, after going on what sounds like a monumental student bender, woke up and told his friends about a dream in which he saw an elderly woman, blacker than soot. She twisted his head in her hands and wrenched it round so his face was looking down the back of his neck, while with her left hand she struck him three times. After this he was afflicted by a shaking of the head, slowly followed by swelling in the throat and loss of voice until he was deaf, blind and mute: and so the story proceeds to his cure.[11]

But the younger a witness, the more likely they were to engage with supernatural women as if they were care-givers. Mutinus was nursed, after a fashion, by the three women who vacillated between giving him death or dumbness: 'What shall we do with this little man? Where shall we take him?'[12] The boy at Thornton Abbey was gathered out of his bed, like a sleepyhead being bundled up for a journey, and carried as far as the door by two women, who apparently finding they could go no further stopped and squeezed his throat until he was dumb.[13] A six-year-old in Fifeshire (he was a Gael, *Scoticus nacione*) was out tending sheep, like Mutinus, when he fell asleep. It was a hot day and he'd got thirsty, such a dreadful thirst that it filled his thoughts, even while he was asleep, and he was glad when four women approached and gave him a drink. He drank and drank, only to find he could not stop, even though his body was distended, and on waking he found a swelling in the throat that blocked his voice. Sixteen years of silence followed until he came to the shrine at Coldingham and saw a lovely bird that flew from the tomb to the altar, and from the altar to his side, turning into the blessed Æbbe and touching his mouth. Running out of the church, he threw up and threw up until the swelling had vanished and he was able to speak again, for the good mother had reversed the work of the bad ones.[14]

The image of the strong otherworldly female is so powerful that it spills over into other genres where the figures are not meant to be malicious at all: the *virago* and angry woman who appeared to Reinburgis were servants of Æthelthryth, but they gave her a hard time for all that. At Minster-in-Thanet, the festival of the translation of Mildthryth saw the abbot providing blessings and a good spread for the locals. After doing justice to this feast, Brihtric the steward bedded down in the abbot's lodgings. That night he dreams of a maiden of glorious appearance and shining garments, who gives him a kick and asks him what he thinks he's doing, to which he answers that he's actually the man in charge. She gives him a nasty look and says that so far her guardianship has been sufficient for both abbey and island, and he's not much of a substitute, seeing as he was asleep and she wasn't. And with that she gives him a hard slap on the face, and her hand burns. That wakes him up, and throwing a cloak around him he runs like someone crazy, into the church, through the psalm-singers in the choir, to prostrate himself at the tomb of Mildthryth and pray for forgiveness. 'Are you mad?' asks the abbot. Brihtric shows the burn-mark on his jaw and tells how he got it. 'That's what happened', he says, 'and though I wasn't mad, by Heaven I was terrified.'[15]

Taken from its pious context, this could be any story of an otherworldly woman inflicting injuries. This time it was Mildthryth herself maintaining standards at her shrine, but hagiography is littered with masterful females whose identity is never made clear: the lovely lady who left scorch marks on the holy man of Bemerton, the strange queen in Christina's vision at Dunfermline, the beautiful pilgrim who joined Godric and his mother on their journey to Rome but never asked where they came from or told them anything of her background, and whom no-one else could see.[16]

Males

There are few masculine figures to match these, which is curious when you remember that medieval writers habitually gendered demons as male.[17] Apart from demon lovers, whose gender is required by the plot-line, when the supernatural took the form of men it came in a crowd, without personality. In the summer of 1403, things like warriors were seen by travellers on the great road that passes Bedford and Biggleswade. They ran out of the trees and as soon as they saw one another, fought like men possessed. These fights began in the cool of morning and lasted till noon. From a distance they could be seen quite clearly, but as soon as anyone approached there was nothing there.[18] At Pointon, a girl had a vision in which she saw herself as a dead woman lying on the high ground between her village and Sempringham, where she watched fighting men struggle in the space between the hills.[19] In Galway troops were seen passing by, sometimes on the march, sometimes fighting amongst themselves. This was witnessed by people on the road or working the land or just walking in the woods: it made no difference, whoever witnessed the strange army immediately became weak and collapsed, and many died.[20]

Sometimes these eerie fights took an emblematic form. The warriors of Bedford battled *sub colore vario*, as if one blason were combating another. In 1327 a pious old man in Westmorland dreamt that he was on Salisbury Plain. (The plain's reputation for uncanny sights seems to have extended far beyond Wiltshire.) Gazing across this English Armageddon, he saw two emblematic armies engage in strife. As usual in these affairs, one had horses, armour and all trappings blacker than pitch (they're the Scots—boo!), while the other, a perfect white in all their accoutrements, carried St George's flag.[21] In the summer of 1361 many who travelled through waste grounds and heaths, both in England and France, saw two castles, from which paired companies emerged ready for war: one with shining banners, the other all clothed in black. They closed, the bright fought the black, and the dark knights won the day, after which each side returned to their castle and everything vanished.[22]

As time passed, these prophetic struggles were seen less often among waste places and more frequently in the sky: aerial battles are a constant of early modern tracts and wonder literature.[23] The same diversion upwards is found in other sixteenth-century troops, hunts and processions: despite the rich mythical resonances of riders on the storm, earlier generations were more likely to expect and experience the supernatural at ground level. The strange company that rose up in the air in 1154 anticipated this later turn of events, though they vanished before they could make much progress overhead. Seen in the lands west of Hereford, this aristocratic party travelled with knights and ladies, hawks and hounds, and a train of carts and packhorses to carry their unearthly goods. The locals, suspicious of any troop that could not account for itself, raised the hue and cry and blocked their path with rustic weapons, but the strangers disdainfully kept silence and floated upwards or, in another account, plunged into the Wye.[24] They were supposed to be the Herlething of Anglo-Norman lore.[25]

Further south, keepers of the royal forests used to hear the cry of hounds and the blowing of horns when night had fallen and a full moon was on the rise. They would see a band of knights out hunting, who unlike their Welsh contemporaries answered when challenged, identifying themselves as the company and household of Arthur.[26] The green riders of Ellingham, three young men of handsome bearing and dignified stature, initiated the conversation, asking young Richard where he was going before carrying him off to their secret realm.[27] The grim riders of Dunfermline said nothing: they galloped after the teenage squire and trampled him down.[28] If there is a common thread, it is the disdainful attitude of noble riders to the people that they pass by. In the mountains of Ireland, two good friars met a sinful man and forced him to reveal his way of life: for thirty years he had served the demon whose brand he bore on his hands. After confession the black seal vanished from his skin and when the demon rode by, followed by a great company on horseback, he demanded to know where his servant had gone. 'Here I am', said the man, trembling. 'You're a liar', said the devil, 'there's no sign of the mark on you', and he rode on.[29] That's the bearing of an aristocrat, right down to his inability to remember the faces of inferiors.

The demon huntsmen of Peterborough, who rode black horses and black he-goats, had no interaction at all with those who saw them, apart from keeping them awake all night with their whooping and horn-blowing.[30] There are common themes in these appearances but reducing them all to a single phenomenon—the Wild Hunt or such-like—obscures more than it reveals; not all these riders were hunting, while Meilyr the prophet and Snowball the tailor knew of phantasmal hunters who were solitary, and on foot.[31]

But the stories have a common theme of crowding: when the supernatural takes shape, it is a multitude. Theologically, this goes back to the spirit whose name was Legion and the swarming, mobbing demons of the Antonine tradition, but such experiences were more than literary. A monk of Rochester woke from confused dreams to a fugue state in which he saw a confused throng all around, some of them monks, some secular clergy, others layfolk, with girls amongst them—every social type that he could imagine, all glaring at him, the more frightening because he was unable to tell what they were doing or what they wanted.[32] Shape-shifting and illusion were part of this effect. The demon masters in the mountains of Ireland appeared to their servant *in diversis figuris*. Chronicling the host, demon after demon, that assailed the forest hermitage at Finchale, Reginald pauses to wonder about the status of one particular apparition. Was it four spirits arriving together, or one spirit manifesting as four?[33]

Size

Among the demons that harried Godric was a plague of little men—the tinier their stature, the more his small cell could contain. They were all very black, and small 'like the little men which are called "half-foot" or pygmies'. Some ran round and round the walls, others descended on him laughing and hissing. Some years later, after he had been tempted into digging for treasure, the empty hole soon filled up with a crowd of these little black hairless pygmies or *semicubitales*. They surrounded him and tossed tiny smoking pellets at him. These smelt horrible—a infernal version of bad little boys throwing puffballs, the medieval stink-bomb.[34]

The bearded goat-riders who harassed Bartholomew of Farne were also *breves staturae*: how short is not clear.[35] Pygmies—the real, or at any rate flesh-and-blood nation described by the classical ethnographers—were supposed to have ridden out each spring on rams and goats to battle with their hereditary enemies, the cranes.[36] This text would have been available to medieval writers, and it describes them as 27 inches tall; Walter Map, who knew his classics, introduces us to a bearded pygmy no larger than a monkey, riding on a large goat.[37] The Greek *pygmē*, at the shorter end of fore-arm units with a length of some 18 inches, could have been described as half of a long cubit; that fits Elidyr's little people, said to be no bigger than pygmies, and riding horses the size of greyhounds.[38] Other writers seem to have remembered an original *semicubitalis* very loosely, as half of something: Gervase describes the *portuni* as only *dimidium pollicis*, half an inch high, which is surprising.[39] True, they had magic powers, and in any case we shouldn't look for scale-model consistency in supernatural stories: the twelve-year-old Elidyr would have towered over his pygmy friends. But a half-inch stature is so impractical, not least for eating frogs, that Gervase or his scribes probably got the words wrong.

Who are these *Gracyous Fayry*, the episcopal commissary asked Marion Clerk of Ashfield, and she promptly answered: 'Little people, who tell me whatever I need to know when I ask them.'[40] Perhaps the miniaturization of her contacts made her more confident when dealing with them, though small was not necessarily biddable. In 1289 John Fraunceys went out to keep an eye on his cattle; he lived near Dalton in Swaledale, where pasture lands merge all too easily with the open moor. John was so concerned for his livestock that even on Sundays he could be found crossing hill and dale when he should have been in church. So he shouldn't have been surprised when one service time he found himself lost in a remote valley and delivered over to the spirits of the air. They clustered around him, a dwarfish crowd, compelling him to join in a parody of the sacrament he should have been attending. First came the dwarf-abbot in robes and cope, with his dwarf-congregation trooping after him with screams of laughter. On either side were the choir, humming in a murmur when they should have been chanting the *Gloria*. Then came the moment of blessing, when the little abbot paraded down the line with a blasphemous *aspergillum*, sprinkling unholy water left and right, with special attention to John. Each drop of water struck him like a stone, so that he was bruised for days afterwards, and when the spirits finally took flight he felt himself rising up with them into the air. Stretched out flat and desperately clutching the grass, he thought of holy things as hard as he could until little by little their power receded, and he could get up and stagger home. But for a week afterwards he was liable to be lifted away, so that four of his farmhands had to hold him down while a fifth fetched the priest.[41]

Elsewhere size varies between tiny and childlike, depending on context. The *lytel spere* of *Wið færstice* is close to invisible, and it implies a corresponding race of little spear-throwers. Demons can be minute, like the one that Meilyr saw dancing up and down on a liar's tongue.[42] But in Coldingham a child was accosted while out pasturing the sheep by a little black boy who wanted to play with him. Uneasy with his new friend, or perhaps with the games proposed, the human boy refused to join in, and was struck dumb.[43] Here the two playmates are evidently of a size. The red man was first seen by William Wynfeld as a *homunculus*, although he then grew in size, at least to a stature where he could pull a horse by the bridle.[44] Malekin, on the one occasion that she appeared to sight, was *in specie parvissimi infantis*.[45]

The experience of nightmare took concrete form as a little heavy figure sitting on its victim's breast, crushing and choking. Arkill the carpenter was afflicted by an Aethiopian dwarf lying on his back, small enough, at least in the logic of dream, to be thrown on the fire when he made a struggle and got himself free.[46] The stalking enemy of *Wið dweorh* is a spider-wight—probably: the textual reading is uncertain but it is fits with a wider tradition of dwarfs as spiders.[47] Certainly it is smaller than the man it bridles, as a rider is smaller than his horse. The nightmare which afflicted Stephen of Hoyland finally appeared to him in the form of a dwarf, *nanus*.[48]

The supernatural routinely manifested as a smaller version of the human, sometimes in unexpected contexts. John de Tregoz was conducting a vigil at the shrine of Thomas Cantilupe in 1287 when, as he kneeled in prayer, he had a vision. A bishop stepped out of the brass frieze beneath the tomb. Robed in white vestments, with a white mitre on his head, he was no more than a foot in height, with a scaled-down white cross carried before him. This pocket-saint came to John, felt his side and cured him, as the *virago* did Reinburgis, by psychic surgery.[49]

At the other end of the scale, spirits could be preternaturally tall. Once again, Godric is our witness. Demons would enter his oratory, and although doing their best to impersonate ordinary worshippers, like all their kind they were attention-seekers: when ignored, they shot up in height so their heads butted against the roof-beam of the church, or extended their necks elastically with heads glaring down on him.[50] This was not just a personal fancy on Godric's part, but something commonly experienced in the neighbourhood. Many years after the hermit's death, a woman from West Rainton was troubled by a spirit that transformed itself into various shapes; finally it stretched its neck right up to the eaves of the house before (like Walter of Kelloe's dog) leaping down her throat, so that she turned demoniac. Her friends kept her under watch and ward, but she broke free and made her way to Finchale and healing.[51]

Tallness in these stories acts as a criterion motif—the narrative sign that we are dealing with a supernatural and not a human being. When Godric received a precognitive vision, it was delivered by something that had looked like an ordinary visitor to the hermitage, but suddenly swelled up to a great height, stretching its mouth into a huge distended grimace and speaking prophecy.[52] The Ayrshire demon who gave moral messages to a toper in 1290 was terrifyingly tall with a repulsive body, fiery eyes and the face of a ghost.[53] That may be literary embellishment, but we are closer to personal testimony with the sick man who saw an immensely tall figure holding a sheet of gold. As he made the sign of the cross, the tall apparition sank into the earth, up to its knees, its chest, then completely.[54] The dancing elf-maidens who entranced Edric Wilde were lovely and taller in stature than mortal women.[55] The apparitions in the water-meadows at Winchester and on Salisbury Plain also featured beings of majestic height.

The last of the many apparitions seen by Snowball the tailor was a tall man, horrible and thin, like one of the three dead who confront the three living in paintings.[56] Alice of Reading saw a figure like a body standing in a winding sheet when she went to milk the ewes.[57] Nothing is said about it being larger than ordinary, but taking the shape of a dead man was another way in which apparitions distorted normal human appearance. Godric was used to bizarre forms, but even he was taken aback by the demon with holly bark for skin, and no back: when you looked from behind, there was nothing to be seen from shoulder to loins but a body cut open, as if you were looking at the inside of an ox's skin.[58]

Shrouded figures would be a staple of later ghost stories, just as the absence of a back would be a give-away feature of fairies in Germany and Scandinavia, long after the motif had been forgotten in England.[59] Another image with a future ahead of it was the headless phantom, like the one on Dunsmore Heath heard shouting 'Bowes, bowes, bowes!'.[60] According to Ranulf Higden, the Isle of Man was full of apparitions, both beheaded and whole. These foreshadowed the deaths of local men, which always happened as the mutilated likeness had predicted. The locals were used to this but strangers could see nothing unless, like Bartholomew of Farne on his travels, they set their foot on the foot of a seer.[61]

Anselm used to tell a story, passed on to him shortly after it happened at Blangy, a cell of Bec in Normandy. A farm lad woke in the night to find that something, he could not tell what, was calling him by name from outside the window. It cajoled him into reaching out his hand, which he thought would be safe enough because the window was only six inches wide, but no! the stranger plucked him through unhurt. It bore the boy away on his shoulder, and when he asked nervously what was going on, said 'Don't bother about who I am, I'm going to show you how the soul can be taken from the body.' Which was surprising, the boy thought, because his captor had no head: where he ought to have had one, there was a mop of hair like a shaggy fleece rounded off into a ball. So he called on God, and was instantly dropped in a wood, at a place he knew well: an old man came up with a boy, the same age as the farmhand himself, and told him to shut up and to go to sleep. Once more he was whisked away, and found himself—apparently dropped from the air, again—on a pile of hay in a barn that he could never have reached through the locked door.[62]

This has the mysterious, unconnected character which we have found in other supernatural reportage. The headlessness, described so exactly; the danger of something at the window, also familiar to us from the experiences of Walter of Kelloe and (by implication) the woman from Devon in the Life of Hugh; the alternation of a dangerous visionary figure with a kindly one; the risks of being carried through the air, as with John Fraunceys and the girl in the *exemplum* who had to be held down by six people; and the way in which aerial flight is brought to a sudden end by invoking the name of God, a trope which would later grow into the tale-type of a bungled trip to the witches' Sabbath.

Animals

Supernatural encounters are full of the unexpected, often with details familiar from later folklore. We have only one instance of a dog dragging a chain round its neck, in Snowball's encounter with the dead man on the Yorkshire moors, yet the motif is so standard in later accounts that it is likely to have been well-known in the fifteenth century.[63] Apparitions like these would later be treated under a heading of the Black Dog, though this may impose a false unity on varied stories. It's true that many people, like Walter of Kelloe or Adelais of Curridge or the midnight traveller who called on Henry VI, met a black dog.[64] In *exempla*, the demon dog is always black.[65] But other stories put more emphasis on the dog's shagginess. The mad Englishwoman who found her cure at Dunfermline was followed by *duo canes horridi et hispidi*; they could not abide sacred space, and halted at the edge of the saint's hospital, allowing her to get away from them.[66] In the same *miracula* a monk dreams of two dogs, again *horridos et hispidos*, one black and the other red. His tale has a developed triadic structure, with the dogs being beaten off by Margaret once, and a second time, and then on the third time with a promise that they will attack her servants no more, as the nightmare bound herself to George and as demons generally promise in charms: this is a more erudite pattern than usual, but then he was a monk who even while dreaming would not forget his daytime studies.[67]

John the clerk just saw a large dog walking in front of him: it was the size which put him on his guard, but he didn't realize that he was dealing with something of another world until it spoke.[68] More tell-tale signs came from the animal encountered by a knight of Penrith. While he was deep in Inglewood Forest, a storm broke out; he was in the thick of it, and just as lightning set a tree ablaze near him, he saw a huge dog, or rather bitch, come loping through the woods with fire darting from its mouth.[69] It ran past him and, as he afterwards learned, kept a steady pace as far as the outskirts of Penrith, where a priest lived with his wife and children. The doors, shut and barred against the storm, were no defence against fire and the dog broke through them in a blaze which burnt down both house and family.

Two runaway peasants of Drakelow dropped dead, testimony to the anger of Modwenna from whose estates they had fled. The day after their funeral, they were back again: in the hour before sunset, when shadows were long, they walked through the village, carrying their coffins. Next night, they took the shapes of animals including bears as well as dogs.[70] Though there were no bears in Derbyshire, people would have known what they looked like, since itinerant bear-keepers had travelled the country since Anglo-Saxon times.[71] Hairy, human-like and able to rise up on its hind legs, the bear was a good stand-in for a demon. A servant at Godric's hermitage was tempted by a stranger that came offering him golden cups and swords with intricately chased hilts; he ran and told his master, but the holy man smiled and pointed to the creature's footprints, which were those of a bear.[72]

Apes, the other man-like exotic animal, are reported from time to time. A judge at the York assizes, spending the night in a haunted room at St Mary's Abbey, had a long struggle with a demonic ape from which he was only rescued by the intervention of the Virgin.[73] A Dubliner who went to check his treasure chest found an ape sitting on the (presumably ill-gotten) gains. His suspicions that this might be something worse than a stray pet were confirmed when it cackled 'Hands off! This all belongs to Colewyn': *id est, diaboli*, our author explains.[74] These are *exempla*, and literary treatment has obscured the original experience, if any: but Ketell of Knaresborough saw little demons in the likeness of apes sitting on his friends' shoulders in the pub. Whenever a drinker mentioned the name of Christ, they would jump off in alarm, but they soon clambered back up again, parodying the excited drunken gestures of the men on which they sat, and slobbering into their beer-mugs.[75]

Only one native creature was a demonic vehicle—the hare. Something about hares made them both funny and uncanny: in the *bas-de-page* illustrations of the fourteenth century, they often appear in human roles, up on their hindlegs, taking aim at the greyhound or his master. When Sir Robert of Edenham went hunting on Sunday, instead of attending Mass like a good parishioner, it was a hare which led him astray until it vanished, proving that it had not been a flesh-and-blood hare at all but something else which, spiritually at least, was hunting *him*.[76] In the years after 1274, when men were arguing whether the late Simon de Montfort was a fallen rebel or a saint in glory, a Herefordshire curate called Philip took the government line and went so as far as to say 'If that Earl Simon's a saint, may the devil break my neck.' Which came to pass: for as he rode home from home, something in the likeness of a hare darted across his path. The horse reared, Philip fell, and from that moment he lost his wits completely and had to be tracked down and tied up.[77]

That might have been an ordinary hare, but the same cannot be said for the animal which had an affair with a woman from St Ives. The sex was pretty much as you'd expect with an anthropomorphic talking demon hare, except that each time he came, the spunk dribbled out of her mouth.[78] This set her thinking that there might not be something entirely normal about their relationship, and she went to confession at the nearby priory, which gave her a little bottle filled with the water that flowed from St Ivo's shrine. Clutching this, she went to the next meeting with her lover, but he kept his distance, rearing up on his hindlegs and complaining vociferously that she was hiding from him behind a wall of water.

Another abnormally vertical creature was the grant, introduced by Gervase as an English village demon. The word is found nowhere else, and as we've already found Gervase's memory playing him false with the *portuni*, it may be a distorted form, or perhaps a very local tradition: but his account is a valuable insight into popular beliefs.[79] The grant looked like a yearling colt, standing up on its hindlegs, with sparkling eyes—a more harmless variation on the fiery eyes seen in demons like the one from Ayrshire. Its appearance would set the dogs of the village into a frenzy of barking, just as elsewhere the walking dead were pursued by a pack of barking dogs.[80] Traditions like these were an easy way to spread stories of the supernatural: any time the local dogs set each other off into a howling fit, people could nod and say that something of another world was amongst them, and none would be so rash as to look out the window and check. The grant was a useful apparition since its manifestations always preceded a fire amongst the houses, so that villagers were warned and could prevent it spreading.[81]

Another horse on its back legs appeared to a labourer at Rievaulx. It was holding up its forefeet, which worried him, so he ordered it in Christ's name not to do him any harm, and the horse walked along companionably before turning into other shapes: at last, when it descended to human form, he conjured it into telling him what kind of thing it was, and was relieved to learn that it was a dead man seeking prayers.[82] This was in the early fifteenth century, at about the time that another traveller from Ampleforth saw a pale horse which, when adjured in the name of the Almighty, turned into a rolling piece of twisted canvas.[83] There was something eerie about a horse in the wrong place at the wrong time. A woman on her deathbed told her confessor that what troubled her most was the grizzled black horse that stood by her bed, staring at her. He suggested it might be an embodiment of her vain desire to have a high-class carriage funeral, but this seems a little stretched.[84] By the thirteenth century, the Old English words *mere* (she-horse) and *mare* (demon) had been fused as Middle English *mare*, and this gave horses a bad reputation in the bedroom.

Supernatural horses were usually black, like those which ran down the young Scottish squire, or the giant horse-demon that ran before the storm at Scarborough, or the uncanny steed from Wandlebury that vanished at cock-crow.[85] The Witch of Berkeley was plucked from the coffin by her tall dark master, who threw her onto a black horse, its back studded with spikes where a saddle should have been, and as they rode off through the night air, her screams could be heard four miles away. First appearing in the 1120s, this story rapidly became a preachers' favourite.[86] The black horse that carries a soul to Hell was such a stock property in *exempla* that people were primed to see one, or at least to suppose that they could be seen.[87] A Dunfermline monk wanted to renounce his profession, which threw all the family into a stir, especially his old nurse. She took him to one side and told him what she had seen on the way to the monastery: a powerful white horse lightly held by a lovely girl, and a jet-black horse grazing nearby. 'Whose are these horses, lady?' 'That black one, he's for a false monk at my abbey of Dunfermline, and soon they will gallop to the master whom he has chosen. But if he returns to my service, I have this white steed for him.' The old woman's vision, or perhaps the love that made her see it, worked miracles on the young man, who returned to his vocation.[88]

Black things came from Hell and white from Heaven. A woman who had lost her mind was brought to the shrine at Coldingham, with two servant girls keeping an eye on her. As she rested in the church, three huge crows burst suddenly through the doorway and set about the woman with their beaks and claws. The servants jumped up, flapping their arms to drive off the birds, but back they came, and again a third time: clearly they were demons, for the woman, who had been quite calm, now fell into a mental agony, twisting herself and blaspheming. But healing, when it came to suppliants at Æbbe's shrine, took the form of a snow-white dove.[89]

These demon crows have their place in *exempla*, providing a touch of drama to match the diabolical black horses.[90] The *Scala Coeli* even anticipates Hitchcock with a flock of crows that mob the miller's boy every time he goes out of doors, descending on him to peck out his eyes until he is saved by confession.[91] Literary influence from sermons might be suspected in the miracle stories: but white and black birds are most frequent in the collections for Æbbe and Margaret, which are also the richest in native details, and they are most often reported by women, the usual guardians of popular lore. So it seems that the contrast of dark and light spirit birds was more than a preacher's commonplace.

In some texts the linkage between spirits and birds is so incidental that it cannot be a deliberate trick of style. Fifteen or sixteen lines after introducing the naked foul-skinned black furies who accosted the citizen of Winchester in the water-meadows, Lantfred casually describes them as *corvinae*, crow-like or raven-like.[92] Shortly afterwards, the tall lady in white describes her black compeers as 'honking after him like geese'. It is as if bird-comparisons had come naturally to the man himself, when he was describing his attackers in Old English, but only made it by accident into the Latin rendition.[93]

The dead man who accosted Snowball on the North York Moors appeared first as a raven (*corvus*) which fluttered round his face, fell onto the ground and beat its wings feebly as if expiring. As soon as he got off his horse to investigate, the bird jumped up and flapped away screaming with sparks of fire shooting out from its sides, only to fly at him further down the road, fast enough to knock him off his horse.[94] This was an attention-seeking bird with a plan of action: it wouldn't go away even when Snowball hacked at it with his sword.

It was hard to mistake a headless man or a horse walking on its hindlegs for anything of this world, but demon-corvids often looked much like ordinary crows. Godric had a servant who, more than any of the other carers, shared the visionary world of the old hermit: like his master, he saw the man with sinister bottles, the human-headed horse and the throwers of stinking puffballs. Being younger and stronger, he would lunge with an axe at their insubstantial forms as soon as he saw the hermit's gaze fixed on something uncanny.[95] This power to see demons came to him suddenly, and lasted until his service came to an end. Walking out of the woods to take up his duties, he saw birds sitting on all the fence-posts which ringed the hermitage garden. They sat on the posts like *corvorum*—crows this time, evidently—very big and very black, cawing with a harsh noise that left him terrified. At once he realized that these were no ordinary birds waiting to scavenge peas and beans from the vegetable patch, but demons lurking just outside the boundaries of the holy plot.[96]

Colour

Blackness is a story-teller's signifier, alerting us to the shift in gear as the supernatural enters everyday life. Green is used in the same way by Richard of Sunderland in his memories of otherworldly abduction. He'd got up early and gone down the road to cut reeds: so far, so normal. Down the road three handsome young men came riding, which is unexpected but still plausible in rural Northumberland. But their clothes were green, and so were their horses—at once this colour warns us that these are no ordinary riders but strangers from a fairy realm, who can throw him with a single twist of the hand up on their crupper, ride away through a valley that magically opens to them and, later on, offer him drink from the green horn that will seal his inclusion among the other crowd.[97] Similarly Bercilak clatters into Arthur's court with a complexion *overal enker grene*; he is *al graythed in grene* and rides *a grene hors gret and thikke*.[98] That detail of the coloured horse appears in both accounts, suggesting a shared body of knowledge rather than authorial invention.

People come in different skin hues, as even the most cloistered medieval writer must have known, so it was not difficult to imagine new ones. The Green Children, according to Ralph of Coggeshall, were not just *viridis* but *prassinum*, a sombre dark green. In all these traditions, colour is a sign that something supernatural has broken into the world. Maybe the stranger has green skin, maybe green hair or eyes, maybe just green shoes or clothing; it is not essential that they should be as impossibly hued as the Green Children.[99] When 'a little green man' appeared to Katharine Gibb of Corstophine and asked if she would be his servant—the early modern equivalent of the demand for homage—it would be a distraction to ask whether he was green all over, or simply dressed for the occasion like the agreeable young yeoman of *The Friar's Tale*, who roams the forest wearing *a courtepy of grene* but is really a fiend whose dwelling is in Hell.[100] It was the choice of colour that should have put Katherine and the Summoner on their guard, not questions over whether it was pigment or sartorial. Godric, who knew his demons, saw one covered in a fresh green skin of holly bark but another simply dressed in green with a black scarf. The second visitor left in confusion shortly before some visiting clergy arrived. Now who was this stranger, Godric asks his guests, and they answer: 'It was the Enemy.' They have passed the test of identifying a criterion motif.[101]

As long as people were primed to recognize colour as a hint that something supernatural was on its way, visionaries and storytellers could vary the actual scheme: it could be black or green, it could sometimes also be red. The pygmy king in Walter Map's story of Herla has a bright red face and a long red beard tumbling down his chest. His head was large, his belly hairy, his feet ending in the hooves of a goat—just like Pan, says Walter, who doesn't want us to think his sources are confined to peasants and jongleurs.[102] But redness and small size were linked with the supernatural in oral narratives, too. It was a little red man who appeared to William Wynfeld in the shaking of the barley.[103] On his first appearance he is a *homunculum rubeum*; later, when tugging at mad William's chains, *rubeus et rufus*. Usually *rufus* means red-haired, occasionally ruddy or sanguine. Bromyard has a story about a *puer rufus*, told very much in the folk style. This boy calls at the miser's house, saying he needs to collect his dues. The wife tells him to run along—evidently he looks like any other red-headed urchin—but her husband takes the news much more seriously and instructs her to make his bed alone in a special room that he's never slept in before. That night the household peek through cracks in the wall to see master and the red boy dividing up the money bags. 'That one's yours, that one's mine'; the counting grows to argument and they are about to fall to blows, so the family break down the door and rush in, and—all is dark! and the miser and the little red boy were never seen again.[104]

Just as the tell-tale motif of green can be introduced indifferently as a skin colour or as clothing, so the storyteller's suspicions of redness are triggered equally by a cloak or a complexion. The *theomacha* in the Life of Samson wears garments of red while when Julian of Norwich saw the Devil, his face was *rede like the tilestone what it is new brent … his here was rode as rust.*[105] The lord of Stackpole in Pembrokeshire gave the post of steward to a young man named Simon, easily recognizable by his shock of red hair. He had many other singular qualities as well—a genius for household administration, an easy-going approach to expenditure (it's not as if you'd live forever, is it?) and a generous attitude to the servants (well, they're the ones who do the work, aren't they?). His anticipation of needs was uncanny: the master and mistress had only to mention something to each other, even just to think of it, and next morning it would be on the table. He didn't live in, and absented himself on Sundays, but always turned up to work on time, until one night a member of the family was walking by the river and heard him talking to his fellow-demons of the mill and the pool.[106] So Gerald tells the story, and there is something of the ethnographer in his description of a migrant from another world, treating short-lived, status-obsessed mortals with the kindly condescension of a *longaevus*. Simon was not a purebred demon, being the son of a local girl by an incubus, but he evidently took after his father.

Shape-shifting

Not that Simon's mother was to blame: the incubus had come to her in the shape of her husband. We have already met with a trick of this kind under the trees of Woolmer Forest where Joan was deceived by something that looked like her boyfriend.[107] There were literary models for this kind of thing. Jupiter had come to Alcmene in the likeness of her husband, a legend of a hero's conception not forgotten by Geoffrey of Monmouth when he made Uther come to Ygraine magically disguised as Gorlois. The story could easily be reinvented, anyway; it is one of those motifs which take natural human feelings (I don't know what he's really like) and raise them to a supernatural pitch (I don't know what he really *is*).

And sometimes story embodied itself as experience. In 1266 the Whitsun fair was in full swing at Ryal in Northumberland. The priest's partner was sitting inside the doorway, watching the dancing and the lads at sport. She'd just had a baby, an addition to their already large family (the doctrine of clerical celibacy was slow to reach Northumberland) and had not been churched yet, so it wouldn't be right to leave the house; but she could sit in the porch and feel she was part of the fun. Here comes her other half (as she thinks). 'You really shouldn't be out here where people can see you', he says, loving but bossy. 'Come back to our room and we'll pick up where we left off.' And in that noontide hour he abused her seven times with such vehemence that she passed out completely. It is evening and the priest—the real one this time—returns home, asking how her day has been. 'Like you don't know', she says. 'Seven times!' But he swore he'd been away all day, and realizing what kind of thing was with her that afternoon, she fell ill, her bowels swelled, a dreadful stink came from inside, and within a few days she was dead.[108]

This story, like many of the *exempla*, has been shaped by the visceral hatred felt by preachers for the priest's concubine, the specific focus of their general misogyny. But it was not always the woman who was fooled. A young clergyman called Oliver died after being deceived by a demon in the shape of his girlfriend.[109] Meilyr the wise man of South Wales acquired his gifts after a girl transformed in his arms into something rough, shaggy, and repulsive beyond words.[110] Here there is no delayed denouement, as in the stories from Ryall and Woolmer Forest: Meilyr realizes instantly what he is with, and runs mad from its touch. The supernatural reached out to take people through the bait of intimacy. It didn't have to be sexual. William Paternoster of Bielby had a childhood friend, a little girl the same age as himself; they'd scramble around on the edge of the village, and though his parents told him off for playing where they couldn't keep an eye on him, he took no notice. One day he saw his friend, or thought he did. She trotted off into the woods, and he ran after her, but somehow he could never catch up, and soon he was lost and tired and could run no further. Uncanny lights shone all around him, sparkling behind the trees in the depths of the wood. He could do nothing, say nothing; there was no sign of his little friend; when he stumbled back home, he had lost all power to speak.[111]

The word *fantasia* recurs throughout these stories, and not in a good sense. The nightmare which vexed Stephen of Hoyland was a *phantasia*; Richard of Sunderland was led into wild places *per phantasie spiritum*; Ieuan of Kilpeck walked at night *cum spiritibus fantasticis*; even that chatty toddler Malekin was *fantastico spiritu*. The sense is never 'unreal' (the power of these spirits was real enough) but 'skilled in illusion, projecting something other than it is'. The fighting men of Bedford—seen from afar, vanishing at nearer inspection— were a *fantastica vel fatalis apparitio*; *fatalis* is not the classical word 'fated' but a Latinization of French *faé*, 'of Faerie'.[112]

William of Aberdeen disembarked at Leith and took the ferry across the Forth. At Inverkeithing he was joined by a little dog. Whatever he did, the dog kept to his side, and as they walked over the hills it suddenly grew to a huge size, turned into a dragon, and tried to swallow him down. Terrified, William lost his wits and threw away his clothes; by the time he ran down into Dunfermline, he was raving mad, driving the people of the town before him and trying to break down their doors with an axe.[113] Nothing from the supernatural world was what it seemed, and nothing seemed the same for long. The dead peasants of Drakelow morphed from men carrying their own coffins, to bears, to dogs, and then into all sorts of other animals.[114] A woman who came to drink from the springs at Wye, in the hope of restoring her health, began vomiting and brought up two large black toads, which had no sooner fallen to the ground than they turned into huge black dogs, and then swelled up and transformed into donkeys. Stepping in between the astonished woman and her inner demons, the guardian of the spring sprinkled around some of its water, on which they flew up into the air, leaving behind only a horrid smell.[115]

The dead man who accosted Snowball of Ampleforth never had the same shape twice running. At first a raven (although seemingly a large one, and with sparks flying from its sides) it reappears as a dog with a chain dangling from its neck, then once he conjures it to speak, the apparition seems to take the form of a man on fire whose innards can be seen glowing through his mouth. After a break in which Snowball commissions masses and draws a protective circle, the spirit returns in the shape of a nanny-goat before falling down to the ground and rising again in the shape of a dreadful dead man. Nearby at Rievaulx the apparition of a horse standing on its hindlegs turned into a spinning haycock with a light in the middle, before being reduced by prayer into the shape of a man.[116]

The *fantasmata* in these Yorkshire stories will not, perhaps cannot, keep the same shape for long. Even the forms that they take seem to be tricks of the sight, not perceptible objects, for when Snowball strikes the raven with his sword the blows fall as flat as if he were hitting a peat-stack. Very often they regress to shapes like haycocks or rolling sheets which have almost no form at all. The moors at Ampleforth were also haunted by spirits in the likeness of a fire, a bush, and the Lovecraftian figure of a bullock without mouth or eyes or ears—its head as close to embodied shapelessness as you can get.

The apparitions which plagued Godric could be just as mutable and formless. On one occasion a spirit burst into the oratory like a robber; the servant who was with the old man, and who had seen him dismiss so many demons, trembled when he realized that his master was genuinely frightened of this one.

It leapt about the church in the shape of a sack stuffed full until, worn out by its deceptions and failing to make any impact on the holy man, it vanished into thin air. Explaining the ways of demons to the monks, Godric said that they could come as a bag of straw, a headless footless limbless thing, a bristling hairy shagginess, a shape shooting up from the ground or squeezing between the bed and the wall. 'All these are silly things, however, and tall tales, wrapped up in falsehood and concealed behind the mask of deception.'[117]

PART II

Places

CHAPTER FOUR

Haunted Landscapes

'*On* Midsummer Eve, *in* the middle of a Ring, and under—right *under* one of my oldest hills in Old England? Pook's Hill—Puck's Hill—Puck's Hill—Pook's Hill! It's as plain as the nose on my face.'

Kipling, *Puck of Pook's Hill*

Place-Names

Through close reading, we can recover something of what it was like to encounter a spirit in the woods and meadows of medieval England. But however it is done, the process always involves some kind of translation: we hear Godric's story through Reginald's words, while even Godric himself was struggling to express ideas passed down in his native English through the tradition of a Latin-speaking Church. Our knowledge would be so much more direct if it came to us through the vernacular, and luckily we have a source which does this: place-names.[1]

Frustratingly, this abundance of material is matched by a paucity of interpretation, for the names as they have come down to us are poor things—labels without the luggage. If we could ask questions of the dead, as a folklorist does of the living, we would be told so much more. Why Fairy Cross Plains, the Reverend John Atkinson asked an old lady of Danby in 1891. Didn't he know? Back in the old days, before roads were made up properly, two tracks used to cross in front of the pub at the Plains: and 'the fairies had a desper't haunt o' thae hill-ends just ahint the Public'.[2] A hundred years earlier, the excavator of a barrow at Cleeve below the Mendips explained that it 'has been immemorially known by the name of Fairy's Toote, and considered still, by our sagacious provincials, as the haunt of ghosts, goblins, and fairies'.[3] But as we work back through the centuries, this sort of antiquarian commentary dies away. There was no need for medieval gentry or clergy to set down what the sagacious provincials knew: they knew it themselves already.

When we use names, they are functionally opaque—no-one stops to think why they say what they say. Over time, with changes in vocabulary and pronunciation, even an intelligible name like Fairy Cross will eventually lose all transparency and become a meaningless string of sounds. But it remains in use—why change what everyone is used to?—and so place-names roll down like weathered pebbles in the stream of time. Many names from Anglo-Saxon charters survive on the Tithe Apportionments of the 1840s.

The appendix at the end of this book contains 900 forms, from the eighth century to the publication of large-scale Ordnance Survey maps, of what can be called elfin names: place-names where the first, descriptive part (the qualifying element, or qualifier) is a word for some sort of supernatural being. Many can be pinned down on a modern map, so that it is possible to match what the names are saying against local geography. Less than half are actual medieval forms—the median date for first attestations is 1601—but the supernatural terms are all rooted in the Middle Ages. Ironically this excludes *fairy* itself, not found in place-names before the seventeenth century.[4] But then it was an innovation of the fifteenth century to use *fairy* for an individual, rather than an otherworldly realm or a state of being, and it takes time for new words to find their home in place-names.

What, exactly, is a medieval place-name? The longevity of names poses problems for anyone trying to assemble reliable data. If we want absolute certainty then the four hundred names antedating 1550 will provide it, but only by short-changing the evidence, for there is no doubt that many later names derive from this period. They preserve early grammatical constructions, or compound with generics which had passed out of use in Modern English, or refer to beings of whom all memory had faded by the end of the Middle Ages; like archaeological finds, they come from a time long before they were collected. Then should we amplify our dataset with those nineteenth-century names which must be medieval, leaving behind those which merely could be? That doesn't work, either: it distorts the statistics. So for the overall corpus I have accepted place-names of all periods as long as they contain the shortlisted supernatural qualifiers. Though two or three of these continued as living words into the early modern period, even these were used in a way that suggests a persistent tradition rather than innovative new senses. When we interpret names, the reliably medieval forms will have priority.

About twenty words for supernatural beings are found as qualifiers in place-names of Old and Middle English origin. But their popularity is very unequal. Far ahead of the rest, forming 43% of the names, is Old English *pūca*, which is found later as Middle English *pouke* and Modern English *puck*: for convenience we can use the Old English form as standard, though that doesn't imply that all its appearances go back to Anglo-Saxon times. The predominance of *pūca* as a supernatural term is even more surprising when you consider that it is confined to half of England. In a southern province, below a line drawn between the mouths of the Dee and the Orwell, *pūca* is the norm and other terms are uncommon. The related word *pūcel*, which must mean 'little puck', is found in 4% of names.

Above this line, in a northern province extending to the Scottish border and beyond, *pūca* is almost unknown while the most frequent qualifier is Old English *þyrs*, or the equivalent Old Norse *þurs*: again, we will use the Old English form as standard when there are cognate words. At the beginning of our period this was thought to be a fitting epithet for Grendel, though by the end it had lost some of its terrors and referred to household sprites. Providing 14% of all names, *þyrs* does not dominate the northern province as *pūca* does the south. It shares the landscape with *ælf*, more common in the north than the south, and appearing in 8% of names overall.

Ælf is the medieval and modern *elf*, and we know something about elves, even if our sources—romances, sermons, charms, books of cures, even alchemical treatises—give conflicting accounts of them. For the *þyrs* we have next to nothing from the Middle Ages, and for the *pūca* nothing at all, apart from pious literature in which the word appears as a vernacular substitute for *demon*. But it would be wrong to suppose that each supernatural term corresponds to a particular kind of being. If the literature of encounters has taught us anything, it is that spirits are forever changing shape. Travellers from Bedford to Doncaster were not leaving behind things that looked like a *pūca* and entering the realm of those that looked like a *þyrs*: they were crossing linguistic boundaries within a common narrative tradition.

The other, less frequent names for supernatural beings also seem to be close synonyms used in varying contexts, rather than a menagerie of different entities. *Scucca* accounts for 4% and Old Norse *skratti* for 3%. The English word is otherwise known only in religious literature, and the Scandinavian one in brief saga allusions, so we have to reconstruct a folk meaning for them as best we can. *Nicor*, featuring in 2% of names, is the exception: it is used distinctively, always compounded with words for watery places, and the *nicor* features in Anglo-Saxon books of wonders, though more often as a sea-monster or hippopotamus than as a supernatural being. Later it competes with French *sirene* as a word for mermaids. Middle English contributes *bugge*, with a general sense of 'terrifying being', accounting for 9% of names; *gobelin*, a loan-word from French, 4%; and the ill-defined *pokere*, 2%.

Below the 1% mark we find a very mixed group of beings. *Dweorg* appears often enough to show that the supernatural adversary of *Wið dweorh* was really present in the landscape, and not just a personification of fever. Then there are words which are unambiguously diabolical, rather than the morally ambiguous fairies of tradition: *dēofol* and *fēond*, our *devil* and *fiend*. *Scinna* meant 'shadow', as *scucca* originally did: it has an evil sense, as does *screawa*, the etymon of modern *shrew*, a word used in the *South English Legendary* to describe predatory elves. These are both epithets for bad things, not specific terms. To people who lived through long firelit nights, the shadow was the sign of a stranger, and strangers did not bode well. Hrothgar describes the creatures that wait outside Heorot as *scuccas* and *scinnas* (*Beowulf* 939), speaking in the idiom of the old pagan world.[5] Christianity used the same language, consecrating church bells in order to drive away the power of everything that lies in wait—the shadows, the spectres.[6]

The Old English *mare* was a creature of the night: the word is not used in place-names but the Middle English compound *niht-mare* occurs sometimes, as does *cangun*, a loanword from Norman French for 'changeling'. One word, *gram* 'the angry one', could be Old Norse or Old English; definitely Old Norse are the obscure *skyrsi* and the better-known *troll*. And at the foot of the list is the *wælcyrige*, cognate with Old Norse *valkyrja* and perhaps, like her, a terror to all except the heroes she loves and takes: but as she is only attested in one name, a meadow at Abbotsbury in Dorset, conclusions must remain tentative.

Just over the border of acceptability lie a dozen terms which have been proposed in the literature as supernatural qualifiers, usually the pet monsters of one particular scholar which have failed to gain wider acceptance in the literature.[7] Filey Brigg is more likely to contain a word for cotton-grass than *fifel* 'sea-monster', and Flawith is the ford of the flagstones, not of the *flagð* 'she-troll'. Otherwise a full spectrum of the Old and Middle English supernatural is present in place-names, with the exception of *wuduwāsa*, ME *wodewose*, used to translate the *satyrus* of Scripture. We know what a *wodewose* looked like, since it is the heraldic term for what art historians call the Wild Man. The absence of this word from the onomasticon, and also from the literature of supernatural encounter, reminds us that a legendary creature could be familiar to medieval people from art and story without ever crossing the boundary into actual waking experience.

Although the list aims to be comprehensive, it leaves out two beings attested in both literature and place-names, the *grim* and the *hob*. There is no doubt that both words were used in place-names to record the presence of spirits, but they were also men's names, and the two categories are not easily separated.

The common word *grīma* (genitive *grīman*) originally meant 'a mask' but was used in Old English to describe a supernatural being, presumably one that hid its face or identity. However, Grima (genitive Griman) and Grim (genitive Grimes) also functioned as personal names. Old Norse does not seem to have used the word in a supernatural sense, but Grímr (genitive Grímar) was popular as a personal name. After 1100, when the English and Scandinavian naming traditions had become fused, men went on being called Grim (genitive Grims). There was another Old Norse word *grima* 'mark or blaze on a tree'; there was also a tradition of naming Odin as Grim, 'the masked one', though that may just have been a poets' convention; there was certainly a medieval hero called Grim, said to have dug mighty ditches and earthworks. In most place-names, the qualifier is appositive—it is not grammatically modified in any way—so that a name beginning *Grim-* could be any of the above. If there is trace of a medial vowel without an *-s-*, then the qualifier would be *grīma*/Grīma, but that still leaves it uncertain whether we are dealing with a man or a spirit.[8]

With *hob* the problems of interpretation are even starker, for this word is not originally supernatural at all: it is simply a familiar form of Robin. Men were called Hob by their friends, and as everyone wanted to be on friendly terms with the spirits of moor and forest, they were called Hob as well. At first the name was a kind of honorary prefix: at the beginning of the seventeenth century you called the *gobelin* Hob Goblin, the *þyrs* Hob Thurse.[9] Further south, where Hob never really took off as a pet-name, spirits were called Tom instead. We meet with places named after Tom Thrush and Tom Pook.[10] As *thurse* fell out of the vocabulary, a unitary *hobthurst* began to replace it, and finally this took on the clipped form *hob*, so that there is a rich folklore about the spirits of Hob's Cave, Hob Garth, Hob Hill and Hob Holes.[11] But without the guiding voice of tradition there would be no way to tell that these place-names referred to supernatural occupants: formally, *hob* the sprite and Hob the man are identical.

These ambiguous place-names are not rare: there are 41 Hob- names in Derbyshire, and 46 in the West Riding.[12] They can't all refer to spirits—if that were the case, references to *hob* in Yorkshire would outnumber all the county's other elfin names together. Editors of the Survey of English Place-Names usually resort to a rule of thumb by which natural places are assigned to fairies and fields to human landowners. That matches up with the Victorian folklore but not with what we know from other place-names, where *land* and *feld* are just as likely to compound with words for the supernatural. Besides, there seems to be little point in making assumptions which prejudge what we are supposed to be finding out from the names themselves. So, reluctantly, I have left *grim* and *hob* out of the corpus.

These fairies had names which originally belonged to people; there were also people who went under names which properly belonged to fairies. As the use of hereditary surnames spread in the early fourteenth century, we find individuals named after the *pūca*, the *pūcel*, the *nicor* and the *bugge*: the adjective *elvisch* also appears, though *elf* the noun does not. Evidently these people resembled otherworlders in their appearance or behaviour, or maybe they were born after a girl's mésalliance while gathering nuts and tactfully fathered on some wood-sprite. As surnames, Pouke and Puckle had a limited distribution, though Bugg was found almost everywhere until it began to be exchanged for something less offensive to modern sensibility. Naturally the personal names were adopted most readily in the areas which already had a lively tradition of the beings themselves, including place-names. The Sussex Lay Subsidies, from the years on either side of 1300, provide us with three people like William atte Pukeneghe, evidently living near an existing *pūcan ēa*; seven like John Pukeput, possibly living at the *pūca pytt* but maybe having carried the name with him when he moved to another village; and eleven taxpayers called Puke or Le Puke, who loved circle dancing or dressing up or inflicting practical japes or whatever other explanation you wish to give the name.[13]

In each individual case, we can never be quite free from a suspicion that the elfin name may reflect Le Puke the local joker and not a genuine *pūca*. But when we come to look at the whole corpus, this is less of a distraction. Just as place-names are more likely to reference knights and earls than Mr Knight and Mr Earl, so the supernatural will appear more often as itself than as a personal metaphor. There is a test case which establishes this: words like *goblin*, *pixy*, *boggart* and *fairy* itself, which entered the common vocabulary too late for surnames to be derived from them. These also gave rise to place-names, and the spread of names in which they appear is much like the compounds with earlier qualifiers.[14]

When Victorian folklorists began to enquire into local lore, they found people still telling tales of pixies and fairies, as they did of boggarts, bullbeggars, dobbies, guytrashes, hyter sprites, kows, lantern men, and shagfoals.[15] But older terms had vanished from the repertoire.[16] Elf, dwarf and goblin continued in educated English, but only as literary words; the other words were unknown. Enthusiasts have claimed to find *scucca* in the name Shuck given to ghostly black dogs in East Anglia, but this is doubtful at best. While Shuck and Shock are found from the 1830s, they belong with other names for a rough-haired dog such as Shucky, Skeffy and Shaggy; as witnesses confirm, these dogs were covered in coarse black hair.[17] This had been a distinguishing sign of the supernatural ever since dogs were described by the miraculists as *horridi et hispidi*, but it is the visual tradition which has survived, not a name.

When did they die out, this elder race of fairies? The presence of a word in place-names is no guarantee that people understand what it means, though some names were updated to keep them intelligible. When people in York stopped talking about *Thurseghele* C13 and started calling it *Thurcelane* 1370, they had evidently forgotten that *geil* meant 'narrow lane' but still remembered that this street was haunted by a *þyrs*.[18] But eighteenth- and nineteenth-century names with this element are frequently scrambled, as if no-one had any idea what the word meant: Thurspittes 1601 becomes Rush Pits 1762, Thursbache 1569/70 is Dustbatch 1839.[19] By contrast most names in *pūca* show little change down to the late nineteenth century, and are often spelt in two words as if both elements of the compound were still intelligible. Some names contain a generic—the second element, the one referring to a kind of place—which did not come into general use until late medieval or modern times. This is certainly true of *pasture*, which appears at Pouke Pasture 1840 at Yazor in Herefordshire and Bugs Pasture 1839 at Capel in Surrey. It is also likely with *piece*, a word for a small field found in Poke Piece 1742 at Bath, Pouk Piece 1838 at Shenstone in Staffordshire, and two Puck Pieces in Worcestershire, as well as Goblin's Piece 1838 at Prees in Shropshire. But then *gobelin* seems later than the other qualifiers, common in the seventeenth and eighteenth centuries but featuring in only one medieval form, *Gobelynshole* 1461 at Portesham in Dorset.[20]

On the other hand, internal evidence shows that many of these names are older—centuries older—than their first attestations. The genitive of Old English *pūca* is *pūcan*, so that the first elfin name in the corpus, dating to 775, appears modified in the landmark *on pucan wylle*.[21] But with the collapse of Old English grammar after 1100, inflection fell into line with other Middle English words: *pouke*, genitive *poukes*. Any name where the qualifier ends in *-n* must therefore date back to Anglo-Saxon times. And yet plenty of these are unattested in the written record until modern times: Puckney 1629 at Shermanbury in Sussex with *eg* 'island'; Pucknold Ditch 1775 at Gotherington in Gloucestershire with *helde* 'slope'; Pucknall 1866 in Braishfield in Hampshire with *halh* 'corner of land'.

The tradition of elfin place-names was evidently rooted in the Middle Ages—and the early Middle Ages at that—even if some terms were added in the fourteenth or fifteenth century, and others remained intelligible and productive up until the eighteenth. The separation of northern and southern provinces must go back to the tenth century, for the boundary between the lands of the *pūca* and those of the *þyrs* corresponds to that of Scandinavian settlement after armies divided up the land in 876–880. Political boundaries fluctuated, but the areas of actual colonization can be mapped through the distribution of village names with Old Norse generics, and these correspond with the distinctive folklore of the northern area, including its extension to Norfolk and parts of Suffolk.

It is not easy to see why this region should differ in its choice of supernatural names from the south, for the invaders knew words—*púki* and *þurs*—which were close cognates to those already existing in Anglo-Saxon England. The elves likewise were familiar to both languages as *ælf* or *álfr*, words so similar that they seem to have been treated as a continuum. In theory, Old English *ælf* should yield *elf* in Middle English place-names, as it does in the literature, and *álfr* should develop into *alf*. But the distribution on the map is not so clearcut, with the occasional form in A- appearing as far south as Dorset and those in E- being common even in the West Riding.[22] The distinction between the two provinces seems to have been cultural, not linguistic. The elves had never been fully demonized, so that in the heathen and post-heathen society of the north, *ælf/álfr* was available as a word to describe beneficent spirits, while the fiercer creatures of fen and crag could be characterized as *þyrs*. In the more intensely Christianized landscape of southern England one word described them all— *pūca*, with its overtones of devil and fiend.

What Do Place-Names Mean?

Place-names are the closest we will ever come to the ordinary language of the past, but names stand at one remove from other language, just because they are names. Once a name has become established, it tends to throw off what are called shift-names—secondary formations in which the original qualifier is applied to a new generic. Is Powke Lane (1591) in Solihull the lane near Puck Grove (1638), or is Puck Grove a grove that happened to be near Puck Lane?[23] Locals may not have cared one way or the other, but we will, if we are trying to analyse the corpus by types of place.

It would be naïve to expect the distribution of elfin names to plot out exactly where the wild things were, like those little gridded maps on which naturalists carefully dot the dormouse or the chough. At the same time we must be careful, as we were with miracles and *exempla* and chronicles, not to become too knowing. Discursive conventions are the frame, not the picture: the selections of onomastics, like those of literature, were taken from real original descriptions.

Yes, but what do they describe? When we find the supernatural on maps of the last two or three centuries, it is at Giant's Grave, Devil's Bridge, Nine Maidens, and Robin Hood's Butts: names which are embedded in story rather than experience. The giants and maidens are not denied but neither are they present in the here and now—instead, we are treated to a local legend about how Robin Hood once held an archery contest, how the maidens were once turned into stone. These names might best be classed as fabulative, since they point to a story of the past rather than a current reality. Often we are dealing with what you might fancy, rather than what is actually there. The Devil's Dell or Dingle or Dancing Ground are spooky, overgrown thickets where you could easily imagine that Devil walks by night. The Fairy Glen is exactly the kind of place where, some enchanted evening, you might think you saw the little people at their revels.

Should we read earlier names in the light of this tradition? Were Thurspittes and Puckney places of imagination rather than experience? It's unlikely. Nineteenth-century field-names can be very sophisticated in their rhetoric, but sophistication implies an original simplicity, and as we work back to the earlier furlong names of the thirteenth and twelfth century, the use of metaphor and irony and personification dies away.[24] Names were originally descriptive statements which through long use became codified into fixed refer-ential labels, and in the Anglo-Saxon period we are still close to the original descriptive stage: indeed it is hard to say whether the landmarks in charters are being named at all, or only described. When a boundary procession toured the outskirts of Canterbury in 993, was their *ælfrucge* Elf Ridge, or just 'that ridge where the elves were seen'?

This is not to say that metaphor and fabulative construction were unknown to the Anglo-Saxons. A number of elfin names in southwest England contain the generic *cirice*, 'church', usually compounded with *pūcel*. These are not parish churches, of course, not even buildings: the only one to be securely identified, Buckle Church 1872 in Sussex, was 'an almost unapproachable cave in the face of the cliff at Seaford Head'.[25] The sequence runs back from Picklechurch Brake 1883 at Oxenton in Gloucestershire through three Wiltshire names—Pucklechurch 1604 at Keevil, Pockle Church 1570 at Winterborne Bassett, and Poculchurchmede 1529 at Lyneham—to *Pokulchurche* 1460 at Wyke Regis in Dorset. The earliest form is *Pucelancyrcan* for what is now the village of Pucklechurch in Gloucestershire, where Edmund was assassinated by a disgruntled outlaw in 946. This has been interpreted as 'church of a man named Pūcel'.[26] But it strains coincidence that the only instance of this name in Old English should parallel what is otherwise a supernatural construction; besides, it is unusual for people's names to be compounded with *cirice*.[27]

It seems absurd that *pūcels*, beings brushed with at least a flicker of hellfire, might attend church. But then there is a Fyndeschurche 1501 at Norton-by-Bromyard in Herefordshire, where the devil might tell his matins at midnight; and the spirits who taunted John Fraunceys of Swaledale were able to mimic the trappings of a service in their moorland home—celebrant, choir, holy-water bucket and all. We can guess from other ironic names in -church that the original *pucelancirice* was a cave or jagged outcrop of stone in some empty place that looked like a mock-chapel.[28] The original Gloucestershire landmark must have been conspicuous enough to name a nearby farm, which became first a royal estate and then a village with an its own real-life church. Metonymic transfers like this take time, so the original coining of the name would be much earlier than its first attestation as a settlement.[29]

In the early eighteenth century, the dwarfs had both a Hill and a Chapel at Lydney, also in Gloucestershire but on the far side of the Severn, where the haunted foundations turned out on excavation to be a Roman shrine. The compound *dweorg hūs* is found at three locations in Lancashire. Already in *Beowulf, hūs* means something very much like 'abode': when Hrothgar takes the hero across hill-tracks that lead to the haunted mere, they pass by moor and cliff and *nicor-hūsa fela* (1411). The *nicors* that the party encounter at Grendel's mere are material enough, slithering on its surface and resting on the ledges below the cliff, easy to bring down with a well-aimed arrow—but that may reflect the poet's own prejudices in favour of a purely physical monstrous, while the 'many nicor-houses' of his earlier reference are closer to the old lore. Enigmatic verses from a lost epic describe a gathering in which some are *ylves*, some *nadderes*, and some *nikeres* that live by the waters.[30] In this company, the *naddere* is not an ordinary adder, but a mysterious serpent, like the Laidley Worm that spoke and wept; evidently these could be taken at first glance for a person, and the *nikeres* too.[31] Slipping between human and not-human, such creatures might well have a *hūs*; the compounds are not merely fanciful, but mark out places where you might actually encounter a supernatural being.

Contrast between the two modes of fabulative and literal meaning is most obvious when names invoke something diabolical. Old English *dēofol*, with *fēond* and Latin *demon*, refer to a devil, one of the innumerable swarm of evil spirits that surrounded the early medieval faithful. By contrast, the Devil of modern English names is emphatically *the* Devil—the gentleman in black, the common enemy of man in Protestant theology and, in folktales, a character as distinct and recognizable as King Arthur and Robin Hood. Modern names in

Devil's- are fabulative descriptors of landmarks so remarkable that only Old Nick could be responsible for them: his giant strength and preternatural malice dug the Devils' Dyke, he threw the Devil's Bridge across an impassable stream and so on. These names depend on a storyteller's suspension of disbelief. The landmarks which they describe are not truly inexplicable and many in fact date from the nineteenth century.[32] The idea that these Devil- names preserve the awe-struck reaction of early Christians to the mighty pagan past collapses as soon as we establish a basic chronology. The idiom that coined them is very recent; Devil's ditches, valleys and caves usually turn out to have had other, more mundane names before the modern period.

By contrast the medieval *dēofol-* names, like those for other supernatural beings, show every sign of being literal: this is the field or lane or pool or wood where there is a devil. Not that he was invariably present there—after all, badgers, wildcats and martens cannot always have featured at the places that bear their names. Some of these are no doubt incident names, the sort that commemorate a one-off event rather than a permanent attribute. If they are like the place-names that reference living creatures, we might expect elfin names to occupy a semantic spectrum from the purely factual—'this is the *denu* where John encountered the *ælf*'—to those where the particular instance has been subsumed into general necessary knowledge—'this is the *pytt* where they say the man saw the *pūca*, and looking at it, I'm not surprised.' People did not name places after fairies because they liked to believe they were present there. They believed in them because these were the places where they had been seduced, abducted, challenged, tortured, maddened, healed and mocked by them.

Outdoors

Isolation was deeply frightening, especially to children despatched to jobs in the fields and pastures, where fear of loneliness could escalate into a full-scale panic attack. When a seven-year-old Welsh girl got lost outdoors, she had to spend the night in a tree; for eleven years afterwards she was unable to speak.[33] Even a single small miracle collection will present multiple variations on this theme. Wulfstan's shrine at Worcester saw the healing of a boy from Abergavenny who fell ill when he was sent to look after livestock in the fields, where he went to sleep. When he woke up, the animals were nowhere to be seen, which doesn't sound very miraculous; but though he searched everywhere, they were gone; and, what with fear of the unknown powers that had snatched them, and possibly also of the family response to their loss, he lost all power of speech and stayed that way for five years. Again, a twelve-year-old went to sleep while he was out in the fields. It was noon, a treacherous time for slumber, and when he woke up, his hands and feet had been twisted right round on the joints. Once more, a boy from Clun fell asleep in the fields while he was in the fields looking after a horse: in his sleep he thought that something came to him, demons it might have been, and with crippling pain they tore out his eyes. He woke up, shivering—he opened his eyes—and could see nothing. For nine years and two months he remained blind, until at last he came to Wulfstan's shrine.[34]

Only the third of these accounts specifies spirits of the air as the cause of illness, but they are clearly lurking in the other tales, their presence signalled by keywords that have survived the transition into Latin—*in agro, meridie*. When the *miraculés* told their original stories in Welsh or English, there would have been appreciative nods and murmurs at this point: no need to spell out what had come to these young people, alone and vulnerable in the fields at noon. Further north, the miracle collections are more explicit. Richard of Sunderland had a nephew—Richard was only a young man, so the nephew must be a child—who was put in charge of the sheep, where he went to sleep in the fields and on waking found that one leg was longer than the other until he hobbled to Farne, where a vigil at Cuthbert's shrine set him right. This, we are told, was done through diabolical illusion—evidently performed by the same beings who had tossed Richard onto their green horses and taken him to the lovely treacherous palace of their otherworld.[35] We have already met with the six-year-old from Fifeshire who dreamt as he slept in the fields, and was given a drink by four treacherous women which destroyed his health.[36] In Dunfermline five-year-old Mutinus slept in the pastures among the browsing calves and saw three ladies, two of whom wanted him killed while the third gave him the apple that enforced perpetual silence.[37]

It was not only children who were at risk outdoors.[38] About Christmas time, a man from Pittington near Durham went out into the open field and was suddenly struck blind in his open eyes.[39] Richard left his village near Wombridge to get some jobs done in a field, but it was Midsummer's Eve, a bad time to venture abroad, and instantly he sank under such weariness that he could go no further but had to lie down in the open air to sleep. And having snoozed for a little, when he got up he found that he could not speak, couldn't even use his tongue. It stuck to the floor of his mouth for months until he was cured by a miracle.[40] The turning points of the year were evidently bad times to be outdoors.

Though the outdoors was dangerous, it was not far from home. A short walking distance was all it took to put the men from Shropshire and Durham at risk, while families are unlikely to have let their children venture miles away from care. When a five-year-old is sent to look after the cows, at an age when you feel the cows should really be looking after him, he might be in a pasture close, or possibly following the animals as they browsed on a green or common, but surely no further than that. These stories do not encourage us to look for fairies in wild or unfrequented places.

The earliest miracle narrative, the one reported by a wealthy citizen of Winchester, is also the most precise geographically. It was near Midsummer Day when he left the city, crossed the bridge over the Itchen, and headed south through the water-meadows to check that all was well with his horses at pasture.[41] The sun stood high at noon when he was overcome by sleep, and waking with a start he realized it was time to get back and began making his way upstream along the familiar homeward path. It was then that he saw the two deformed dark naked women waiting for him on the riverbank, and next, as he hurried nervously up to the Winchester road, the third woman, dressed in shining white and immensely tall, who stepped out from behind a hill and confronted him. When she had struck him down with the blast of her waving sleeve, all three women leapt into the river. This spot cannot have been far from the city, for despite the apoplexy suddenly inflicted on him, the stricken citizen was able to lean on his spear and stagger up to the East Gate.

All this happened within a mile or so of Winchester—the leading city of Wessex, and the nearest thing that tenth-century England had to a capital.[42] This is no wild landscape. The horses, valuable enough to be a personal concern of their owner, would have been penned safely in a field off the common meadows. The closest toponymic parallels would be with names whose generics mean 'small field, enclosed field'. *Pukelecroft* C12 at Elmore in Gloucestershire is the earliest name in this group. At Milverton in Somerset there is an *Alve Crofte* 1322, *Buggiscroft* 1316 at Taverham in Norfolk, Pokerscroft 1506 at Crowhurst in Surrey, *Thrissecroft* c.1228 at Shrewsbury, and *Pukecrofte* C13 at Bruton in Somerset, followed by several other *pūca-* compounds with the same generic.

The variety in generics shows that there was no one standard supernatural experience at these places; everyone visited by these visions had to make what sense they could of them—though it is tempting to link the *Valgirimede* 1357 of Abbotsbury in Dorset with the experiences of the man from Winchester, given that his assailants have been speculatively identified as *wælcyrige*s, or maybe *hætses*.[43] But they are completely different from the pale figure with a man's face and shrouded body that confronted Alice of Reading in the early morning light as she went to the sheepfold to milk the sheep, or the horrible black men that crowded the orchard in Mersington where a girl had gone to pick an apple.

They hung her up on a tree and, as it seemed, cut off an arm; the pain was so bad that she lost the power of speech, not to be recovered till after many journeys she drank of Æbbe's well.[44] The apparitions are always different but the environment is the same, a small field near home, secure to all outward appearance, but dangerous when there is no other human being in sight and other things come clustering round.

Croft is Middle English; earlier words for enclosures are *geard*, found in *Deilȝerde* 1427 at Wingerworth in Derbyshire and *Scratȝord* 1417 at Nantwich; *hæg*, in *Poukhey* C14 at Kemerton in Gloucestershire and *Pukehaye* 1436 at Wellington in Somerset; and *haga*, in *Scrathawe* 1256 at Weston in Nottinghamshire, which has many other doublets down to Scrat Haigh 1891 at Kexborough in the West Riding. Scrat- names are often found with generics that mean some kind of field, making up about half of the attestations for a word which is otherwise absent from the literature about fairies, spirits, demons or anything else. There was an Old English *scratta*, *scrætte*, but in all the written texts this means 'hermaphrodite', understood specifically as a medical condition. Old Norse *skratti* was much more polysemous and could be used for both goblin and wizard—one of many words bridging that fiercely guarded boundary between human and otherworlder. Evidently the underlying sense of 'something not quite right, a being who exploits the power that comes to those who do not fit' had been reduced to a doctor's diagnosis by the same Anglo-Saxon literalism which turned the *nicor* into a hippopotamus. It may be that Old Norse *skratti* was adopted as Middle English *scrat*; the word could also have been borrowed, or at least strongly influenced, by German *schrat*, another reflex from the Common Germanic original, used for spirits of the wild.[45]

Arable Land

When people met fairies in the fields, *in agro*, it was usually while they were in charge of livestock, but that was not necessarily on permanent pasture. Half or a third of a village's open fields would lie fallow each year for crop rotation, with cattle ambling over the ridges to pick what grazing they could. Sometimes encounters took place among strips that were still under cultivation. William Wynfeld was riding by a field of ripe barley when the little red man emerged from between the stalks, took hold of his bridle and led him into the crop.[46] Gwestin Gwestiniog looked out from his hall by the banks of the Llyfni; it was a serene moonlit night, clear enough for him to make out the forms of women as they danced in the field where his oats grew. When he went out to chase them off, they slipped away, plunging at last into Llyn Syfaddon. Like the terrible women of Winchester, these sisters took refuge in water, but they cannot have been so formidable, for Gwestin was able to pursue them that first night without harm, and the second, and the third; as they plunged under the water he overheard one tell the other how lucky it was that the mortal had not done the one thing that would have enabled him to keep hold of them, and on the fourth night he took advantage of what he had heard, and caught himself a fairy bride.[47]

There is abundant place-name evidence for fairies among the arable strips of the old common fields. The most common generic is *feld*, which by the end of the Anglo-Saxon period had become the standard villagers' term for a large unified block of land in the open field. *Pokefelde* c.1190 at Leverington in Cambridgeshire is followed by other names in Essex, Berkshire and Hertfordshire. Though it is the most common compound, this simply reflects the overall frequency of *pūca*, for other elfin qualifiers are present: *þyrs* in Tursfield Crosse 1699 at Scawby in Lincolnshire, *dweorg* in *Dwerefeld* 1421 at Maghull in Lancashire, *dēofol* in *Dewelfeld* 1487 at Sowerby Bridge in the West Riding. There is a *Buggenfeld* 1433 at Coventry and *Elvenefeld* 1467 at Hartlip in Kent, both qualifiers marked with what seems to be an adjectival *-en*.[48]

Next in frequency is *land* which, although retaining a more general sense in Middle English, was used in agrarian names for a single holding of arable land, ploughed up into a ridge some 220 yards long. Again *pūca* is the most common qualifier, beginning with *La Poclond* 1200x90 at Preston Candover in Hampshire, and again there is a scattering of other terms for spirits: *Thirslande* 1268 at Marr in the West Riding and *Therslande* 1207 at Cowley in Oxfordshire, a rare instance of *þyrs* in southern England; *Elflandes* C13 at Eakring in Nottinghamshire, with adjectival forms in *Alvenelond* 1318 at Downham Market in Norfolk and Elfylands 1703 at Colne in Lancashire.[49] There is also a *Buggelond* c.1300 at Lamarsh in Essex although here some local context would be helpful, since *bugge* was also used for 'scarecrow', and scarecrows belong in arable fields by definition.[50]

The rare *niht-mare* appears in *Negtmareslond* C13 at Barton in Cheshire. Other instances of this qualifier are compounded with terms from the management of the open fields, also in Cheshire: *Nahtmare furlang* 1300x20 at Coddington and *Nachomaresforlong* c.1312 at Macclesfield. The only other name in this group—*Naughmarethorn* 1290—comes from Cannock, fifteen miles away in Staffordshire; it seems to be a very regional tradition.

A *furlang* was a block of *land*s, usually a subdivision of a *feld*. We find it in *Pukefurland* C13 at Radipole in Dorset and *Pukefurlong* 1288/9 at Silverstone in Northamptonshire, which also has a later name Goblin Furlong 1775 at Crick.

In the eastern counties, Old Norse *deill* was used for blocks of this kind: the trio of *Thyrsdal* 1342 at Anwick in Lincolnshire, *Elvernedele* 1316 at Holme next the Sea in Norfolk and *Puchedole* 1419 at Walton in Suffolk shows the variation in qualifiers as we move from the northern to the southern province.[51]

The *æcer*, a strip some 22 yards wide making up a *land* or part of a *land*, was the base unit of the open fields. Here again we find the *pūca* in *Pokacre c.*1250 at Coulsdon in Surrey, and even a *Pokehalfacre* 1399 somewhere in Essex. A *land* which lay at right angles to the rest on the short end of a *furlang* was a *heafod* or *heafod-land*, found with *ælf* in *Elfhede* 1452 at Piddlehinton in Dorset, *scucca* in *Scucheved* 1216x72 at Little Casterton in Rutland and, under Scandinavian influence, *skratti* in Scrathewed 1579 at Ingleton in the West Riding and *troll* in *Trolleheudland* 1309 at Goxhill in Lincolnshire.

The testimony of these place-names cannot be denied, but it is hard to see how they were coined and remembered, for a *land* or an *æcer* barely counted as places at all. They did not stand out like a tree or a stone; they were just lines drawn across the undulation of the open field, an unbroken landscape only demarcated by counting strips up and along from a starting point. And whereas pasture saw the comings and goings of people who were alone, and therefore open to fairy encounter, most work in the open fields was communal.

But to emphasize working practice in this way overlooks the geography of openfield. Because it lay all round the nucleated villages, paths ran along or across its ridges; it was a space through which people were always on the move. The people who saw the burning plough and its devil ploughman in the fields of Strubby were not there to cultivate the land themselves; they were passing through, presumably on their way to somewhere else, when noontide came and revealed the damned sight.

People oriented themselves among the open strips by keeping their eyes fixed on reference points outside the field itself. They named sections of arable after the landmarks that lay beyond them—hillocks, pits and wells, some of them with supernatural reputations, so that we find additive names such as Bugbarrow Furlong 1764 at Portesham in Dorset, Goblin Pit Furlong 1625 at Carlton in Leicestershire, *Poukewallefeld* 1389 at Bishopstone in Herefordshire and *Thirswelleflat* 1345 at Whiston in the West Riding. The wells and hillocks cannot have been in the field itself, or they would have been ploughed out of existence. They stood just outside the sown land at the point where meadow and pasture began; the arable strip, the path that led by it and the spot to which it was heading were equally likely to receive an elfin name.

We are so used to seeing fairy landscapes through the eyes of Romanticism, to idealizing places that are wild and fierce and undefiled, that we lose sight of how different things were in an age when the supernatural world clung much closer to the human. Medieval fairies were not children of the mountain and the flood: the Home Counties have a higher density of elfin names (4.6 per 250 square miles) than Yorkshire (3.3).[52] Take all the generics that mean different sorts of fields and enclosures, either pasture or arable—take *hæg*, *haga* and *hecg*; *falod*, *geard*, *clos* and *croft*; *stede*, *tūn* and *tyning*; *orceard*, *parc*, *plat*, *nest*, *piece*, *pightel* and *place*; *grene*, *læswe*, *leah*, *pasture* and *walke*; *rod*, *ryde* and *ryding*; *end*, *halh*, *hop* and *hyrne*; *banke*, *bryce*, *ersc*, *intak* and *vangr*; *æcer*, *butte*, *deill*, *feld*, *flat*, *furlang*, *heafod* and *land*: collectively these account for 25% of elfin names, the highest proportion for any landscape category.

Roads

There was not much to choose between a road and an open space, for travellers typically followed rights of way not surfaced highways; the *exemplum* of the bailiff of Turvey begins with him on the road, but by the time the demonic creature lollops towards him, he is in the midst of the fields.[53] The most common generic in these cases is *lane*, an informal word for routes better suited to walkers or riders than wheeled transport. Of the 46 compounds with this element, more than three-quarters have *pūca* as generic, so there was evidently something about the trickster spirit which seemed particularly appropriate to them. The *portuni*, who might be a confused memory of late twelfth-century *poukes*, liked to attach themselves to men who rode late at night though the uncertain shadows, only to make fun of them by leading the horse into some muddy slough, and vanishing with derisory laughter, the *ho ho ho* that later tradition attributed to Robin Goodfellow.[54] These are the victims that were *led al ny3t with gobelyn, and erreth hider and thider ... after the sunne is downe, and the ni3t is come*, in the preacher's simile for spiritual deception.[55] This is how the devil leads us astray, the *Fasciculus Morum* explains. Doesn't he specially target men who sneak out at night for no good purpose—to see their mistress perhaps? (We remember John the clerk and his girlfriend). Victims wandered round and round all night long, circling endlessly around a wood or a farm while convinced they were heading straight to where they needed to be. Then the sun rises, they see with bewilderment that they are trampling in their own tracks, and with a burst of invisible laughter the demon called Goblin lets them be.[56]

These supernatural confusions took place, not in remote or waste places, but near familiar farmsteads and woods: that was what made them so inexplicable. If so, we might expect haunted lanes to be on the outskirts of a village, but in fact the earliest records come from towns. We have *Pukelone* C12 at Gloucester, *Poukelane* 1250x99 at Chichester, *Pokelane* 1310 at Windsor, *Pokelane* 1317 at Shaftesbury, *Poke Lane* 1382 at Guildford, *Poukelane* 1384 at Dorking, *Pokelane* 1455 at Axbridge, and *Pukkelane* 1479 at Warwick. The first name to come from something like a village is *Pouklone* 1395 at Tillington in Herefordshire. In the sixteenth century, towns and villages are about equally balanced; from the seventeenth, the attestations are mostly from villages. This suggests a tradition that had spread out into the countryside but was urban in origin, although the towns are modest places even by medieval standards: Gloucester and Warwick the only county towns, Chichester the only city. At Gloucester, Eynsham and Witney, the lanes are short, lined with old houses, just away from the town centre and linking two busier streets.[57] The lane at Guildford is an alley off the High Street, that at Witney a path running between the backs of properties.[58]

There must have been something about the small-town environment that fostered these names—an old, untenanted house with a spooky reputation, or a side-street known for its shady inhabitants, etherial or otherwise. Otherwise *lane* is found with qualifiers that overlap with *pūca*: three instances of *bugge* beginning with Bugg Lane 1602 at Laindon in Essex, two of *pūcel*, and two of *gobelin*. Curiously, although *troll* may be present in Trow Lane Head 1817 at Lynesack in Durham, *þyrs* is rare with *lane* or its northern counterpart *gata*. Instead, there is an unexpected *þurswege* c.1174 as far south as Abbotsham in Devon.

We might expect *strǣt*, originally meaning 'paved highway', to be found in urban centres but by the late Middle Ages the word was more widely applied: *Buggestrete* 1394 at Burton in Staffordshire, *Poukestrete* 1482 at Milborne Port in Somerset and Puck Street 1676 at Woodmansterne in Surrey seem to belong with the villages and small towns.[59] It was because they lay near to settlement, not far from it, that these roads were haunted. People had to venture down them if they were to go anywhere at all. The supernatural lurked close to home, especially for women, whose world was already circumscribed. Agnes Watson of St Dunstan's in the East was out with her mother in the dusk when the rage of an unclean spirit attacked her in the churchyard.[60] In Warwickshire a girl, sent out on an errand by night, was seized by such fear that as soon as she was back inside she lost her mind and dropped down in a fit.[61]

For those who ventured further, the generalised threat of the outdoors had its focus in particular places. It is no coincidence that Pucklewood 1841 at Limpley Stoke in Wiltshire lies on either side of a highway, exactly the situation which threatened the priest and his clerk returning south from Taunton to Pitminster.[62] They passed through a wood that stretched on either side in a hollow valley: this would be Old Combe, where the road climbs up to the Blackdowns. The tree-lined belt along the slope of these hills was no more than half a mile wide but that was enough for the clerk to lose his way and for the three eerie women to find him and throw him down. A traveller passing through a wood would do well to scan the gloom behind the trees, one hand on a charm and the other close to his sword, for criminals and fairies were not always distinct to the frightened mind. As thieves beguile people down wrong paths in the forest, says Bartholomew the Englishman, so the devils lay a false trail for souls in the wilderness of this world.[63] For Lucian of Chester, demons were interchangeable with the low-lifes lying in ambush along Watling Street.[64] The citizen of Winchester, fleeing from two otherworldly females who meant him no good, was accosted by the third who had been lying in wait for him behind a hill, a little way from the road—just as in thirteenth-century Oxfordshire, evil men used to lie in the hollow of the barrow at Cutteslowe before jumping out to rob and murder travellers.[65]

The qualifiers for *wudu* are very mixed, and mostly attested late: *Bugewde* c.1250 at Stogumber in Somerset and *Dyulesewude* 1254 at Ashover in Derbyshire are the only medieval forms, followed by Pokewodde 1530 at Nettlecombe in Somerset, Thrushwood 1567 at Kirkleatham in the North Riding, Puckle Wood 1698 at Cobham in Kent and Goblins Wood 1758 at Bellingdon in Buckinghamshire. The general term *wudu* often gives way to more exact descriptions such as *grafa* in *Buggryfftt* 1409 at Scarborough, *Poke Grove* 1472 at Downe in Kent, and Elfes Grove 1543 at Garsdon in Leicestershire. Unusually Old Norse *skógr*, 'shaw, belt of trees', is found three times with *gram*: in the West Riding, *Gram'skebanch* 1225 at Hebden, and in Westmoreland, Gramskeugh 1721 at Hartley and Gramshaw Head 1842 at Nateby. This word *gram*, never found compounded with any other generic, is homonymous in Old Norse and Old English (Grendel is a *gram* in *Beowulf* 765), although it properly means 'angry' and using it substantively to describe demons was a poetical convention.[66]

The traveller was at most danger, from elves or from outlaws, wherever pathways converged on a single point at which an enemy could wait.[67] That would explain the uncanny reputation of fords and bridges. The earliest form is *Turesfort* 1086, now Thursford in Norfolk, likely to have been a major crossing if it gave name to an estate in Domesday. Other names in *þyrs* are *Thrusbrige* 1272x1307 at Whitby and Thrush Brigg 1846 at Priest Hutton in Lancashire.[68] For *pūca*, we have *Pokeford* 1199 at Chiddingfold in Surrey, *Poukebrugge* 1406 at Eynsham in Oxfordshire and Puckbridge 1803 at Churcham in Gloucestershire; for *scucca*, *Shokeforth-brooke* 1412 at Soyland in the West Riding; and there is one attestation each for *bugge*, *pokere* and *skratti*.

River crossings, like roads in themselves, are liminal places: neither quite here nor there. That might seem particularly appropriate to spirits who linger ambiguously on the boundaries between life and death, this world and the other, and who liked to appear at the crossing-points of time. Medieval people were afraid of what might come at twilight, as can still be readily appreciated; they also felt menaced by the chill hour before dawn, which has less resonance now, probably because we don't get up so early.[69] For us, midnight is the witching hour, but this had much less significance in an age without chiming clocks, when there was no easy way you could tell you were halfway through the night. But everybody reckoned time by the sun's passage, almost without being aware of it, so they knew when it was noon: that was when you expected something of another world to break into this one.[70]

Other crossing-points such as gates and stiles shared the uncanny reputation of the bridge. We have a *Poukhacche* 1400 at Crowhurst in Surrey and a Poke Hatch Gate 1642 (explaining the now obsolete word *hæcc*) at Lingfield in the same county; a Scradgate 1673 (with *skratti*) at Hensingham in Cumberland, a Thirst Gate 1769 at Kaber in Westmorland, a Dwarf Gate 1771 at Dallington in Sussex, and a Goblin Styles 1842 at Newnham in Shropshire.

At Puckthorne Yeate 1574 at Milverton in Somerset, with dialect *yeat* for 'gate', travellers would have seen the thorn tree marking where the road went through—a ragged silhouette against a darkening sky. At Chiddingfold in Surrey, that fairy-haunted parish, *Thurstrehacche* 1250x99 was a similar combination. There are nine other place-names referring to trees, half of them thorns: the medieval forms are *Succhethormam* 1154x9 (with scribal *m* for *n*) at Crich in Derbyshire, *Elvene Tres* c.1200 at Hook in the West Riding, *Buggehesel* 1248 at Cookham in Berkshire, *Naughmarethorn* 1290 at Cannock in Staffordshire, *Fendeshok* 1301 at Barrow in Shropshire, and *Alvysch Thornys* 1319 at Milton Abbas in Dorset. Most of these are field-names, referring to isolated trees or stands of trees in the fields. Elfelders 1647 at Kings Bromley in Staffordshire, Suckethorne Nooke 1666 at Wormhill in Derbyshire and a Goblin Oake 1680 somewhere in Middlesex make up the total. It is significant that, unlike most elfin names, this group does not include any nineteenth-century attestations for the typical medieval qualifiers. More recent times have seen the coinage of new names in *fairy*, but these are not at the old sites.

Stones were more durable. There are eight possible attestations, though only those in *pūca* are truly convincing: *La Pukestone* 1275 at Bitterne, a boundary mark overlooking Southampton, *Pokeston* 1415 at Duffield in Derbyshire, Puketon 1585 at Studland in Dorset, and Pokestones 1688 at Fareham in Hampshire. Nineteen names, 2% of the corpus, is not very much when you consider all the denunciation that trees and stones receive in the homilectic literature. If people really were slipping away to these places to offer candles in homage to the spirits of the land, there is little to show for it in the onomastic record.

Another place for illicit ritual, the crossroads, barely registers in elfin names.[71] Encounters certainly happened here, as we learn from Matilda, who came to a crossroads in the Lindsey countryside where a violent whirlwind suddenly broke upon her. It clutched at her, whipped her round and threw her to the ground, when she instantly became blind.[72] No explanation is offered by the miraculist, but we can fill it in from later lore, in which the fairies travel in whirlwinds.[73] Other tales of strange meetings set the scene at a roadside cross. At Haydock in Lancashire a man lived with a woman as his wife; they had two sons, but the woman died, and after that the man took another wife. One day in 1373, as the story tells, he went to the blacksmith to get a new coulter for the plough. The forge was at Hume, which is some miles from Haydock, so it was dark when the man walked home, his coulter in his hand. And as he came to Newton Cross, he saw a shadow in the shadow of the cross. When he had got the strength to speak, he called out and demanded its name. 'Do not be afraid', it said. 'I was once your woman; if you loved me then, help me now.' He asked how things stood with her, and she said, 'Not well. I will suffer until the last prayer is said: reach out and touch me, reach out, do not be afraid.' And he held out his hand and touched a woman's head with long tresses of hair, and as he felt them they came away in his hand.[74]

The *exemplum* continues in exemplary style, with the man saying masses for his dead mistress until, one by one, each black hair turns to gold.[75] But behind the preacher's text there are hints of a more brutal popular version, in which the dead threaten the living. Remember that folktales do not go in for gratuitous realism; every feature of the story is there for a purpose, and if in this tale the man is carrying a piece of plough equipment, there must be a reason for it. I suspect that in the original version, the ghost said something like 'If it were not for the iron you hold in your hand, I would tear you as a cat tears a mouse.' If so, it would the first mention of a theme common in later tradition, that cold iron protects you from supernatural beings; but the story has been softened into a more sentimental tale of rescue from purgatory.

Travellers were fearful, and with good reason. It was late on a Wednesday night when William of Birdforth was walking home from Ampleforth to Newstead. As he went, he heard a terrible cry from the fells to his right; he shivered and walked on, but the next time he heard the cry, it was closer; and the third time, it came from the crossroads ahead.[76] There was nothing to do but to go forward, though in the darkness he saw something ahead of him, like a pale horse. His dog ran forward and barked at it, then suddenly returned in terror, sheltering between his legs. But William adjured the spirit in the name of the Lord and the blood of Christ not to block his way, and it took off, turning over and over like a twisted piece of canvas.[77]

Marshes and Mires

Not all haunted places were to be shunned. There was a *þyrs haga* near York, mentioned in 1416 when the master and brethren of St Leonard's Hospital wrote to Henry V soon after his return from Agincourt. They wanted the royal council to summon John Langton, esquire, who had muscled in on the common at Heslington, sending men to Thurshawe and Thirspole and cutting turf which belonged by right to the hospital. Langton was of too great lineage and alliance for the brothers to tackle but they hoped that the king might be able to bring him to heel.[78] The resource was worth fighting over because it was so convenient—Heslington is only two miles from the centre of York, an easy trip to bring back turves for fuel. Evidently there was nothing to be feared from the resident *þyrs*, at least not compared to the city's overweening esquire, and if peat was being cut from around his *pōl*, then the waters in which he had originally dwelt were shrinking, perhaps drying up completely.

This is not the kind of setting we would expect, at least not if we are primed by the early literature of the supernatural. *þyrs sceal on fenne gewunian, ana innan lande* say the eleventh-century Maxims: the *þyrs* will be found in the fen, alone in the land.[79] The literary *þyrs* is a solitary, like the hermit saints who venture far from human society to contest his demonic realm. But a fiend hardly counts as *ana* when his home is in a busy and contested peat-cutting half an hour's brisk walk from the city gates of York.

In vocabulary, at least, elfin names match the landscape of the Maxims: there is even a *Thursefen* 1200x50 at Stainburn in the West Riding.[80] There's also a *Poukwan* 1321 somewhere in Essex, with East Saxon *fœnn*, and an *Elvenfen* in Lincolnshire: as we have previously found, the varied names for spirits turn out in practice to be interchangeable.[81] Yorkshire has a *Thirskerr* 1382 at Methley and Lancashire a *Turssekar* 1190x1212 at Hindley, both with *kjarr*, the modern dialect *carr*, a piece of swampy ground matted with alder and other trees that tolerate wet around their feet. Several names have a generic *mýrr*, whose meanings range from swamp through bog to miry place. From *le Thursmyre* 1256 at Windermere onwards, these names are found in the West Riding, East Riding and Lincolnshire; some forms, like *Thrysmer* 1484/5 at Gimingham in

Norfolk, formally suggest Old English *mere* although this may represent a fusion of the two words at the limits of the Scandinavian speech area, rather than a genuine difference.[82] However, there is a *Pukemere* 1283 at Bray in Berkshire, which is a West Saxon region: nothing could be more southern English than these lush fields cupped in the valley of the Thames.[83]

Here, of all places, it seems strange to find an onomastic match for the dark waters of epic, for *mere* is the word consistently used for the monstrous lake in *Beowulf*. Not that this makes the scene clearer: the haunted mere of the poem is not a realistic body of water but a landscape chimaera, at once swamp, tarn and fjord.[84] But if close reading fails to yield a coherent sense for these dark waters, there is another authority to which we can turn, the English landscape. For over a century it has been claimed that the *Grendlesmere* is not a place of myth but an actual location you can visit. Just follow the Pewsey–Hungerford road, turn off before Doves Farm, take a left at Ham village and carry on till you get to a dogleg in the Spray Road.[85] If a landscape really came this close to the Old English epic of the supernatural, we would have a clue that opened up meanings for the *Thursmyre* and the *Elvenfen* and many other places. But it may not be so straightforward.

The men and women of *Beowulf* belong to the heroic lore of the old north: the audience would have recognized their names as soon as they were mentioned. But Grendel is unique. We are told, twice, that he is *called* Grendel (102, 1354) as if this needed explaining. The name never appears again and there are no analogues in subsequent tales or other languages. But confusingly there are several place-names that resemble it, beginning with the river *Grendel* 961 in a charter from Clyst St Mary in Devon, *Grendel* or *Grindel* 1280x95 at Ashley in Cambridgeshire, *le Grindel* 1280x95 at Norton in Suffolk, *atte Grundel* 1365 and *le Grundel* 1391 at Welton in Northamptonshire, *the Grendyll* 1463 at Bury St Edmunds, and then a trio of Grindles from seventeenth-century Leicestershire and the Grindle Syke 1679 which runs through several Rutland parishes.[86] Clearly there was some particular landscape feature that could be described by this word, and to judge from the first and last instances, it was a feature in a river. The best fit would be a word **grendel* (perhaps also **gryndel* with *y*>*i* or *y*>*u* in later forms), an *l*-formation from words for gravel and grinding.[87] If this is right, *le Grindel* would be the place where you went to dredge gravel from the shallows, pools or pits.

Like many elements, **grendel* appears not just on its own (a simplex) but as a qualifier. The river in Devon is also the *Grendelbroc* C13, and a dredging place (*delf*) along its banks was *Grendulf* c.1200 (with syncope of an original **Grendeldelf*). We find the *Grindelmere* 1216x72 at Throckenholt in

Cambridgeshire, *Grundelford* 1248 (now Grindleford Bridge) at Eyam Woodlands in Derbyshire, *Grenlington* 1250 (with connective *-ing-*, now Grindleton Brook) at Great Mitton in the West Riding, *Grendelbury* 1330 at Chudleigh in Devon, *Grendelhull* 1340 at Ashwell in Hertfordshire, and Grindelapitt 1645 at Sidmouth.[88] Still mostly associated with water, these clearly contain the same element as the simplex names.

As usual in compounds, the qualifier is appositive: the elements *grendel* and *mere* are shunted next to each other without any grammatical coupling. But many other names take the form *Grendelsmere* with a genitive *-s*, and you wonder if this is at last 'the mere of Grendel', because in Modern English compounds we only use the genitive for people (or, stretching a point, warped hell-guests in human shape). But Old English idiom was different, and Anglo-Saxon place-names employ the genitive, as we use 'of', for things as well as individuals.[89] So a gravelly feature could be behind *grindeles pytt* C10 (notionally 708) at Abbots Morton in Worcestershire; *grendeles pytt* C10 (notionally 739) at Crediton; *grendlesmere* 931 at Ham in Wiltshire (afterwards Grindells 1649); *grendelsmere* 951x5 at Oldswinford in Staffordshire; *gryndeles sylle* 957 at Battersea; *grindles bece* 972 at Alfrick; *grendeles gatan* 972 at Hendon in Middlesex (now Barnet Gate); *Grendelesmere* C12 at Felstead in Essex (now Gransmore); *Grundeleswelle* 1295x1317 at Worthington in Leicestershire; *Grundelespole* 1327 at Compton Bassett in Wiltshire; *Gryndeliscombe* 1339 at Stoke Climsland in Cornwall; and *Grundleswell* c.1400 at Misterton in Leicestershire (afterwards Grindle mid C17).[90]

None of these names can be drawing directly on *Beowulf* itself.[91] Anglo-Saxon charters were documents hedged with anathema and majesty, not a platform for fan-fiction from a scribe impressed with the latest manuscript he'd read: besides, we have little evidence that anyone ever read *Beowulf*, apart from the enthusiast for monsters who commissioned a copy and the two bored scribes who transcribed it.[92] Perhaps there was such a thing as 'a grendel', a vernacular monster standing in the same relationship to his literary exemplar as the *pūca* does to Shakespeare's Puck.[93] But if so, the *Beowulf*-poet does not expect us to know it, introducing the name Grendel as something unfamiliar to his audience. Were there really two homonymous words, *grendel*[1] 'gravel' and *grendel*[2] 'water monster'? It seems unnecessary to posit one element for all the simplex names and appositive compounds and another for all the genitival compounds, especially as the latter have the same range of generics and seem to survive in modern form as simplexes. And besides, there are too many *grendel-* names to carry conviction as haunted landscapes. When we consider that there are four possible instances of *ælf* in charters, three of *pūca*, three of *scucca* and two of *þyrs*, it strains credulity that a common noun **grendel* for a monster should appear seven times in charters when it is absent from any other Old or Middle English text.[94]

Pools and Streams

The horror of the dark fen explains much about elfin names in *kjarr*, *mersc*, *fenn*, *mor*, *mýrr*, *mere*, *pol* and *ponde*. Stagnant waters were eerie places, death-places. Grendel drags his victims to the mere, and dying throws himself into the bloodstained depths. The link between standing water and corpses was not just a literary theme: it played out in real life.

James Tankerlay, former priest of Cold Kirby, was not a spirit and when he got out of the grave at nights and rambled back to his old home, it was the physical presence of their dead rector that troubled the villagers. But like many wandering corpses in medieval England, he took on attributes of other supernatural beings. Just as the dead men of Drakelow became shapeshifters in animal form, so when Tankerlay broke into a house to terrify his mistress, he blew out one of her eyes.[95] In *exempla*, this nasty trick is credited to demons.[96] It appears in miracles, too: a fisherman was setting nets off the Isle of Wight when the wind got up against him, and a mist flowed over his face, leaving him stone blind. His boat bobbed helplessly here and there on the waves until his mates saw there was something wrong, and got him back to shore. No-one knew what had been in that wind until at last its malice was overcome by the holy power of Aldhelm at his shrine in Malmesbury.[97] In later stories it is the fairies who blind people because they are angry at having been seen. The migratory legend of the midwife to the fairies, found throughout Europe and already known to Gervase of Tilbury, concludes with an uncanny stranger thrusting his finger into a woman's eye.[98]

Tankerlay's reign of terror came to an end when he was exhumed from his grave at Byland, coffin and all, and hauled away from the world of men. Nobody wanted to do this but Roger Wayneman got the job. Apparently he was a professional carrier; at all events he had a waggon and a team of draught oxen. They dragged the coffin four miles to Gormire, a black lake on the slopes below Kirby Moor, where the oxen trudged into the morass and almost drowned while Roger was pitching the coffin off the cart.[99]

This is what you did with the bodies of the bad dead: consigned them to the clinging mud until they found fit company among the *þyrs* or *scucca* or whatever it was that haunted these fetid places, and forgot that they had ever been men. Leofstan the shire-reeve of Suffolk was a ruthless judge and in the closing years of the tenth century he condemned a defendant who was innocent, and also a client of St Edmund's abbey at Bury, which in the eyes of the monks was more or less the same thing. After the woman fled to sanctuary, he had her dragged from the altar, sneering at her prayers, but God is not mocked; Leofstan fell mad and died. The demons who had possessed his mind now took hold of his body and he climbed out of his grave at nights to trouble the people of Bury until they disinterred his corpse, sewed it up in a calf's skin and sank it in a lake.[100] Written down about a century after it happened, this story appears to be historical in its broad outlines, which is more than can be said for the fate of Cwœnthryth, wicked stepmother of the saintly toddler Cynehelm. Her funeral rites were a mockery, for the coffin would not rest underground— neither in the church nor churchyard, nor even in the bare fields. At last a hermit stepped forward to say that he had seen a vision of a brilliantly shining child who ordered that her body should not have burial, but be cast into some remote deep.[101]

The *Vita Kenelmi* is a fairytale, but its ending faithfully reports tenth- and eleventh-century practice: bodies of the despised and outcast dead were thrown into a bog or fen, a mark of disrespect but also, tacitly at least, a ritual that consigned them to somewhere far from the walks of men.[102] In modern times, when the physicality of the Anglo-Norse walking corpse had dwindled into an insubstantial phantom, it was not the body of the dead which was consigned to water, but their ghost. Storytellers from the West Country tell, again and again, of a parson who knew a thing or two and despatched the local ghost to a pit or a pool in the nearby river, where it remains howling in the performance of some endless task.[103]

These modern stories give us a clue to interpret medieval place-names. Bugmore 1563 at Salisbury, *Dewelepole* 1285 at Beaminster in Dorset, *Dwarewmere* 1200s at Fenny Compton in Warwickshire, Pokemershe *c.*1500 and *Pokemore* 1463 somewhere in Devon, *Pukpole* 1232 at Bishopstrow in Wiltshire, *Pokelmour* 1399 at Portesham in Dorset, Skinsmeare 1601 at Broughton Astley in Leicstershire, and *Shukmore* 1200s at Coventry, along with all the *þyrs* names—*Thirspol* 1305 at Cringleford in Norfolk, *Thrusmyre* 1400s at Wighill in the West Riding: they can best be understood as the equivalent of the Lumb Mouth, Black Anne Pool, Amstell Pond or Homersfield Bridge where recalcitrant ghosts were laid in more recent times.[104]

A migratory folktale, found in medieval sources, may give a context for these banishings. Bromyard compares the self-important priest to that demon who worked the quern, and was rewarded by the head of the household with a gift of clothing, upon which he broke off work forever, saying as he quit the place a couplet which, with the help of later versions, we can reconstruct in English: '*Now ich habbe cote and hode/Never more will ich do gode*'.[105] Bromyard calls the demon Gerard, a devil-name with a long history.[106] But Master Rypon, whom we may suspect of being a Yorkshireman, tells a version in which the demon is a *thrus*, and his parting words are given as *Suld syche a proude grome grynd corne?*—the use of alliteration, rather than rhyme, reflecting a northern setting.[107] Such is the tale of The New Suit of Clothes, F381.3 to the folklorists. Grendel has come down in the world by the fourteenth century, if he is reduced to grinding at the mill, but there is still a common thread linking him with his later avatar: a wild, shaggy being, immensely powerful even when that power is bent to help human ends. If we want to know how the *þyrs* was imagined at the midpoint of the twelfth century—tall, hairy, effortlessly performing household tasks—then the demon which dug over Godric's smallholding, performing a fortnight's worth of work in an hour, may be the closest approximation.[108]

The point of the story is that the demon servant goes away—it sounds very much as if he is driven away. But where is he driven to? Something of the *þyrs* was still present in early modern brownies, whose shagginess, strength, and latent violence made them uncomfortable servants, so it was with some relief that they were at last banished or exorcized.[109] And they were usually despatched into water, returning to the stream or pool from which they had originally come. If this theme goes back to the Middle Ages then we can match it with the *Thirspol* and *Thrusmyre* of onomastics.

Place-names are so stubbornly resistant to interpretation, and the modern archive of fairy folklore is so rich, that it is tempting to use other modern stories as a key for interpreting old names. But it is probably wiser to take medieval evidence on its own terms. Some tale-types and motifs have crossed the bridge that separates the Middle Ages from modernity, others have not, and we should be prepared to map a supernatural landscape that is very different from our own.

It is unclear, for instance, how much of a distinction was made between fens and ponds—stagnant water with matted vegetation that pulled you down if you fell in, and open water where you could safely cool off on a hot day. In the dictionaries, *mýrr* belongs to the former class, *mere* to the second, but outside the library it is not so clear. Gormire, for instance, is a lake; you can swim across it. Most supernatural qualifiers seem to be allocated equally to both kinds of feature, but *nicor* is different. As we saw earlier, this was the only kind of spirit to be found exclusively at one kind of landscape: with the exception of a solitary *Nikeresaker* 1313 somewhere in Cambridgeshire, they are all wet places, as you might expect of a creature whose name derives from

Old Germanic *nikwazaz*, ultimately stemming from Indo-European words for 'washing' and 'water'. And clear water, for preference: there are five names in *pōl* to one in *mersc*—*Nikerespol* 1200s at Passenham in Northamptonshire, *Nikerpoll* 1263 somewhere in Sussex, *Nikerpole* 1272 at Mildenhall in Wiltshire, *Nikerpole* 1296x8 at Lincoln and *Nikerespool* 1309 at Sutton in Cheshire, as against *Nickersmarsh* 1687 ('a marsh island') at Kirton in Suffolk. In Lincolnshire there was a spring, *Nikirwells*, perhaps feeding a pool.[110]

Mapping these names is not easy, as there are no modern instances to guide us: this is one supernatural element that cannot be reliably separated from its homonyms in field-names.[111] But we know that the Mildenhall *Nikerpole* lay within a bend of the river near the village. The Cheshire *Nikerespool* was in another river, the Weaver, not far upstream of Winsford. At Lincoln the pool was formed by the junction of the Sincil Dyke and the Great Gowt, two waterways which join just beside the main entrance to the city from the south.[112] At King's Lynn the *Nikeresfleet* 1390 lay within the town itself, one of several streams canalized east–west to drain into the Ouse.

Many of these pools lay near bridges, perhaps deepened by the swirl of water downstream of the piers. They are no lonely monster-haunted tarns: all the same, there was something about dark pools that gave unease, however close to the lights of home. The woman on her way back from Haddington fair stopped by a stream only a little way from her village, yet it was there she met the girl that was not a girl, pale and savage and armed with a hand like a horse's hoof that ripped into her arm and tore flesh off her back.[113] That threat from something which was at once water-animal and human reminds us that by the fourteenth century, *nykeres* were no longer lake-monsters but '*a ssewynge of þe ze ... þet habbeþ bodyes of wyfman/and tayl of uisssse*': in other words, mermaids.[114] And if there was one thing that mermaids liked to do, it was to tug at the bodies of those who ventured into water, drag them down, drown them. We expect mermaids to be sea-women nowadays, but there is nothing in the tradition that requires this, and their name betrays a link with the *mere*. Inland mermaids appear in both folklore and toponymy, the earliest attestation coming from Colchester, where in 1563 John Colt the miller was presented for fishing in Marmaydes Hole.[115] Evidently a deep place in the Colne, and not far from the town, this is a good match for the Lincoln *Nikerpole*. These names do not reflect experience, not even story, but fear of what might happen. Not far from Colchester, a folklorist wrote in the early nineteenth century that the mermaid was 'a bugbear to frighten children from the water'.[116] There were people other than children who might have benefitted from these warnings—overbold swimmers, incautious fishermen—and names in *nicor* would address them all.

Running water had different hazards from stagnant fens, although in some regions the dividing line was thin. A few miles from King's Lynn, the 'newly-made' *Pokedych* ran into the Wash in 1423, sluggishly draining twelve miles of marshland from Emneth to Clenchwarton.[117] This ran along an earlier ditch which had existed since at least the late thirteenth century when Terrington people had rights to fish there.[118] Such a large and carefully engineered undertaking is unlikely to have been called *Pokedych* at random, so we may be looking at a rare example of a deliberate name, decided on by a landowner or syndicate rather than just coming gradually into use. Perhaps they hoped to disarm fate by putting their work under the nominal protection of a trickster spirit.

Another substantial earthwork is the Pouke Ditch 1572, a boundary earthwork crossing the valley of the Alne to run across four miles of Warwickshire countryside. It later became the Hobditch, suggesting that the association with spirits still held good even while the name was updated.[119] There are several other compounds of *dīc* with *pūca* and two with *þyrs*, both oddly in the southern province where such names are rare: *Thorsdiche* 1327 at Sparsholt in Berkshire and *Thursdyche* 1451 at Preston in Dorset.[120] Goblin's Ditch 1726 is recorded from Loughton in Buckinghamshire, adding a touch of menace to the future Milton Keynes.

Several compounds with *brōc* show that the *pūca* was associated with small streams, the earliest being Polebrook in Northamptonshire, *Pocabroc* 1076. There are also compounds with *lacu* (*Pucchelake* 1470 at Chideock in Dorset), *rīð* (*Poukerithe* 1327 at Cuckfield in Sussex) and *ric* (*Pukerich* 1294 at Standon in Hertfordshire).[121] All these words belong to small streams or rivulets, and many are minor dialect terms. The rare *ric* was routinely assimilated to *hrycg* 'ridge'; at Cuckfield, *rīð* was unintelligible by 1582, so that a crossing was renamed Pookeborne Bridge; while *lacu* never really took off outside the West Country, although we find the cognates *læc* in *Thurseliic c.*1200 at Raithby in Lincolnshire and *læce* in two Cheshire names. There are no wide waters named after the supernatural, perhaps because the major rivers of England already had long-established names; even so, the streams which were given elfin qualifiers are surprisingly shallow. All the more curious, then, that the second most popular word for naming these was *scucca*, with its demonic connotations. Shobrooke Lake in Devon, recorded as *sceoca broce* 924x39; Church Shocklach in Cheshire, *Socheliche* 1086, and a Shocklach Field 1650 at Lea Newbold in the same county; Shuck Lake 1755 at Porlock in Somerset; these names suggest that the *scucca* was not always trailing hell-flames. Shobrooke Lake had a tributary, the Poke Water 1760, as if the older qualifier was being updated.

When he appears in hagiography and scriptural paraphrase, the *scucca* has more personality than other demons: not a shapeless threat in the dark, but someone you can have a conversation with. 'Get thee behind me, Satan!' (Matthew 16: 23) is addressed in Old English to 'you *scucca*!', and in early paraphrases of Job 1: 6 it is the *scucca*, not Satan, who appears in the court of Heaven among the sons of God and talks freely with the Almighty.[122] If there was a pre-demonic figure behind these pious uses of the word, it might be something like the green riders who spoke to Richard of Sunderland as he set out to the water to cut rushes, or perhaps the grim horsemen who ran down the young squire at Dunfermline, at the time of sunset, while he was taking a walk by a little stream.[123] In some of these stories, it is the sound of water that initiates encounters, which would explain why little trickling streams feature more often than wide flowing rivers. Snowball of Ampleforth had his first troubling encounter with the dead when he was riding back one night from Gilling and in the darkness heard the sound of ducks washing themselves in the beck—a detail so bizarre it must surely have been taken direct from testimony.[124]

People heard strange sounds in rivers. A thirteenth-century charter from Dunsford in Devon grants all the land between *Pokachurna* and the water which flows down from the house of William, an address which was clearer then than it is now; but we seem to be following the river Teign, south of the village, and the name cannot mean anything but 'the churn of the *pūca*'. In the rocky bed of this Dartmoor stream there were many hollows, and the noise of the water breaking over these or rolling rocks inside them was the sound of the *pūca* pounding butter in his churn. In the same way a later generation perceived the *proude grome* at work in Hob Thrush's Mill Nick, 'a deep fissure in Callaly Crags, near Callaly Castle, where spates bring down stones which rattle in the pot-holes like the grinding gear of a mill set in motion', while others heard the water roar and gush against some rocks in the stream at Kirkby Stephen, and called it the Devil's Mustard Mill.[125] The Devil of modernity has taken over the domestic tasks that were once performed by spirits, just as *pūcel cirices* have become Devil's Chapels.

Pokachurna is a fanciful name, of the sort that were rare in the Middle Ages though they are much more common now. Then, the default interpretation was literal: after all, even a monitory name like *Nikerpole*, which you suspect was intended to keep the rash and young away from deep waters, pointed to something that could actually happen. Pale murderous females really did lie in wait for men and women beside streams, as the Lanercost Chronicle bears witness.

In a world so full of encounters with supernatural beings, when people talked about them it was not easy to distinguish the picturesque from the practical. At South Creake in Norfolk there was an *Elfringhe* 1347; at Little Hadham in Hertfordshire an *Elfringemad* 1220x70.[126] These elf rings were what we call fairy rings, a circle of bright growth in the grass, caused by the radial expansion of *Agaricus campestris* or some other mushroom: a herb book of around 1300 gives the name *elferingewort* to a flower that flourished in the mycelial zone.[127] But we don't know how literally people took their supernatural explanation of the botanical fact. When Chaucer talks of days when

> *The elf-queene, with hir joly compaignye,*
> *Daunced ful ofte in many a grene mede*

this is the language of romance, and of nostalgia—*I speke of many hundred yeres ago*—and anyway we should not look for realism in a tale of chivalry told by a fictional character.[128] But people did find elfin ladies dancing in wild places, or at least those who reported they had done so were received with nothing more sceptical than surprise: Gwestin Gwestiniog, Edric Wilde and the knight who snatched his wife out of a dance.[129] *Ofte in forme of womman · in moni deorne weie/ Men sieþ of hom gret companie · boþe hoppe & pleie*, says the *South English Legendary* of the *eleuene*.[130] These are the same beings—'in our native tongue called *elves*'—that night-time travellers ('superstitious wretches' in the judgement of the preacher) saw dancing in circles, a ring of girls around the most beautiful queen.[131]

So the name *Elfringemad* commemorates something possible, not imaginary, although the immediate motivation of the name was not a sighting of the queenly company itself but observation of the imprint left by their dancing feet. In these names, *mǣd* evidently means a rich pasture field, not a hay meadow, for the grass would have to be close cropped by grazing animals before fungal rings could be noticed. Attributing them to supernatural revellers was not unreasonable when the markings were unquestionably there, and no-one else had a better explanation for them: fairy rings remained a scientific mystery until well into the modern period.[132]

The same explanation, with Old Norse *eng* rather than Old English *mǣd*, would account for *Elf Enge* 1373 at Wath in Derbyshire and *Elfe Ynge* 1583 at Swinton; possibly also for *Elfonenghouses* 1308 at Dacre, also in the West Riding.[133] Like the meadows at Winchester haunted by the ugly black furies and commanding woman in white, these would have lain alongside a stream. Other words for riverside grazing include *hamm*, and there is an *Alfham* C13 at Merston in Warwickshire. There is also *Poukham* 1418 somewhere in Sussex, a genitival *Poukesham* 1341 at Godalming in Surrey, and a *Bugeham* 1267/8 at

Chatgrave in Norfolk. The frequency of *pūca* as a qualifier with words for 'meadow' simply reflects its overwhelming frequency in southern England: *Poukemede* C13 somewhere in Devon, *Pokemede* 1240 at Malden in Surrey, and *Puckmede* 1493, but also Pokelmede 1547 at Shaw cum Donnington in Berkshire and, to round off the series, Goblin Meadow 1840 at Shifnal in Shropshire. What at first seemed a simple explanation—meadows named after elves are places where elf rings grew—becomes less certain on closer inspection. Some of these probably were fields where fairy rings had been seen and attributed to the dances, if not of the elves then of other uncanny beings: the dialect *puckstool* for 'mushroom' suggests that tradition was flexible on this point.[134] But other names, like those compounded with *croft* or *hæg*, may come from direct experience, or at least a conviction that in lonely places such experiences were possible.

Valleys

When people coin names, they are influenced by all the other names that they know, sometimes to the point of imitation. Place-names in Old Norse *gil* exemplify this. This is a generic for 'a deep, narrow valley, a ravine', found in the Scandinavian-speaking regions of Yorkshire and Cumbria. And unusually among elfin names, *gil* has limited collocation: it only compounds with *þyrs*, *troll* and *skyrsi*. Furthermore, *skyrsi* never compounds with any other generic but *gil*. This is a much narrower range of language than that found in the names for fields and wetlands.

Of the thirteen instances of *þyrs gil*, eight can be identified on the map today: all of these originally referred to streams, though the name may have been subsequently transferred to a farmhouse or wood. But the streams do not necessarily run through steep valleys. Pilgrims of the eerie will be disappointed if they look for the *fyrgen-strēam* of *Beowulf* (1359–61) running deep below the windswept crags, a torrent under rock. The closest match in the landscape for the original meaning of *gil* is the Thrushgill Beck at Whinfell (*Thrusgyll* 11770x84) which tumbles off Whinfell Beacon through a steep wooded incline. The Thursgill at Sedbergh (*Thursegilmos* 1220x50) is also a considerable stream, although its setting is only steep on one side as it skirts the eastern foot of the Howgill Fells. The Thrushgill at Wray (*Thursgyll* c.1350) feeds the Hindburn, falling steeply at one point where it enters the main river. All the other rivers are very modest affairs. At Garsdale the Thrushgill is just one amongst a dozen small streams running off Baugh Fell into the Clough River; at Milburn, a tributary of the Crowdundale Beck, falling rapidly off the moors; at Selside, in

Horton in Ribblesdale, a stream off Simon Fell which soon joins the Ribble (or did, before the railway line was built in its way); at Arkholme, a feeder stream of the Lune running through farmland and a wood, not precipitous at all; and the Thorsgill Beck at Startforth wriggles through flattish ground and straggling woodland to meet the Tees.

Significantly, the three earliest Thrushgill names are also the closest geographically to a Scandinavian *gil*. It looks as if the others were not independent coinages, but imitations from the older names made by people who had lost any understanding that the word meant 'ravine' and were instead applying it to small streams flowing off the fells, or ultimately to any stream at all. If the generic had lost its topographical sense, the qualifier may also have become obscure: a Thrushgill was no longer a *gil* haunted by a *þyrs*, but a recurrent name used for some particular kind of stream—running off a hillside, perhaps, or lined with woods. Like many recurrent names, it is confined to a very small part of the country: not only is the compound unknown outside a few counties, but it is found in tight local clusters—Askham and Bampton, Whinfell and Milburn, Sedbergh and Garsdale and Selside, Arkholme and Wray and Capernwray.

What goes for Thrushgill may also apply to Skirsgill, another recurrent name which is found in much the same area—indeed, the parishes of Askham and Horton in Ribblesdale have examples of each. The attestations tend to be late—Skirse Gill at Rylstone in the West Riding, *Skircegayle* C12, is the only medieval form—but *skyrsi* is a good Scandinavian word, evidently naturalized in England before the phonetic change to *skyssi* in the homeland. It is a curiously empty expression, semantically. The *skyrsi* left no reflex in Middle English or North Country dialect; even in Old Norse literature, it does not mean a particular kind of goblin or fiend, but something ill-defined yet ominous. It is hard to see how such a loose term could be repeated seven times in conjunction with *gil*, and never with anything else, unless it had acquired a new sense which was something to do with hillside streams rather than the supernatural.

At first sight, Old Norse *skugga* 'shadow' seems to resemble *skyrsi* in its uncanny vagueness. The North Riding has three matching names—*Scuggedale* c.1190 in Guisborough, *Schugedale* 1228 in Whorlton and a late Scugdale 1856 in Bulmer.[135] This looks like a recurrent name, and it has been suggested that it should be understood literally: a *skugga dalr* was a valley so deep that it was always in shadow, like the Dimmings Dales found elsewhere.[136] But the valleys are not particularly deep, and do not run north–south as you would expect of a cleft that shut out the sun. In any case *skugga* is the Scandinavian cognate of *scucca*, which as we have seen was not a physical shadow but a spirit of brooks and streams, and by extension of valleys. There is a Shagdale 1850 at Upper Elkstone in Staffordshire, which looks very much a hybrid with the Old English qualifier and Old Norse generic.[137] Shugden Head at Queensbury in the West Riding, *Shukden* 1492, is purely English, with *denu* as generic: *dalr* and *denu* seem to have been interchangeable in areas of English-Norse contact for long, gently sloping valleys.[138] If supernatural names were worth transmitting across the language barrier, it was because they were not poetical fancy but hard fact. A shadow-spirit had been seen on the slopes and might be seen there again; you took care when you went there, not resting under the trees at noon, carrying a herb or charm in your pocket; this was information that the new Scandinavian settlers learnt from Anglo-Saxon precursors, and repeated in their own language.

Two names in *fēond*—*Fendesdale* 1325 at Tilston in Cheshire and Finsdale Nab from Bowland Forest in the West Riding—paint a picture of supernatural contact that is less neutral than usual. *Fendesfell* 1479 at Skirwith in Cumberland has been Cross Fell since 1608, as if a cross had been raised (if so, it must have been before the Reformation) to counteract the rage of whatever it was that brooded on the slopes.[139] This fell has the dramatic setting which is lacking in most supernatural topography; it is the point from which fierce winds sweep down into the valley below 'and certainly the violence of the Helm Wind, whirling down chimneys, uprooting trees and lifting haystacks from one field to another must ... have suggested it was due to supernatural powers'.[140] It may be that the small corpus of names unequivocally meaning 'devil'—five examples of *fēond* and seven of *dēofol*—come from places where a tradition of spirits was interpreted more harshly than usual, because of the harm they did, or because they had been exorcized in some way, or simply because a priest or landowner accepted John Bromyard's line that all uncertain spirits were of Hell, and was able by sheer force of personality to impose it on the local namescape.[141]

Other spirits could be associated with valleys: *bugge* in Bugden 1597 at Herriard in Hampshire and Bugdale 1752 at Fangfoss in the East Riding; *þyrs* in *Thursdene* 1271x81 at Grantley in the West Riding and *Thirsedeneheved* 1324 at Briercliffe in Lancashire; and *ælf* in *ylfing dene* 956 at Welford in Berkshire (with connective -*ing*-), *Eluedena* 1086 now Elveden in Suffolk, *Alvedel* c.1200 at Bramhope in the West Riding, *Aldenehevet* 1234 at Tottington in Lancashire, and *Ulvenden* c.1240 at Goring in Oxford.[142] The association with elves remained vivid well into the twelfth century, when a miraculist explains that Elveden is to be understood in English as *vallem nunpharum*: *nympha* was the standard Latinization of *ælf*.[143] Another enthusiast for putting English place-names into Latin dress mentions a *vallis demonum c.*1195 along Watling Street east of Chester.[144] The original name is lost, although the likeliest reconstruction would be *þyrs bæc*, from the word ('stream, valley with a stream running through') found regionally in *Thurbatchker* 1327x77 at Rainow, also in Cheshire; *Thursbacheheved* 1216x72 at Charlesworth in Derbyshire; and Thursbache 1569/70 at Highley in Shropshire.[145] In these names, *heafod* does not mean 'headland' as it does in openfield names, but refers to the head of the *bæc* or *denu*, which may have been where the haunting took place, unless these are additive names distinguishing one part of the valley from another.

What marked these valleys as the place of spirits? An ingenious explanation comes from Dwarriden to the south of Stocksbridge, *Dueridene* 1272x1307, the only *denu* name to be compounded with *dweorg*. 'I paid a visit to the spot in the spring of this year, just when the larches were putting out their fairylike buds of green ... I shouted, and echoes on all sides answered me.'[146] A remarkable echo—and the Icelandic for 'echo' is *dvergmál*, literally 'voice of the dwarfs'.[147] Perhaps, then, the place-name is grounded in observable fact: just as people looked at fungal circles, thought of dancing places and named Elfe Ynge, so they heard echoes, imagined voices answering them back from the hill, and named Dwarriden.

Like many explanatory stories for place-names, this has caught the imagination of scholars and been copied elsewhere. Elvendon lies in 'a quiet valley with low wooded heights on each side, quite the sort of place you might expect elves to lurk in. It may be added that there is a very good echo all through the valley.'[148] At *Pokeput* in Sherington the pit has not survived, but the local historian is confident nonetheless that it echoed powerfully.[149] A theory is not invalid just because others have worked it to death, but there are reasons to be cautious about deriving Dwarriden from *dvergmál*. We do not know that this expression was current among tenth-century Scandinavians in Britain, and if used at all, it must have been communicated to their Anglo-Saxon neighbours, for all of our place-names are derived from Old English *dweorg* not Old Norse *dverg*; the *g* is soft, not hard. There is a cluster of these names in Lancashire, where one might expect Scandinavian influence, but they extend far down into Warwickshire, to *Dwarewmere* C13 at Fenny Compton and *Dwarfeholys* 1490 at Aston. There must be explanations for *dweorg* names other than echoing valleys, as there are twelve instances of the qualifier of which only one compounds with *denu*. And the *denu*, as we have seen, could be home to a *bugge*, *þyrs* or *ælf*, beings that had no literary or lexical association with mysterious sound.[150]

Pits and Hollows

But the expression *dvergmál* highlights the mysterious way that spirits concealed themselves among the cliffs, in gaps and crannies. 'It was a commonly received opinion among our Saxon ancestors', says an antiquarian, 'that all caves, and remarkable hollows in the earth, were inhabited by fairies.'[151] He is describing a crevice under a stone slab in Calderdale and his conclusions owe more to observation of the Awfe Hole than they do to Old English literature, but the toponymy is sound.

The *Dwarfeholys* were apertures cut into sandstone cliffs by the River Tame as it wore through the soft rock of the Birmingham ridge. The river was crossed by a ford, afterwards superseded by a bridge which kept the old name of Salford, earlier *Scraford* C13, with *Scrave Medwe* 1319 nearby.[152] Evidently the original name for these features had been *scræf* 'cave', which suggests that they were not renamed as holes of the *dweorgs* until later in the Middle Ages.[153] Throughout its life as a generic—and it remains formative from Old to Modern English—*hol* is always the hollow where something lives; usually, in earlier names, some sort of animal, but more recently holes have been named after dobbies, boggarts, bogles, clabberlabbers and many another eerie thing.[154]

Like *denu* or *bæc*, *hol* may appear under a Latin disguise. At Acton Grange, south of Warrington, wetland was granted *c.*1249 to make a millpond for Grange Mill; it extended from the mill upstream to the *caveas nanorum*, which must be dwarf holes.[155] This is flat country without either cliffs or caves, but the dwarfs may have occupied a ruin, as they did on Lydney Hill.

It does not seem surprising that dwarfs should live in places cut out of the cliff-face, but the associations that we now bring to the word are conditioned by the re-importation of dwarf lore in the nineteenth century after it had died in native English tradition.[156] The Scandinavian *dverg* is synonymous with rock—out of which, as the Edda tells us, Durinn and his folk grew like maggots. The German *zwerg* occupies the characteristic jewelled otherworld of Faerie, accessed through caves and openings in mountains. These traditions offered the raw material for a mythology of dwarfs as diminutive stocky underground craftsmen but this was not fully realized until they took their place in modern romantic and fantasy literature.[157]

They saw things differently in the Middle Ages, when the natures of different spirits overlapped. We would not associate the *pūca* with caves, but *le Puchschroneaker* 1326 at Effingham in Surrey can hardly derive from anything but *scræfen*, a derivative of *scræf*. If we followed convention by translating him as 'giant', the *þyrs* would be hard to fit into a rock crevice, but epic tradition took a very loose approach to these matters—Fafnir in the Sigurd cycle is a giant, his brother Reginn is a dwarf—and there is a *Thurse Hole* 1429 at Bulkeley in Cheshire and a Threshole 1766 at Saxilby in Lincolnshire.

'A Thurs-house or Thurse-hole', says White Kennett, is 'a hollow vault in a rock or stony hill.'[158] He may have got his information from Robert Plot, who knew a Thurse-house in the Peakstone Rock at Alton in Staffordshire which was large enough to accommodate a family. He had been to another place of the same name—though the people sometimes called it Hob-hurst Cave—at Wetton. This was a long cave, 'from the mouth to the further part, about 44 yards and is in the middle, as near as I could guess, about 30 foot high, the roof being supported by a rough natural pillar, which also in a manner divides it into several partitions or rooms: where I was shewed in the roof, the natural effigies of a Man with a curled beard, looking out of a hole, not very unlike what it was said to represent, though I suppose wholy casuall, and never designed by nature.'[159] Was this the shaggy-haired *þyrs*? After the cave-dwellers had departed, he seems to have moved back in, for twentieth-century lore remembered the fiddling hobthurse of Thor's Cave; *fiddling* meaning 'screeching' rather than instrumental music, a wailing counterpart to the echoes of the dwarfs.[160]

People and spirits yielded to one another, like light and darkness: as one left, the other returned. Before Christian time, Farne was the unchallenged haunt of demons. But when Cuthbert came, he ordered the spirits to withdraw, and the island became habitable, with water, shelter and fields of barley.[161] Then Cuthbert was appointed bishop and left his calm islet for the comparative hubbub of Lindisfarne; the demons slid back in, and even in the twelfth century were still vexing Bartholomew of Farne as they tried to regain their old domain. Meanwhile Cuthbert, needing a place of quiet prayer away from his episcopal duties, made a hermitage on a small islet just off the coast of Lindisfarne, sometimes called St Cuthbert's Island. But after his death the hut and chapel fell into ruin and from its new occupants it was called *Thrusheland*, the island of the *þyrs*.[162] Gerald of Wales tells an odd story about this place. On Holy Island itself, women could not give birth; they could get pregnant, and carry the babies to term—but that was as far as it went. So when their time came, they would take passage to this *Thrusheland* and as soon as they stepped off the boat, they would go into labour and nature would take its course. If for any reason they could not leave the main island (and apparently some heartless relatives had tried the experiment), they were in agony, the contractions continuing to the point of death, unless they could get away, when at once they would give birth.

Notoriously, Cuthbert had issues with women and his female tenants may have preferred the easier yoke of the *þyrs*. The alternation of saint and spectre is recognized in an English verse *Life* of *c*.1450, which tells us that

> *Þis lyf contemplatyue þan*
> *Cuthbert in a priue place began,*
> *In a place withoute his cell*
> *Now calde þe thrus house as men tell.*[163]

This ruined chapel, like the Staffordshire caves, was only a house in an ironic sense, just as the unapproachable cavern at Seaford Head was figuratively the church of a *pūcel*: these lairs of wild things were to them what homes and chapels were to men. Demons loved ruins. When Isaiah (34: 13–14) prophesies the desolation of Edom, he foresees nettles and brambles on the crumbling city walls and creatures of the desert stalking in the ruins, as one might expect, but then (in the Vulgate text, at least) introduces some less substantial fauna: demons shall meet onocentaurs, one satyr shall cry out to another and *ibi cubavit lamia*, which the Wycliffite Bible of *c*.1382 helpfully glosses as *there shal lyn lamya, that is, a thirs, or a beste hauende the bodi lic a womman and horse feet*.[164] There were ancient precedents for this horror of an animal-footed woman, although it is also a good description of the thing that emerged from the waters and savaged the housewife of Haddington.[165]

There was another *Tursthous* 1417 at Chelmorton, in the heart of the Peak and therefore probably a cave. At Bristle Bridge in Myddle, Richard Gough noted in 1700 that 'there is a certain cave in the rock near this bridge, this cave was formerly a hole in the rock, and was called the Goblin Hole, and afterwards was made into a habitation, and a stone chimney built up to it'.[166] At Tipton in Staffordshire there was a Bughouse 1849, another in 1804 at Mettingham in Suffolk, and a Powkhouse 1839 at Stoke Bliss and Pookhouse 1842 at Lucton, both in Herefordshire.[167] Association of dwarfs with caves or hidden spaces is confirmed by three names in Lancashire—*Dweryhouses clyf* *c*.1250 at Parbold, *Dwerihouses* 1349 at Wrightington, and The Dwerry House 1755 at West Derby—together constituting 25% of the not very large corpus of *dweorg-* names.[168]

In sandstone regions these holes were extensive enough to be converted into cliff-dwellings. They may have had other uses. Two names from Essex— *Congeonshole* 1287 at Stebbing and *Canyoneshole* 1401 at High Easter—use the word *cangun*, found also in Congin Pits 1842 at Linton in Derbyshire. This is not a common qualifier, and Coniuncros 1216x72 at Derby is the only other medieval instance. There are three hollows, three fields, a wood, and three landmarks (Quanguins Oak 1609 at Cookham in Berkshire and Conjins Gate 1764 at Tideswell in Derbyshire, with the cross at Derby). Three examples come from Essex and four from Derbyshire, suggesting a very localized distribution of the term.[169]

But what is a *cangun*? Unlike other supernatural terms, which however ambiguous do indicate some kind of being, this word represents a situation. The Norman French *cangun*, indigenized as Middle English *conjeoun* and sometimes half-heartedly Latinized as *cambio*, is a changeling: the result of an exchange in which the fairies took one of our children and left one of theirs, an unwanted elfin thing in the cradle, characterized by voracious appetite, foul temper and a refusal to grow as a good baby should.

So the changeling was real, and in more recent times doctors have been able to inspect them, as mycologists have examined fairy rings and archaeologists looked at fairy arrows. Nineteenth-century folklorists were told many stories of how the exchange was reversed and the human child brought back, usually by some sort of violence or abandonment; these overlap with reports of what was actually done, although our evidence is imperfect, most informants thinking it wiser to entertain members of the magistrate class with folktales rather than reminiscences of infanticide. From the Middle Ages we have one local, almost ethnographically detailed account from Lyons in 1312, where the unwanted babies were laid at the foot of a tree on the edge of the forest while two inch-long candles burnt out.[170] Grafting this narrative onto more recent accounts—a questionable methodology, but the only one we have—would match it with reports of children being exposed in the fields, or at a well, or in a stone trough.[171] If the parents did not get back their original desired baby at these places, at least they were no longer burdened with the fairy substitute. On this reading, *cangun hols* would be analogous to the mires and marshes in which spirits and the restless dead were laid: places where you got rid of something otherworldly that had intruded into the home.

That explains many features of this group of names, such as the bias towards holes and landmarks, and there is no plausible competing theory, for the changeling was not otherwise linked with the landscape; it simply arrived in the cradle, so you wouldn't encounter one in the fields as you might meet dancing elves or deceptive goblins. On the other hand, the *cangun* names which have been identified in the landscape do not seem very suitable places to abandon a baby. *Congeonshole* is at TL 680 238, near two roads and easily visible from some old farms; Quanguins Oak is at SU 888 854, north of Cookham Rise and within hearing distance of the busy Thames.[172] Perhaps abandonment was never contemplated, for rituals to annul changeling status often end with the child being taken back home. It is easy when classifying other people's beliefs to draw an absolute distinction between the changeling (bad, to be banished) and the fairy-struck child (innocent, to be healed), but distraught mothers may not have seen things in such a clearcut way.[173]

Hollows are ambiguous features—places where something can be pushed away, but also portals through which it can come. This was remembered well into modern times. The name of the Awfe Hole at Soyland proves that this remained a site of living tradition, for if the name had become opaque, the *-l-* of *ælf* would have been retained, whereas the 1773 form has the phonetic reduction which produced *awfe, oaf* in Midlands dialect. Eighteenth-century tradition speaks of fairies coming out of hiding-places like this to dance and play music. Elfhole 1753 at Selby in the West Riding looks as if it remained a transparent name. At Allendale in Northumberland, the Elf Holes of the 1859 OS map are by the river below Elfa Green. Elfe-hole 1631 was near Elfe Cragge 1631 and Elfgate 1633 at Millom in Cumberland, where the Elf Hall of the modern OS is either a fourth name in the group, or a gentrified version of Elfe-hole. All these names are from upland country where locals evidently liked to point out a crevice in the rocks from which elves emerged.

Elvescarebrec 1300x25 at Marton in Cleveland, from *sker* 'a rock, a rocky cliff', suggests that this was an old tradition. Also in the parish—or perhaps another name for the same place—was *Scincliff* C13; another *Scinneclif c.*1125, now Shincliffe in Durham, is a steep wooded scarp rising above the Wear. It was in a hollow bank like this, somewhere in the Gower, that Elidyr found the entrance to another world; he said it had been down by a river, evidently overgrown by vegetation, because after the path to happiness had been closed to him he spent a long time searching for the exact spot where once he came and went.[174] As with many stories of Faerie this has a split perspective. Externally, we are looking at a crevice in a riverbank; but on the other side, as soon as we pass through into another reality, a long dark tunnel leads into the delightful twilight land of the people of truth. The Green Children followed a similar route, but in reverse: happy in their half-lit home, they decided to explore a cave and wandered too far down its passages until they emerged confused under the cruel sun. Like Elidyr, they searched desperately for the opening that would lead them back again, but could not find it. In Ralph of Coggeshall, they are found next to a pit, *fovea*; William of Newburgh calls it a *fossa*, usually 'ditch' but here evidently 'excavation', for he uses it to translate the *pytt* of *Wlfpittes* (Woolpit).[175]

Ralph was a friend of Gervase of Tilbury, who told him a story about the heretical Publicani. They may have shared other tales, for Gervase knew about paths to the underworld, including one near Catania in Sicily where the bishop liked to show off the presents sent to him by Arthur, now monarch of that shadowy realm. This was a time when supernatural tableware was in vogue, including the cup retrieved for Henry I from a fairy hill and the silver spoon used at table by Henry Sandford, Bishop of Rochester, which a man had handed over to the devils in sign of homage, and which tumbled out of the air the minute Henry heard his confession.[176] Arthur's gifts arrived more innocently, after a horse went astray on the slopes of Etna and ran into the dark recesses of the mountain. The servant chased after it down a narrow path until he emerged into a level land full of wonderful things, where the legendary king returned his palfrey with the gifts that were part of gentlemanly good relations.[177]

Exchange of presents is a mark of good breeding in Walter Map's story of Herla, who is armed with gifts when he pays a return visit to his opposite number the pygmy king. They are led away from familiar territory to a cave in a high cliff, enter it, and after a time in darkness emerge into a sunless land that is lit by glimmering torches.[178] But we are moving into literature here, and could draw instead on personal testimony, such as that of the swineherd of Derbyshire, which was passed on (through how many removes is not clear) to Robert, a local cleric.[179] Like his counterpart in Sicily, the servant lost a prized animal, in this case a sow, and following her trail he entered a cavern and made his way for a long time through blackness until suddenly he saw light and emerged into a field where the reapers were gathering the harvest, though it had been bitter winter when he left the world above.

And as he returned with his sow and her piglets, they passed from the mysterious geography of the antipodes into a much more familiar landscape, for the cleft through which he entered the otherworld was not some mysterious aperture seen only at fairy command: it was the Peak Cavern, a tourist spectacle then as now, though not known until 1586 by its present name of the Devil's Arse.[180] The Devil as so often, has usurped a landscape previously belonging to the fairies. Imagination revels in the thought of that monstrous bulk bending over Buxton and presenting his rear towards Castleton, but that may misunderstand the place-name, which in its first form appears as *Pechesers* 1086: the arse in the Peak, not anybody's arse in particular.[181] Many other words for body parts are used metaphorically for hollows in the landscape—*ceafl* 'jaw', *ceole* 'throat', *nafola* 'navel', *wamb* 'womb'—and we don't have to imagine a body to correspond with them.

This raises questions about the other *Develeserce* 1448 at Lechlade in Gloucestershire, *le Fendesers clogh* 1407 at Witton in Cheshire, and a pair from Yorkshire, *Trollesers* 1335 at Lockton in the North Riding and Trollers Gill

1812 at Appletreewick in the West. The Gill is not a cavern, but something very close: 'a winding but nearly perpendicular fissure in the lime-stone rock, about half a mile in length, a very few yards in width, and, upon an average, about sixty feet high.'[182] The other names are not so easily located, but they all come from regions where a chasm in the rock is topographically plausible, so that *Fendesers* may be better understood as an *ears*, arse-cleft, haunted by an actual demon, rather than a fanciful fiend's fancied arse.[183]

Even if it does have a fictive sense, this is a rare element. That can hardly be said for *pytt* which with 104 instances is far and away the most frequent generic in the corpus. The runners-up—*lane* with 46 instances and *wella* with 36—are less than half as common, and they are the standard expressions for the things they denote, whereas *pytt* has to share conceptual space with *hol*. A *hol*, as we have seen, could be a sideways break in the landscape as well as vertical: sometimes a hollow, but just as often a crack or cave or hole in the cliff-face. But a *pytt* always led down. Beyond that, it is not so easy to tell what it might be.

Latin *puteus* meant more or less what *pit* does now, though it was also applied to diggings for water, what we would call wells; there has been a semantic game of musical chairs in which Old English *wella* 'water springing from the ground' came to mean 'draw-well, hole dug for water' while Modern English *spring* moved to denote 'natural well-spring'.[184] In classical times *puteus* was adopted as a loanword by Common Germanic, so the Anglo-Saxons already had the word when they arrived in Britain.[185] But our attempts at visualization are not helped by their single-minded focus on landscape form and outline, regardless of the two questions that preoccupy us now. Was a *pytt* large or small? And was it natural, or something manmade?

Both, apparently. We find *pytt* applied to features as large as the Manger below the White Horse of Uffington. Charters sometimes seem to use it for valleys—but then a hole in the ground would be lucky to survive ten centuries of agricultural improvement, so maybe the original document pin-pointed a smaller feature within the larger hollow. Sometimes we are told what the pit is for, usually something dug out of it: clay, sand, marl. Pits could be working hollows to make charcoal or lime; saw-pits let a man stand underneath the log placed over him; pit-falls and wolf-pits must have been small, deep and steep-sided. These terms all suggest small features, places where you could stand on the edge and take in everything at a glance. They must often have been dangerous, and one of Wulfstan's miracles involved the cure of a man who was working in a sand-pit when he was suddenly taken by a malign spirit and lost his mind.[186]

What was in the pit? The choice of qualifiers turns out to be limited, much more so than with fields or meres. In early names, with four exceptions, a *pytt* is always the home of a *pūca*, *þyrs* or *gobelin*.[187] Since *gobelin* looks very much like an expression used to replace *pūca* in the Midlands, as *pixy* did from the seventeenth century onwards in Devon, the choice is between *pūca* and *þyrs*, with the southern *pūca* as usual outnumbering its northern competitor by 3 to 2. Evidently the range of stories that might be told about a pit in the ground was more limited than those appropriate to a stream or a hill or a pathway. In later names, features of this kind are typically Hell Holes.[188]

Unexpectedly, these names are often in the plural: one in three of them refers us to *pytts*, not an individual *pytt*. Plural generics are very rare in major toponymy. They are commoner in local nomenclature, where farmers and herdsmen have to distinguish clusters of things from isolated features, but they are not often found in the elfin names: we have met with plural holes and dells and (metaphorical) houses, though these seem to be in a similar semantic field to pits, but also with names which refer to multiple lands in the openfield, and two which describe groups of clearings (*Alueridinges* C13 at Farnley in the West Riding and Puck Reddings 1840 at Churchdown in Gloucestershire). The only pre-Conquest instance, *elfaledes* C11 from Corse in Gloucestershire, may contain the plural of *falod* 'enclosure', but this is contested.[189]

The Thurst Pyttes at Holmesfield near Sheffield were fed with water; in 1595 a tenant of the manor had diverted the channel from its old line, but the court told him to set it in its right course again.[190] They may have been dug for drainage, or to provide somewhere for the livestock to drink. This was certainly the purpose of the *Therspettes* at Dinnington north of Newcastle, which provided a watering place (*aquatorium*) on the Seaton Burn between the manors of Weetslade and Mason, so that in 1256 a lawsuit was needed before the two rival landowners could agree shared access for their cattle.[191] These pits provided a convenient place where the animals could stand and drink; they are water features like the meres and fens, but on a more domestic scale.

Clearly a *pytt* could be many things, and the few which can be identified on modern maps do not narrow down the range of reference. *Pukeput* 1263x84 at Maisemore in Gloucestershire is a large valley folded into the hills overlooking the Severn, while *Poukepitte* 1447 at Wool in Dorset is a square steep-sided quarry hole at the corner of a field.[192] The ponds called Goblins Pit 1775 at Walsall seem at first sight to belong with other water features; but local geology shows a band of limestone near the surface here, so they are probably quarry pits which flooded after extraction came to an end.[193]

It is not easy to visualize these mundane cuts and hollows as a tradesman's entrance to the pit of hell. Was it simply a turn of phrase to ascribe them to the *pūca* and the *þyrs*? It's true that children can imagine the most frightful things in any abandoned pond or quarry, but these place-names come from lawsuits and boundary surveys: they must have had a meaning for the adult world, though unlike the names for fields and pathways this does not seem to have referred to supernatural encounters. While some pits remained in use, especially the watering places, the most plausible common denominator for these sites is dereliction. They are places where something was quarried or trapped or mixed or made, and when the job was done the pit remained; it was nobody's business to fill it back in, so it would soon have acquired the spooky feeling of places where people were once busy and have since moved on.

Wells

An overgrown pit is a shadow of the work that was done there, as a ruined cottage is of a life once lived. Once their original purpose was forgotten, along with the owner's name, there is not much that you can say about these places except that they are haunted. By contrast, water sources can be described in many ways—by the strength, colour and temperature of the spring, the rocks from which it rises, the trees that grow over it and the plants below, the landscape around and the activities nearby: so elfin names in *wella*, though fewer than those in *pytt*, must have been chosen to mark something important about the place. No-one could afford to neglect a source of good drinking water, which meant that wells were never off the beaten track as a rock or hollow might be. When Repton Priory was found in 1172, the *Pukewelle* was one of the monks' prime assets, with freedom of access and a right to channel its waters by any convenient route to the conventual buildings.[194] *Poukewalle* at East Luccombe near Minehead was prominent enough to give name to a local family in 1299/1300 and 1315.[195] In Northamptonshire, the Puck-well 1712 was a landmark in Aynho Park—bubbling up like a boiling pot and rich enough in chalybeate water to redden the surrounding vegetation.[196]

As with *pytt*, the southern names in *pūca* outnumber the northern ones in *þyrs*, in this case by about 2 to 1. The West Riding, where Scandinavian influence on the language lasted longest, has two names where the generic is Old Norse *kelda*, also meaning 'well-spring': *Thurskeld* C13 at Long Drax and *Ruskall Springe* 1579 at Hebden.[197] A few other qualifiers feature in these names. There is an *Elfwelle* c.1240 at Garsington in Oxfordshire, while the modern Elfa Hill at Uldale in Cumberland has an Elfa Well just north of it. Bugwell 1672 at Barnstaple in Devon and Pucklewell 1841 at Dyrham in Gloucestershire attest other qualifiers. But *pūca* provides the earliest forms, both *pucan wylle*: one from a charter of 772 for Bexhill in Sussex and the other from one of 946 for Weston in Somerset. It doesn't necessarily follow that there was a special association of *pūcas* with wells. Though the *þyrs* names begin later, with two thirteenth-century forms from Lincolnshire—*Thruswelker* at Stallingborough and *Tuswellsic* at Langton-by-Partney—that is because all names are recorded later in the northern province, where charters were not preserved as they were in the Midlands and the South.

How should we read these names? The literature on haunted and magical wells is immense, but one tale may give a clue. In an episode from the outlaw tales about Hereward the Wake, he breaks out from his fenland camp to discover the enemy's plans.[198] Knowing that disguise is vital he dresses shabby and, when he meets a potter, takes his wares and sets off for the headquarters of the enemy at Brandon near Thetford. A poor potter must take what lodgings he can, so Hereward spends the night in the house of a humble widow. But this is no innocent old lady: she is a friend of the witch, *venefica mulier*, who has come to support the Norman assault with her diabolical arts. All that evening the two women sit chattering in French, with many snide remarks about the witless country potter, and he takes care to act dumb as if he can't understand the language; soon he has learnt everything about the attack that threatens the Island of Ely.[199] Eventually they all bed down, but at the silent hour of midnight Hereward hears the rustle of someone getting up. In the garden there is a little stream, running eastwards, and the witch is making her way to the spring at its head.[200] Hereward creeps after her. He can't get close but he hears her talking to… something. A guardian of the spring, it seems; he can hear that she is asking questions, and waiting for a long time in anticipation of a reply.

The witch got her come-uppance in the end, but she was not the first or last whose incantations called on a *custode fontium*.[201] Three generations before Hereward, the practice of honouring springs was denounced in a canon that goes on to forbid omens, charms, and magic involving dead bodies.[202] These were not just private superstitions, but something carried out under the supervision of ritual experts; Ælfric's denunciation of people who make offerings to wells warns them against doing what witches teach.[203] For a moment the veil of clerical contempt is twitched aside to reveal another world with its own native shrines and teachings, defiant of the official Church and yet oddly similar to it. It is this parallelism which makes it so hard to tell magical rites from orthodox ones. The landscape trio of wells, trees and stones, always denounced together as the places where people go to practice heathenism, were also the locations for honouring folk saints. People automatically translated the familiar rituals of worship—candles, offerings—from one sort of place to another.

There is only one custom which belongs to magic rather than religion, and that is divination. Although Christianity affirmed the saints' power to do most of what divine beings do elsewhere—heal, protect, make the crops grow tall—it never made any accommodation to our desire for knowledge of the future. Any shrine that claimed a power to predict was therefore illicit. Wells did it more than most.

Many have names compounded with *freht* 'divination'. There are medieval attestations for *Fertwelle* 1086, now Fritwell in Oxfordshire, *Frethewell c.*1210 at Morton in Nottinghamshire, and *Frythwell Gate c.*1320 at Billingham in Durham, with later field-names from Tadcaster in the West Riding, Gumley and Hallaton in Leicestershire, and Chetton in Shropshire.[204] The name may also be suspected in *Frewell* 1316 at Chicheley in Buckinghamshire and the field-names Freckwell at Hartshead in the West Riding and Friswell at Bexley in Kent.[205] If *freht* is a loanword from Old Norse, as has been suggested, then these names must all postdate the tenth century, but it would be unusual to find Scandinavian vocabulary being used in Oxfordshire, Buckinghamshire and Kent, so there may have been a cognate Old English word.[206]

It was certainly familiar to Old Norse speakers in England. The Laws of Cnut forbid witchcraft and the sinister practice of encompassing death *oððon on blote oððon fyrhte*, where *blót* is the specifically Viking ritual of blood sacrifice.[207] An earlier English tradition is represented by spring-names with the qualifier *hǽl* 'fortune, omen' such as Elwell near Upwey in Dorset and Holywell in Lincolnshire.[208]

A similar meaning has been suggested for places called Runwell. The earliest form is *runweolla c.*940, now Runwell in Essex. The same etymology probably applies to *Runewelle c.*1250 at North Carlton in Lincolnshire, and *Rounwellesic* C13 at Swinton in the West Riding.[209] The qualifier is usually taken to be *rūn*, which has a wide range of meanings—'whisper, counsel, secret, rune'.[210] The core sense seems to be what we mean when we speak of 'a quiet word': literally, one in a low voice, but also confidential advice, while for medieval people, muttering something softly and inaudibly suggested incantations. That takes us back to our witch at the well, with Hereward straining to hear what she has asked and what the demon guardian replies.

Hills and Mounds

Encounter with the otherworld never ends well in encounter stories, though these may suffer from selection bias, given the miraculists' insatiable demand for tales of illness and its cure. *Ofte in forme of womman· aday and eke niȝt / Hi leteþ men hom ligge bi*, the *South English Legendary* warns us, but *hore members toswelleþ somme … and somme fordwineþ al awei*. These shapeshifters *ofte comeþ to toune/ And bi daie muche in wode beoþ· & biniȝte upe heie doune*.[211] It is as if hills are their natural starting point, the place where they first landed when cast out from heaven, or where they *aliȝt adoun* from their home in the turbid lower air, and then proceed to *som deorne stude … in wode and eke in mede*: secret places where they can dance, play and seduce.

The *eleuene* of the *Legendary*, with their retreats upon *heie doune*, are matched by place-names where *dūn* is most frequently qualified by *ælf*. *Elvedonne* 1283 at Chevening in Kent, *Elvedon* 1285 in the Peak Forest, *Alfedon* 1403 at Ropley in Hampshire make up half the attestations for this generic, with two compounds in *pūca* and one in *bugge*. A *dūn* was a long low hill, often appearing as a ridge above flat land in the foreground, so it is not unexpected that the two names in *hrycg* both have *ælf* as qualifier: *ælfrucge* from the Canterbury charter of 993, and a late Elvrigg 1836 (influenced by Old Norse *hryggr*) at Scalthwaiterigg in Westmorland. Shroner Wood at Martyr Worthy in Hampshire, *scrēawan ōra*, may belong here, for an *ōra* was a flat-topped ridge.[212]

The Life of Collen presents us with a fairy stronghold on a hill: the geography is uncertain, even by the standards of a late hagiography strongly influenced by romance, for we are told that events happened at the hill of Glastonbury (by which we are to understand the Tor) although the original story came from Dinas Bran at Llangollen.[213] Invited to dine at the table of Gwyn ap Nudd, Collen passed through the drawbridge of the finest castle he had ever seen. Within its walls, all was music, sport and laughter, with Gwyn himself presiding at the high seat. He greeted Collen courteously, and invited him to join the feast, but the saint said 'No: I do not eat the leaves of a tree.' Gwyn rallied and asked his guest, 'What do you think of the livery of my servants, so red and so blue?' Collen said, 'They are well for what they are. The blue is for eternal ice, and the red is for the endless burning.' Then he pulled a flask of holy water out of his robes, and sprinkled it all around him. Everything vanished, and Collen found himself alone on the close-cropped turf.[214]

In place-names, *hyll* like other words for high places compounds with *ælf*: *Elueshyll c.*1300 at Edgefield in Norfolk, *Elvehull* 1359 at Carlisle, and two later examples, to which we can add *Elfknolle* 1310 at Rawdon in the West Riding. There are more names in *pūca*—thirteen of them, beginning with *Pokehill* 1268 at Berry Pomeroy in Devon—but that is to be expected: it is the relevant frequency of *ælf* that stands out. There is also a *Pokelshull* 1305 at Worthen in Shropshire and another later *pūcel* name, two names in *bugge* and three in *scucca*, two of which—*Schuchenhulle* C13 at Artington in Surrey and *Shokenhulle* 1377 at Weston Beggard in Herefordshire—contain a remnant Old English genitive. There is a Shinnel 1795 at Burton Overy in Leicestershire, with *scinna*, and a *Schrewenhulle c.*1330 at Badsey in Worcestershire. Alternative interpretations of the word *screawa* are possible, but remember the *ssrewen* of the *Legendary* and their fondness for congregating on *heie doune*.

But how many of these were high hills, dominating the low ground as Shincliffe does the valley of the Wear, or Shucknall Hill that of the Frome, or Eldon Hill the lands south of the Peak? We are dealing once more with the Anglo-Saxon tendency to use generics for shape or situation irrelevant to the size of the thing being named. Poukehill 1661 near Walsall stood out in the landscape, a conical hill of hard bluish-black basalt with veins of calcite of white quartz, but it was only three or four hundred yards in circumference, and has now been obliterated entirely by quarrying.[215]

More hillock than hill, you might think. The same is true for the *collis* behind which the domineering white-clad figure lies in wait for the citizen of Winchester after he has escaped from ragged black furies in the water meadows. He is hurrying away from his pursuers up onto the road that leads back to the city when she steps out of hiding. The hillock is large enough to conceal someone—admittedly someone of majestic supernatural stature—but small enough for her to climb quickly to the top and cripple him with the air that wafts from the folded sleeve of her tunic.[216]

Gervase conveniently tells us the dimensions of the fairies' hill in the Forest of Dean: as high as a man. It stood alone in a glade, a familiar landmark to knights and hunters who, when dry-throated after a day's chase in the woods, would leave their companions—you had to be alone for the magic to work—and climb up the mound. When you said 'I'm thirsty', a cupbearer would be at your side, elegantly dressed and handing out a bejewelled drinking horn of the old English kind. As soon as you drank, all the heat and the sweat of the day vanished and you felt like a new man, handing back the horn to your attendant—who suddenly wasn't there anymore. This lasted until an ungracious knight took the horn, drank, but refused to return it. When news of this got out, Robert, Earl of Gloucester, confiscated the horn and not wishing to retain stolen goods— especially those robbed from Faerie—he presented it to Henry I.[217]

Robert was created Earl in 1121; the horn must therefore have been handed over between that date and 1135. According to William of Newburgh, Henry had just received a cup of unknown material and strange form snatched from revellers in a Yorkshire hill. Though there was a ready market for fairy vessels in those days, it is hard to believe that two of them came into the hands of the same king in the same decade, and Gervase may have transferred the original report to a new location. As he retells it, the story has moved from legend to romance: it involves a knight, rather than a peasant, the presentation of a drink by an attendant rather than joining a party, criticism of the bad manners of the thief rather than celebrating his opportunism, and an easy confidence that the otherworld can pose no risk to highborn people: far from being toxic, the cup contains refreshing nectar.

Unlike the *monticulus* of Dean, which lies under suspicion of never having existed at all, the fairy hill in the valley of the Gypsey Race still stands and can be visited, whether you take it to be Willy Howe or, as I suspect, Duggleby Howe. Both are large Neolithic barrows, about twenty-five feet high, so that it would be possible, as William says, for a man on horseback to look in through an open door and see the table spread for a banquet inside, and the brightly lit faces of men and women. The mounds are called howes, using the usual North Country reflex of Old Norse *haugr*, and this generic features in more than twenty elfin names.

Elveshov C13 is the earliest form, now Ailcy Hill to the east of the minster at Ripon.[218] Also in Yorkshire we have the early forms *Alfhov* 1216x72 at Rimington in the West Riding and Elfahall 1544 at East Witton in the North Riding; to the west, *Elfowebek* 1377 at Hutton-in-the-Forest and Elvinhowe 1577 at Gosforth, both in Cumberland, and Elfhowes 1687 at Hartley and Elfhow 1694 at Over Staveley, both in Westmorland. In the further reaches of the Danelaw we find *Alvehoghe c.*1250 at Little Ryburgh in Norfolk, and *Heluhou* 1467x84 (with inorganic initial *h*) at Barkby in Leicestershire.

Since *haugr* is a specifically northern element, *pūca* is absent from these compounds. But it is curious to find that *þyrs*, usually the prime qualifier for elfin names in this region, only appears twice, against sixteen examples in *ælf*. It is present in *Thirshowe* 1292 at Barmston in the East Riding and Thrushhowe 1578 at Wasdale in Cumberland. There are also five names in *skratti*, the early forms being *Scrathou* C13 at Hayton in the East Riding, *Scrathowe* 1388 at Thimbleby in the North, and Scatthowe 1601 at Bradley in Lincolnshire.[219]

In the Scandinavian homelands, *haugr* had meant 'burial mound'. Although the word developed new meanings on English soil, it still has its original sense in *Thirshowe*, now Trusey Hill facing Bridlington Bay, a disc of earth rising a few feet in flat lands where nothing much rises at all. At least one burial has been excavated here.[220] By contrast, Ailcy Hill at Ripon is a natural hill of glacial sand and gravel, more than thirty feet high; a cemetery of the sixth or seventh century was dug into its slopes and the practice of burial continued down to the tenth.[221]

The corresponding Old English words were *beorg*, used for old mounds as well as new ones, and *hlāw*, which was largely reserved for newly raised tumuli.

You would expect these generics to feature in the elfin names of the south, as *haugr* does in those of the north, and so they do, but as with other words for hills, the choice of qualifiers differs from what we have come to expect. On average, in the southern counties, *pūca* is found in about half the names, but it only features in three of the twenty-four compounds in *beorg* and *hlāw*: two Gloucestershire names, Puck Berries 1838 at English Bicknor and Pucklow 1838 at Newent, and one from Dorset, *Puckysbarry* 1451 at Winfrith Newburgh, though that may be a shift-name from the nearby *Puckysway*.

The earliest attestations are for *scucca*, not otherwise a very common element. There is *scuccanhlau* 792 at Little Horwood in Buckinghamshire, *Socheberge* 1086 now Shuckburgh in Warwickshire, *Succhelauefurlong* c.1210 at Steeple Barton in Oxfordshire, *Shokeburew* 1285 now Shugborough in Staffordshire, *Shuckeburgh* 1333 at Hollowell in Northamptonshire, Shuggborowe Leys 1601 at Burton Overy in Leicestershire and Shuckbarrow Field 1670 at Hamstead in Staffordshire, with two later examples—very much a Midlands distribution.[222] One name in *scinna*, Shinborowes 1552, appears at Wethersfield in Essex. But the commonest qualifier, expecially in the south-west, is *bugge*. *Buggenb'h* 1277 (presumably contracted for *bergh*) is the earliest form, at Pottlebury in Northamptonshire, with *Bugebur* 1400x50 at Chard in Somerset and *Buglawe* 1478/9 at Darlaston in Staffordshire.[223] After the medieval forms come Buglow 1501 at Bollington in Cheshire, Buckeborough 1563 at Ryme Intrinseca in Dorset, Buckbarowe 1617 at Bere Regis in Dorset, Bugberie 1630 at Kirk Langley in Derbyshire, Bugber 1705 at Clifton in Bedfordshire, and Bugbarrow 1764 at Portesham in Dorset, with two later names.

It is difficult to place these names because neither *haugr*, *hlāw* nor *beorg* were used exclusively for burial mounds in early and medieval England. The archaeological term *barrow* is a false-friend translation of *beorg*; needing a word to describe the funereal landmarks they were looting, antiquaries took what had originally been a Wessex dialect term for hillock and gave it a meaning more precise than its original users ever meant. For the Anglo-Saxons, who valued clarity about shape over classification by size, a *beorg* was simply a rise with a round profile.

Regional preferences influenced the semantics of these words. North of a line from the Mersey to the Humber, *hlāw* or its medieval reflex *low* is used for natural hills. In the Lake District *haugr*, as *howe*, is the standard term for peaks and mountains. In all the identifiable locations called *ælf haugr*, the generic has this sense. Elfa Hill at Uldale is a knoll north of Green Howe; Elva Hill at Setmurphy, a prominent knoll at the end of a spur; Elfhow at Over Staveley, one at the end of Millrigg Knott. Elfa Green in Allendale is a secondary name but the original Elfa would have been on the hills west of the river. At Elfa Hall in East Witton, the deserted site of the hall is on low ground, and must be named after an original Elfa on the ridge to the south. All of these hills are craggy uplands where the plough never drove, where ancient dykes and enclosures still survive; if there had been burial mounds or cairns here, we would see them, and we don't.

The only name in this group that undoubtedly refers to a tumulus is Elfhow in Folkton, and here the barrow stands on the end of a ridge much as in the Cumbrian fells.[224] Ailcy Hill is a natural hill, tall even after centuries of quarrying.[225] Certainly people were interred here, and their burial would still have been within memory at the time when the name was coined; their resting place remained one of the key points in the sacred layout of the town, but *haugr* cannot in this case literally mean a mound raised over the dead.

In lower-lying land, there is always the possibility that a barrow was ploughed out during the expansion of openfield. Even so, it is remarkable how few can be identified today. Scratters in Hayton is a large area of low-lying land, and Scrathowes in Thimbleby is low ground at the foot of a hill; neither of them the kind of place where you would expect to find a barrow. At Shinborough the ground is flat, although we could imagine a very low burial circle as at Trusey Hill. Shagborough at Bibury is a low hill, and the hill at Upper Shuckburgh is distinct though not steep; here *beorg* seems likely to refer to the hills themselves and there is no need to suppose lost barrows. Shucklow Hill, *scuccanhlau* 792, is a low rise, hardly a hill at all, so the *hlāw* must have been near its top in the field now called Shuckla, but there is nothing to be seen.[226] Bugbarrow at Bere Regis is an impressive mound but probably natural.[227]

Of the sixteen recorded instances of *aelf haugr*, thirteen seem to have the generic in the sense 'peak, hill', while the meaning of the other three cannot be established. They are still supernatural names, but they align with the *ælf dūn* group—heights onto which the elves descend from their home in the upper air, not hillocks inside which they live, as they do in William of Newburgh's story. Of the other names in *haugr*, *beorg* and *dūn*, so few can be located on the ground that no conclusions can be drawn geographically, but onomastically they stand apart from all the other categories of elfin name in the infrequency of the usual qualifiers *pūca* and *þyrs* and the preference instead for Old English word *scucca* and Middle English *bugge*, both carrying implications of a shadowy, indistinct fear: nothing like the fairy revellers of the story.[228]

That is not how barrows were understood by the Scandinavian tellers of tales. They retained a lively sense of the dead man within the mound, seated in the dark earth-hall with his treasures around him, ready to fight whoever ventures in. The pagan dead live on in the space where they were buried, sometimes alone, sometimes in the company of their kin.[229] Sometimes the mound is the home of the dead; sometimes it is full of elves. In *Kormáks Saga*, Thordis the wise woman tells how a man's wounds can be healed. A bull is to be killed, and the body dragged to a mound nearby in which elves live. If the bull's blood is sprinkled on the surface of the mound, and its flesh cut up as a feast for the elves, then the man will get better.[230] Throughout Scandinavia the dead, especially the ancestral dead, live on in their earthen halls as elves, or like elves, receiving a similar cult and credited with similar powers. None of this is attested in English sources; and even if we were to assume a native Anglo-Saxon tradition that has been utterly erased from the written record, we would still have to explain why place-names, the paradigmatic source for vernacular knowledge, show no sign of it either.

Except in the Yorkshire Wolds, where one midnight hour in around 1130, a boozy *rusticus* rode past a *haugr* and saw what any Norwegian or Icelander would have recognized: a spacious, brightly lit room, full of people singing and enjoying themselves, seen through an open door that led into the hill. The rest of the story, with the snatching of the cup and the madcap ride to escape from the elves, can be paralleled in any number of Scandinavian folktale collections but (if we except the probably derivative story in Gervase) there is no parallel to it in English sources.[231] Of the peasant's background, nothing is known, but the rural working class did not usually present gifts directly to kings; he must have been represented by an intermediary, and perhaps both cup and story were collected not from a barrow but from the wharfs at Bridlington. There was much traffic across the North Sea, in stories as well as goods. We have already seen the hermit Bartholomew telling demon tales from Norway, and a Norwegian crippled by supernatural encounter finding his cure at Durham.

The idea that elves inhabit a mound—living inside it, rather than just haunting it, or descending onto it—is a distinct tradition: if it was imported from Scandinavia, then it arrived late in the development of the English fairy tradition, after the Middle Ages. A fair woman in fine cloths appears to a man, leads him to a little hill, knocks three times, and as the hill opens before them, they come to a fair hall: this is in 1653, significantly in Yorkshire.[232] The Scottish witch trials are full of stories like this. Katherine Ross went into hills to speak to the elf folk, 1590; Isobel Haldane was carried to a hillside, where the hill opened, and she entered, 1623; Isobel Gowdie went to the hills, they stood open and she came to a large fair room, 1662.[233] The scene is often laid at a prehistoric mound, but we should not let the antiquity of the site blind us to the comparative modernity of the motif. Medieval fairies did not live in barrows.

Afterword

'If you ask me the cause and the explanation of an event of this sort, I do not know what to answer', remarked Gerald of Wales when confronted with the Pembrokeshire poltergeists.[1] Familiar with all the sprawling Gormenghast of medieval learning, he had the honesty to admit that he had encountered something beyond its boundaries. The modern historian is not so privileged. As we come to the end of a survey covering nine centuries, with a cast list that extends from kings to cowherds, you might expect a conclusion about who the fairies were, why they appeared, and how they came to be part of the medieval world. But it is not as easy as that.

We can say what they meant for individuals. William Wynfeld lost and recovered his mind and turned from an ambitious young retainer in a gentry household into a humble village priest. Christina went through a crisis that refashioned a troubled teenager into a postulant at the Cistercian house of Elcho. Richard the son of Roger grew in the respect of those who mattered through his commanding account of dreams and visions. In these microhistories we can see not just how the supernatural touched their lives but what they made of it afterwards. And as we move out from the individual to the general, broader patterns become clear: amongst them, the empowerment of women. Those whom no-one had taken very seriously—Reinburgis, Marion Clerk, the maiden of Dunwich and the matron with St John's-wort down her bosom—they all emerged from encountering the supernatural with an unexpected accession of authority, an ability to command attention that they could never have achieved alone. This sudden influx of power to the humble was not just for women: it appears in the shrewd judgements of Meilyr as much as the healing rituals of Agnes Hancock, wherever the fairy touch opened up an alternative system of belief beyond the rule of clergy. And Meilyr, like Elidyr and Edric Wilde and Ieuan ap Gwilym, lived on the marches of England and Wales, in territory where kingly and ecclesiastical authority broke down, a geographical correlative to the borderlands of sense and madness in which so many of the seers suffered and grew powerful. All of these patterns are present in the evidence, and I have touched on them lightly as they appeared.

But it is not as easy as that: yes, we can follow the personal and social consequences of encountering spirits, but in each case the chain of events traces back to the encounter itself, and at this point history breaks down. Historians—and this is what distinguishes us from annalists and copyists and journalists—ask *why*. Without causation, there cannot be a historical narrative. And supernatural events are not caused. They have no antecedents: they break into our world at will. This is not a comforting thought and both religion and superstition are rich in schemes of pseudo-causation, endowing the otherworld with motives and intentions, just like ours. In medieval times, the belief in demons, patron saints and purgatorial ghosts functioned in this way: while such beings might be malignant, at least they were not motiveless. Fairies were disturbing because they were capricious—and even that imposes a causality that is not there: they came from a place that has no 'because'.

And yet fairies do have a timeline: their appearances in the Middle Ages differed from what they had been in the pre-Christian past, and would be in the post-Enlightenment present. So we can, after all, write a history of the small gods—or of the great ones, if we prefer—but only by treating them as the product of human minds. Take that step, and we can find plenty of reasons why elfshot or changelings or pixyleading should happen in one culture but not another: but at the cost of believing, or writing as if we believed, that fairies are something which people have just made up. I know many people who have seen things which, they tell me, they didn't make up, and I do not think they are wrong. This has been a book of things that happened, not of fables or traditions or fictions, though these all had a part to play in the overall story.

If there is a way out of this impasse, it lies in the traditions of anthropological history. Much writing about the past, especially the medieval past, deals not with changes over time but with the functioning of society at some given moment. Here the insistent *why* of causation is softened into an inquiry about what events meant at the time, how they played out within social relations. And the fairies were certainly social. We do not need to dismiss their status as independent actors—nor to affirm it, either—if we look back on the evidence in this book as reports from a world in which people mingled with spirits, and both had something to say.

Elfin Place-Names: A Corpus

This is a list of English place-names containing Old English and Middle English words for spirits, listed alphabetically under each county first by qualifier and then by place, following the base units—parishes or townships—used in the English Place-Name Survey. Names are included if it is likely that they contain the 21 qualifiers discussed in this book, though not all etymologies are certain. The first attestation is given for each name, though that is not necessarily the current form. Where different compounds with the same generic are recorded from a single parish, only the earliest is given, on the assumption that the others are shift-names. Adjectives such as *elven* and *elvisch* appear under the corresponding noun. Earlier volumes from the English Place-Name Society mentioned some names without any location: these go at the beginning of a section. Names on a parish boundary are allocated to the first parish alphabetically.

Forms appear as in the sources, except that Old and Middle English have been italicized, Modern English not. Names are given capital letters except for forms from Anglo-Saxon charters—identified by their Sawyer (S) numbers—which appear in lower case as a marker of their possibly appellative status. The convention 1210/11 is used for documents dated to a split year, and 1210x20 for those from a date range.

Names are credited to volumes of the English Place-Name Society, other publications, Ordnance Survey 6-inch maps (with grid reference) and record office document numbers (or, in the case of tithe awards and maps, the abbreviation TM).

Bedfordshire. Uncredited references from Bedfordshire Archives

ælf. Elvinsloe 1700 (Cople: R6/14/12/11)

bugge. Bugber 1705 (Clifton: V231/1–2), Bugg's Close 1725 (Wrestlingworth: S2172)

gobelin. Goblin's Hole 1707 (Turvey: GA1827)

pūca. Pucks Pightle 1838 (Colmworth: X284/22/3), Puckhay 1731 (Crudwell: L19/128–129), Pugg's Lane 1675 (Harrold: GA1410), *Poukeruding* 1254x64 (Renhold: R6/47/1/4)

skratti. Scratteye Wood 1566 (Cardington: W70)

scucca. Sucke Hill 1642 (Podington: OR25)

Berkshire. Uncredited references from *PN Berks* and Berkshire Record Office

ælf. Elven Close 1600s (Cookham: 1 p. 86), *Alfletegore* 1432/3 (Steventon: 2 p. 421), *ylfing dene* 956 (Welford: 3 p. 665; cf. S 622)

bugge. *Buggehesel* 1248 (Cookham: 1 p. 83; cf. Derby, *Cookham* p. 54), Buggrow 1547 (Radley: 2 p. 457), Bug Lane 1848 (Winkfield: 1 p. 39)

cangun. Quanguins Oak 1609 (Cookham: 1 p. 87; cf. Derby, *Cookham* p. 73)

pūca. *Pukemere* 1283 (Bray: 1 p. 46; cf. *VCH Berks* 3 p. 101), Pug Pightle 1842 (Burghfield: 1 p. 209), Puckneys 1623 (Buscot: 2 p. 355; cf. D/ELV/ T12/1–52), *Pokestede* 1355 (Cookham: 1 p. 79; cf. D/QR22/2/193), The Pug Pits 1840 (Enborne: 2 p. 297), Powkecrofte 1547 (Hamstead Marshall: 2 p. 301), Pugdown Hill 1843 (Hurley: 1 p. 65), Puckhayse 1717 (North Moreton: 2 p. 526), Pugg's Eyott 1849 (Radley: 2 p. 458), Pokefeld 1551/2 (Reading: 1 p. 183), Pokelande 1547 (Shaw cum Donnington: 1 p. 265), *Pokebrok* 1413 (Sonning Town: 1 p. 135; cf. D/EE/T1/1/6), *Pokesden* 1439/40 (Steventon: 2 p. 420), Pug Field 1838 (Stratfield Mortimer: 1 p. 219), *Pokelane* 1310 (Windsor: 1 p. 35)

pūcel. Pokelmede 1547 (Shaw cum Donnington: 1 p. 265)

scinna. Shinmoor 1840 (Didcot: 2 p. 518)

þyrs. *Thorsdiche* 1327 (Sparsholt: 2 p. 491)

Buckinghamshire. Uncredited references from *PN Bucks* and Buckinghamshire Archives

gobelin. Goblins Wood 1715 (Bellingdon: D-LO/1/6/1–30), Goblin's Ditch 1726 (Loughton: *Buckinghamshire Sessions Records* 5 p. 150), Goblins Pittes 1625 (Marlow: D-CE/M592)

pūca. *Pokeputte* 1300s (Princes Risborough: The National Archives C 146/6686), *Pokeput* 1328 (Sherington: Chibnall, *Sherington* p. 11)

scucca. *scuccanhlau* 792 (Little Horwood: p. 69; cf. S 138)

Cambridgeshire. Uncredited references from *PN Cambs* and Cambridgeshire Archives

bugge. Buggs Pond 1726 (Ely: P68/18/2)

nicor. Nikeresaker 1313 (p. 311)

pūca. Pokle 1570 (p. 337), *Pokelodelake* 1397 (p. 335), *Pokemilne* 1260 (p. 339), Pokes Nest 1712 (Chippenham: 71/P3), *Pokefelde c.*1190 (Leverington: p. 272), *Pokedych* 1386 (Wisbech: 604/T28)

screawa. Schrewehirst 1207 (Upwell: p. 289)

scucca. Schokepet 1431 (p. 341)

þyrs. Þrispit 1250 (p. 341), *Thurspit* 1200s (p. 341)

Cheshire. Uncredited references from *PN Cheshire*

bugge. Bug Hall 1839 (Alsager: 3 p. 4), Buggely Well 1831 (Appleton: 2 p. 100), Buglow 1501 (Bollington: 1 p. 191), Buggfeilde 1650 (Brereton: 2 p. 277), Bug Spit 1896 (Heswall cum Oldfield: 4 p. 278), Bug Fields 1840 (Moston: TM), Bugmoor Hill 1841 (Shurlach: 2 p. 211), Buggler 1848 (Tytherington: 1 p. 215), Bug Hole 1800s (Witton: 5:1i p. xxx)

dweorg. Dwarf Wood 1831 (Somerford Booths: 1 p. 64)

feond. Fendesdale 1325 (Tilston: 4 p. 60), *le Fendesers clogh* 1407 (Witton: 2 p. 197)

gobelin. Goblins Croft 1840 (Alpraham: 3 p. 301), Goblins Hole 1831 (Buerton: 3 p. 87), The Goblin's Tower *c.*1650 (Chester: 5:1i p. 27)

nicor. Nikerespool 1309 (Sutton: 2 p. 258)

niht-mare. Negtmareslond 1200s (Barton: 4 p. 70), *Nahtmare furlang* 1300x20 (Coddington: 4 p. 87), *Nachomaresforlong c.*1312 (Macclesfield: 1 p. 125)

skratti. Scratley Field 1842 (Dodcott cum Wilkesley: 3 p. 100), *Scratʒord* 1417 (Nantwich: 3 p. 41), Little Scratley 1841 (Woodcott: 3 p. 119), Scratley 1841 (Wrenbury cum Frith: 3 p. 121)

scucca. Socheliche 1086 (Church Shocklach: 4 p. 62), Shocklach Field 1650 (Lea Newbold: 4 p. 121)

þyrs. Thirs Pits 1848 (Brereton: TM), *Thurse Hole* 1429 (Bulkeley: 4 p. 20), Thurshaugh Brook 1690 (Daresbury: 2 p. 149), Thrush Butts 1838 (Moreton cum Lingham: 4 p. 321), *Thurbatchker* 1327x77 (Rainow: 1 p. 141)

Cumberland. Uncredited references from *PN Cumb*

ælf. Elfe Hill 1578 (Aspatria: 2 p. 262), *Elnehill* 1355 (Carlisle: 1 p. 50), Elvinhowe 1577 (Gosforth: 2 p. 397), *Elfowebek* 1377 (Hutton-in-the-Forest:

1 p. 209), Elfe-hole 1631 (Millom: 2 p. 418), Elva Hill 1864 (Setmurthy: 2 p. 435), Elfa Hill 1863 (Uldale: OS at NY 258 378)

bugge. *Bugmyre* 1357 (Seburgham: 1 p. 154)

feond. *Fendesfeld* 1340 (Skirwith: 1 p. 243)

pūca. Poukes Moss 1860 (Ennerdale: 2 p. 387)

scinna. *Skyneburg* 1175 (Holme Low: 2 p. 294)

skratti. Scradgate 1673 (Hensingham: 2 p. 401)

scucca. *Skukkerhouses* 1332 (Carlisle: 1 p. 149; cf. Kristensson, 'Scugger Ho')

skyrsi. Skirsgill Wood 1859 (Culgaith: OS at NY 595 302), Skirs Hill 1603 (Dacre: 1 p. 189)

þyrs. Thyrspoone 1568 (Ainstable: 1 p. 171), *Thruswell* 1479 (Alston: 1 p. 174), *Thursgill* 1384 (Hesket in the Forest: 1 p. 207), Thrushbank 1662 (Loweswater: Lancashire Archives WRW/C/R224A/13), Thirspott 1616 (St John's: 2 p. 315), Thrushhowe 1578 (Wasdale: 2 p. 442)

troll. Trowyshaw Rigg 1864 (Kingwater: OS at NY 630 746)

Derbyshire. Uncredited references from *PN Derbs* and Derbyshire Record Office

ælf. *Alveleg'* 1205 (Crich: 2 p. 441), *Elvedon* 1285 (Peak Forest: 1 p. 160), *Elfe Eng* 1373 (Wath: D7676/Bag C/856)

bugge. *Buggehalowe* 1415 (Duffield: 3 p. 556), Bugley 1879 (Hartshorne: 3 p. 638), Bugberie 1630 (Kirk Langley: 2 p. 478)

cangun. *Coniuncros* 1216x72 (Derby: 2 p. 454), Congin Pits 1842 (Linton: 3 p. 640), Conjins Gate 1764 (Tideswell: 1 p. 173), Conghen Flats 1610 (Wirksworth: 2 p. 420)

dēofol. *Dyulesewude* 1254 (Ashover: 2 p. 191), *Deilȝerde* 1427 (Wingerworth: 2 p. 333)

pokere. Poker Pittes 1603x25 (Matlock Bath: 2 p. 394)

pūca. *Pokeston* 1415 (Duffield: 3 p. 555), Poke Lane Close 1792 (Mickleover: Fraser *Field Names* p. 97), *Pukewell* 1172 (Repton: Fraser *Field Names* p. 125; cf. Dugdale, *Monasticon* 6i p. 430), *Pokecroft* 1308 (Shirland & Higham: 2 p. 301)

skratti. *Scratteharde* c.1570 (Little Longstone: 1 p. 142), *Scrattehaghe* 1327 (Scarcliffe: 2 p. 296)

scucca. Suckstones 1841 (Bradbourne: 2 p. 350), *Succhethormam* 1154x9 (Crich: 2 p. 437), *Shucktone* 1330 (Hulland Ward: 3 p. 576), Shuckshorn 1825 (Spondon: 3 p. 607), Suckethorne Nooke 1666 (Wormhill: 1 p. 182)

þyrs. Thurspitt Hole 1642 (Bonsall: 2 p. 348), *Thursbacheheved* 1216x72 (Charlesworth: 1 p. 72), *Tursthous* 1417 (Chelmorton: 1 p. 75), Thrusley 1842 (Doveridge: 3 p. 552), *Thurspyttys* 1491 (Holmesfield: 2 p. 268), Thrush Pits 1779 (Osmaston by Derby: 2 p. 490; cf. *Derby Mercury* 11 June 1779)

Devon. Uncredited references from *PN Devon* and Devon Heritage Centre

bugge. Bugwell 1672 (Barnstaple: North Devon RO 1142B/0/T/3/110), Bugg Parke 1680 (Georgeham: North Devon RO 1142B/0/L/28/1), Bugbeare Mills 1604 (Morchard Bishop: 3799M/0/T/10/1), Buggehedbeme 1519 (Moretonhampstead: 4912M/T/1), Buggy Hill 1819 (Northam: North Devon RO B127/6/83), Bugesford 1509x47 (Stoke Fleming: 1 p. 331)

pokere. Puker's Meadow 1777 (Chulmleigh: QS/4/1777/Michaelmas/CO/18), Pocker's Ford 1761 (Plympton St Mary: QS/4/1761/Michaelmas/PM/1)

pūca. *Poukemede* 1200s (2 p. 691), Pokemershe *c.*1500 (2 p. 691), *Pokemore* 1463 (2 p. 691), *Pokepytte* 1473 (2 p. 691), Pocombe 1761 (Alphington: QS/4/1762/Easter/HI/6), Pookhole Cottage 1888 (Arlington: OS at SS 638 415), *Pokehill* 1268 (Berry Pomeroy: 3799M/0/ET/3/2), Pugshole 1840 (Burlescombe: TM), Puckie Stone 1848 (Chagford: Rowe, *Perambulation* pp. 80–1), *Pokepark* 1468 (Clyst Honiton: The National Archives E 40/12315), *Pokeswylle* 1386 (Colyton: 123M/TB/262), *Pokachurna* 1200s (Dunsford: Devon Heritage Centre Z1/16/4), Pokelakes Plantation 1886 (High Bickington: OS at SS 602 212), Pugshole Cottage 1888 (Luppitt: OS at ST 171 078), *Puckland* 1330 (Pancrasweek: 1 p. 157), Poke Water 1760 (Shobrooke: QS/4/1760/Midsummer/HI/4), Pokeyne 1556 (Southleigh: 123M/L/1008)

pūcel. *Puchelahole* 1301 (Hartland: 1 p. 75)

screawa. *scræwanleg* 924x39 (Stoke Canon: S 389)

scucca. *sceoca broce* 924x39 (Shobrooke: 1 p. 12; S 387)

þyrs. Þurswege *c.*1174 (Abbotsham: Finberg, *Tavistock Charters* p. 363)

Dorset. Uncredited references from *PN Dorset*

ælf. Elvelands 1838 (Buckland Newton: 2 p. 251), Elvelands 1841 (Chideock: 4 p. 381), Elveland 1840 (Lydlinch: 2 p. 352), *Alvysch Thornys* 1319 (Milton Abbas: 2 p. 225), *Elfhede* 1452 (Piddlehinton: 1 p. 313)

bugge. Buckbarowe 1617 (Bere Regis: 1 p. 278), Bagbarrow 1840 (Cann: 2 p. 96), *Bogeley* 1275 (Gillingham: 2 p. 11), *Biggputtlane* 1462 (Holnest: 2

p. 340), Bugbarrow 1764 (Portesham: 4 p. 33), Buckeborough 1563 (Ryme Intrinseca: 4 p. 221), *Buggeshaghe* 1327 (Sherborne: *Dorset Lay Subsidy* p. 34), Bugdowne 1545 (Stockwood: 4 p. 227)

dēofol. *Dewelepole* 1285 (Beaminster: 4 p. 250), *Deoulepole* 1216x72 (Caundle Marsh: 2 p. 317)

gobelin. *Gobelynshole* 1461 (Portesham: 4 p. 35)

pokere. Poker's Pool 1888 (Lyme Regis: 4 p. 398)

pūca. Pug's Plantation 1876 (Alderholt: 2 p. 198), Pook Marsh 1778x88 (Arne: 1 p. 80), Puckway 1842 (Beaminster: 4 p. 249), Puckmoor 1838 (Cann: 2 p. 98), Pokershe 1540 (Cheselbourne: 2 p. 207), *Pucchelake* 1470 (Chideock: 4 p. 386), Puckhay 1842 (Compton Abbas: 2 p. 100), Pook Acre 1625 (Godmanstone: 4 p. 144), Pucklake 1684 (Halstock: 4 p. 205), Pucklake Mead 1838 (Langton Matravers: 1 p. 38), *Pokemour* 1371 (Motcombe: 2 p. 54), *Poukepitte* 1447 (Osmington: 1 p. 214), *Pokeput* 1428 (Puddletown: 1 p. 328), *Pukefurland* 1200s (Radipole: 1 p. 243), *Pokelane* 1317 (Shaftesbury: 2 p. 149), Pug Pit 1841 (Stour Provost: 2 p. 77), Puketon 1585 (Studland: 1 p. 49), *Puckysbarry* 1451 (Winfrith Newburgh: 1 p. 185), *Poukepitte* 1447 (Wool: 1 p. 192), *Pokesyde* 1354 (Yetminster: Somerset Heritage Centre DD/SF/2/106/16)

pūcel. *Pokelmour* 1399 (Portesham: 4 p. 35), *Pokulchurche* 1460 (Wyke Regis: 1 p. 272)

þyrs. *Thursdyche* 1451 (Preston: 1 p. 238)

wælcyrige. *Valgirimede* 1357 (Abbotsbury: 4 p. 12)

Durham. Uncredited references from Mawer, *PN Northumberland & Durham* and Durham Record Office

pokere. *Pokerlege* 1242 (Urpeth: p. 158)

scinna. *Scinneclif* c.1125 (Shincliffe: p. 178)

troll. Trow Lane Head 1817 (Lynesack: D/X 1392/9/1), Trow Point 1858 (South Shields: OS at NZ 385 667)

Essex. Uncredited references from *PN Essex* and Essex Record Office

bugge. Bugg Lane 1602 (Laindon: Q/SR 159/117), *Buggelond* c.1300 (Lamarsh: The National Archives E 40/527), Bugg Field 1606 (Wakes Colne: Q/SR 175/54) *cangun*. *Canyoneshole* 1401 (High Easter: p. 639), Congous Grove 1848 (Pleshey: p. 640), *Congeonshole* 1287 (Stebbing: p. 634)

gobelin. Goblin Grove 1825 (St Osyth: D/DHw T99)

nicor. *Nikersmadwe* 1313 (p. 598)

pūca. Pokefelde 1513 (p. 587, three instances), *Pokehalfacre* 1399 (p. 587), *Pokemelne* 1302 (p. 586), *Pokemulne* 1302 (p. 587, four instances), *Poukwan* 1321 (p. 587), *Pucheacre* 1200s (p. 587), *Pokefelde* 1373 (Foxearth: p. 628), Poke Field 1621 (Great Leighs: D/Q 14/33), *Pokepet* 1319 (South Fambridge: p. 183), Pooke Mill 1622 (Sturmer: HA517/B17), *Puchisland* 1356 (Waltham Holy Cross: p. 33)

scinna. Shinborowes 1552 (Wethersfield: p. 466)

scucca. Suckmoreheath 1604 (Lawford: p. 243)

Gloucestershire. Uncredited references from *PN Glos*

ælf. elfaledes 1000s (Corse: 3 p. 147; cf. S 1551)

dēofol. *Develeserce* 1448 (Lechlade: 1 p. 43)

dweorg. Dwarfs' Hill 1723 (Lydney: Bathurst, *Lydney Park* p. 3)

gobelin. Goblin Ledge 1881 (Henbury: OS at ST 539 864)

pūca. Puckwell 1575 (Alkington: 2 p. 211), Puckpool Farm 1802 (Arlingham: 2 p. 176), The Puckpitt 1709 (Aston Somerville: 2 p. 3; cf. East Riding Archives DDRI/36/5), *Povkesdiche* 1445 (Awre: 3 p. 254), Puck Mill 1882 (Bisley: 1 p. 123), Pockhill 1738 (Bourton-on-the-Water: Somerset Heritage Centre DD/HYD/36), Pughill 1841 (Brookthorpe: 2 p. 162), Puckbridge 1803 (Churcham: 3 p. 197), Puck Reddings 1840 (Churchdown: 2 p. 122), Puck Acre 1837 (Daglingworth: 1 p. 70), Puck Moor 1848 (Dymock: 3 p. 171), *Pukeputteswey* 1282 (East Dean: 3 p. 224), Puck Berries 1838 (English Bicknor: 3 p. 213), Puckpits 1838 (Filton: 3 p. 103), *Pucheacre* 1245 (Fretherne & Saul: 2 p. 180), *Pukelone* 1100s (Gloucester: 2 p. 131), Pucknold Ditch 1775 (Gotherington: 2 p. 89), *Poukesplace* 1380 (Hawkesbury: 3 p. 35), Pug Pits 1839 (Henbury: 3 p. 135), *Poukhey* 1300s (Kemerton: 2 p. 60), *Pukeput* 1263x84 (Maisemore: 3 p. 162), Pucklow 1838 (Newent: 3 p. 180), Puckhame 1635 (Newland: 3 p. 240), Pug Pitt 1839 (Quedgeley: 2 p. 189), Pucks Hole 1830 (Randwick: 2 p. 190), Pughill 1863 (South Cerney: 1 p. 59), Puck Pitt 1839 (Standish: 2 p. 192), Puck Pits 1837 (Stoke Orchard: 2 p. 94), Puck's Well 1883 (Sudeley: OS at SP 023 256), Puck Lane 1600x50 (Taynton: 3 p. 188), *Poukepitteʒ* 1487 (Tredington: 2 p. 70), Pucksmoor 1840 (Twyning: 2 p. 73), Puckpit Field 1840 (Upton St Leonards: 2 p. 172), Pukpite 1575 (Walton Cardiff: 2 p. 74), Pugpits

1837 (Wheatenhurst: 2 p. 205), Puckpit 1815 (Winchcombe: 2 p. 37), Puckpath 1558x1603 (Wotton under Edge: 2 p. 261)

pūcel. Pucklewell 1841 (Dyrham & Hinton: 3 p. 50), *Pucelecroft* 1100s (Elmore: 2 p. 163), Picklechurch Brake 1883 (Oxenton: 2 p. 61), *Pucelancyrcan* 946 (Pucklechurch: 3 p. 64; cf. S 553)

scucca. Shagborough Barn 1830 (Bibury: 1 p. 28)

þyrs. Thursditch 1801 (Kempsford: 1 p. 40)

Hampshire. Uncredited references from Coates, *Hampshire PNs* and Hampshire Archives

ælf. Alfedon *1403* (Ropley: DC/A2/32)

bugge. Bugden Cops 1597 (Herriard: 44M69/E2/14), Buggesmore Woode 1632 (Preston Candover: 44M69/D1/8/7), Bugromede 1533 (Sherfield on Lodden: Surrey History Centre LM/345/72)

cangun. Congellons 1840 (Durley: Field, *Field-Names* p. 53)

gobelin. Gobley Hole 1781 (Nutley: 15M84/2/1/14/1)

pūca. Pukenhale 1300s (Ampfield: *VCH Hants* 3 pp. 421), *La Pukestone* 1275 (Bitterne: DC/M4/8/1), *Pokesdoune c.*1300 (Bournemouth: p. 132), Pucknall 1866 (Braishfield: OS at SU 386 249), Pokeland 1567 (Buriton: Attree, *Post-Mortems in Sussex* p. 64), *Pucknall* 1331 (Chilcomb: DC/A2/20), *Pokeryche* 1189x99 (Crondall: Austen & Hill, 'Boundaries of Itchen'; cf. S 1559), Pook Poll 1831 (Eling: 11M70/B1/2/10), Pokestones 1688 (Fareham: 16M74/E/ T1), *Pukebroc* 1213x15 (Farlington: p. 135; cf. *Cartularies of Southwick Priory* 2 p. 68), Pug's Hole 1871 (Frenchmoor: OS at SU 279 281), *Pokepole* 1337 (Hambledon: DC/A1/12), Pooksgreen 1871 (Marchwood: OS at SU 376 104), Puckpits 1863 (Minstead: OS at SU 255 097), Pucknalls 1797 (Newton Valence: 26M64/118–119), *La Poclond* 1200x90 (Preston Candover: 29M82/40), Puggs Mead 1653 (Sherborne St John: 31M57/102), Pooks Meadow 1815 (Soberton: 31M57/102), *Pugdells* 1263 (Wield: Reaney, *Origins* p. 223)

pūcel. Pookles Lane 1870 (Worldham: OS at SU 755 385)

Herefordshire. Uncredited references from Coplestone-Crow, *Herefs PNs*

bugge. Bugs Yard 1843 (Woolhope: TM)

fēond. Norton-by-Bromyard 1501 (p. 153)

gobelin. Goblins Field 1843 (Ross: TM)

pokere. Puckers Field 1843 (Brinsop: TM), Poukers Meadow 1846 (Kilpeck: TM), Puck a Piece 1843 (Michaelchurch Escley: TM), Puckers Orchard 1840 (Peterstow: TM)

pūca. Puck Hill 1840 (Acton Beauchamp: TM), Puckhill Coppice 1884 (Bishop's Frome: OS at SO 679 494), *Poukewallefeld* 1389 (Bishopstone: The National Archives C 146/6734), Puckley Field 1802 (Bodenham: Enclosure Award), Pouke Lane 1842 (Canon Pyon: TM), Puck Holes Close 1722 (Credenhill: Bannister, *PN Herefs* p. 158), Powke Meadow 1840 (Kimbolton: TM), Puckmore Rise 1606 (Kings Caple: Wiltshire and Swindon History Centre 1720/315), Puck Meadow 1839 (Kinnersley: TM), Powk More 1846 (Leintwardine: TM), *Pukedich* 1200x25 (Leominster: Bannister, *PN Herefs* p. 158; cf. Dugdale, *Monasticon* 4 p. 54), Powke Croft 1839 (Linton nr. Ross: TM), Pookhouse 1842 (Lucton: TM), Pokewell 1842 (Madley: TM), Little Puckmore 1653 (Much Marcle: Wiltshire and Swindon History Centre 1720/353), Powkes Close 1840 (Norton Canon: TM), Poukes Hole 1842 (Orcop: TM), Poke Field 1840 (Pembridge: TM), Puckmore House 1839 (Putley: TM), Pokewall 1844 (Stapleton: TM), Powkhouse 1839 (Stoke Bliss: TM), *Pouklone* 1395 (Tillington: Bannister, *PN Herefs* p. 158; cf. *Registrum Johannis Trefnant* p. 34), Pouk Lane 1838 (Upper Sapey: TM), Puckmoors 1840 (Upton Bishop: TM), *Poukeputte* 1369/70 (Wellington: The National Archives C 146/2854), Pouke Pasture 1840 (Yazor: TM)

pūcel. Puckle Field 1839 (Lugwardine: TM)

scucca. Shukway Meadow 1839 (Bosbury: TM), *Shokenhulle* 1377 (Weston Beggard: Bannister, *PN Herefs* p. 171; cf. *Registrum Johannis Gilbert* p. 130)

Hertfordshire. Uncredited references from *PN Herts* and Hertfordshire Archives

ælf. *Elfringemad* 1220x70 (Little Hadham: Hadley, *Hollow Places*, p. 307; cf. DE/Sr/T12)

pūca. Puchley 1571 (Preston: 72183), *Pukerich* 1220 (Standon: p. 198; cf. *PN Oxon* 1 p. 1), Pokefelds 1584 (Therfield: 25427), Little Poknest 1616 (Ware: DE/Fo/T62)

pūcel. Pokyllyshedge 1556 (Bennington: p. 286), *Pucheleslee* 1211 (Great & Little Munden: p. 288)

skratti. Scratched Piece 1638 (Bengeo: DE/AS/489), Scratch Spring 1843 (Flamstead: p. 34)

Huntingdonshire

bugge. Bugg Grene 1543 (Abbots Ripton: *VCH Hunts* 2 p. 204)

Kent. Uncredited references from Wallenberg, *PN Kent*, and Kent History Centre

ælf. *ælfrucge* 993 (Canterbury: Wallenberg, *Kentish Place-Names* p. 347; S 877), *Elvedonne* 1283 (Chevening: U1590/T5/3), *Elvenefeld* 1467 (Hartlip: U771/ T36), *helfesdene* 944 (Sibertswold: Wallenberg, *Kentish Place-Names* p. 265; cf. S 501)

bugge. *Buginherst* 1279/80 (Leigh: U1007/T283), Buggs Field 1894 (Sitting-bourne: UD/SM/S4/165)

pūca. *Poukeland* 1339 (Chevening: U1384/T1/7), Pookden 1747 (Chiddingstone: U908/T193), *Poke Grove* 1472 (Downe: The National Archives C 146/5019), Pukkell 1538 (Frindsbury: U601/T96), Pookhale Wood 1767 (Goudhurst: U2627 P1), Pook Well 1797 (Rolvenden: U86/P19), Puxtye 1869 (Sandhurst: OS at TQ 808 285), Puckland Wood 1872 (Shepherdswell with Coldred: OS at TR 242 479), Puck Croft 1686 (Southborough: Hampshire Archives 4M56/248–256, 305), *Powkelane* 1424 (St Paul's Cray: p. 23)

pūcel. *Pukeleshala* 1181/2 (Bapchild: p. 265), Puckle Lane 1774 (Canterbury: U1879/T1), Puckle Wood 1698 (Cobham: p. 111), Puckles Wood Farm 1723 (Eastling: U624/T26), Pugglestone 1817 (Hernhill: U229/T129), Puckle Hall 1690 (Lewisham: U1590/T31/3), Puckle Hill 1860 (Shorne: p. 118), *Pucleston* 1198 (Stodmarsh: p. 526), *Pukelsrede* 1312 (Wye: Cavill, *New Dictionary* p. 342)

Lancashire. Uncredited references from Mills, *PN Lancs* and Lancashire Archives

ælf. Elfa 1846 (Carnforth: TM), Elfylands 1703 (Colne: DDB 80/96), *Aldene-hevet* 1234 (Tottington: Ekwall, *PN Lancs* p. 64)

bugge. Bug Mire 1840 (Preston in Amounderness: TM), Bug Meadow 1844 (Trawden: TM)

dweorg. *Dwerefeld* 1421 (Maghull: DDIN 31/3), *Dweryhouses clyf* c.1250 (Parbold: p. 80), The Dwerry House 1755 (West Derby: DDBB/5/5), *Dwerihouses* 1349 (Wrightington: DDSC/63/16)

nicor. Nikerhole 1603 (Radcliffe: Greater Manchester Record Office E7/13/1/3)

pūcel. Pucklecroft 1746 (Widness: DDX 3/46)

þyrs. Thrushgill Wood 1845 (Arkholme: TM), *Thirsedeneheved* 1324 (Briercliffe
with Extwistle: Ekwall, *PN Lancs* p. 85), *Thursgyll* c.1350 (Capernwray:
Ekwall, *PN Lancs* p. 182), Thrushay 1735 (Cartmel: DDX 243/3/3),
Thrushland Meadow 1838 (Heysham: TM), *Turssekar* 1190x1212 (Hindley:
Chartulary of Cockersand 2ii pp. 647, 649), Thrush Brigg 1846 (Priest Hutton:
TM), *Thyrsewalkehyrst* 1295 (Worsthorne: DDTO/O/(1)/3), *Thursgyll* c.1350
(Wray: p. 140)

Leicestershire. Uncredited references from *PN Leics* and Leicestershire Record Office

ælf. *Heluhou* 1467x84 (Barkby: 3 p. 27), Elfes Grove 1543 (Garsdon:
26D53/1434)

bugge. Bugnall 1849 (Carlton: 6 p. 64)

gobelin. Goblin Pit Furlong 1625 (Carlton: 6 p. 65), Goblin Hole 1601
(Netherseal: 7 p. 274), Goblin Pit 1601 (Twycross: 6 p. 315)

pūca. Pookehole 1631 (Barkstone: 6 p. 43), Puck Lane 1888 (Evington: OS at
SK 625 030), *le Pukhirst* 1477 (Lockington: 7 p. 106)

scinna. Skinner Flatt 1625 (Appleby Magna: 6 p. 20), Skinsmeare 1601
(Broughton Astley: 5 p. 44), Shinnel 1795 (Burton Overy: 4 p. 24)

skratti. Scrat Hawes 1554 (Newtown Linford: 7 p. 161)

scucca. Shuggborowe Leys 1601 (Burton Overy: 4 p. 26), Shuckbry 1843
(Lockington: 7 p. 105)

þyrs. Thurse slade 1601 (Ashby Parva: 5 p. 15), *Thirspittes* 1449 (Belvoir: 2
p. 19), *Tyrspitwong* 1253 (Bottesford: 2 p. 32), *Thursputwelle* 1343 (Catthorpe:
5 p. 56), Thurspitt Leayes 1601 (Croxton Kerrial: 2 p. 109), *Thurspyt*
1272x1307 (Donisthorpe: 7 p. 281), Thurspittes 1601 (Lutterworth: 5
p. 144), Thrush Pits 1850 (Measham: Field, *Field-Names* p. 233), Thruspits
1605 (Saltby: 2 p. 255)

Lincolnshire. Uncredited references from *PN Lincs* and Lincolnshire Archives

nicor. *Nikerpole* 1296x8 (Lincoln: 1 p. 31)

skratti. Scatthowe 1601 (Bradley: Bower, 'PN Lindsey' p. 406), Scratting Close
1829 (Swinderby: Nottinghamshire Archives DD/CT/2/429–430)

scucca. Shucdale 1655 (Haxey: Bower, 'PN Lindsey' p. 554)

þyrs. *Thirspol* c.1190 (Alvingham: *Cartulary of Alvingham* pp. 29–30), *Thyrsdal*
1342 (Anwick: Nottinghamshire Archives DD/A/21/18), Thrushpit Furlong

1750 (Ashby: 6 p. 21), Thurspits 1679 (Bottesford: 6 p. 27), Thrusmyre 1579 (Edlington: Bower, 'PN Lindsey' p. 492), *Thyrspittes* 1280x90 (Foston: Thompson, *Wyggeston* p. 227), *Thirsewell* 1220x30 (Glentham: 6 p. 163), Thursedale 1577 (Hemingby: Bower, 'PN Lindsey' p. 493), Thuswelle Closes 1670 (Hemswell: 6 p. 183), *Tuswellsic* 1200s (Langton-by-Partney: Bower, 'PN Lindsey' p. 506), Trusdall 1577 (Nettleton: 2 p. 244), *Thurseliic* c.1200 (Raithby: 2ANC1/29/2), Threshole 1766 (Saxilby: 7 p. 91), Tursfield Crosse 1699 (Scawby: 6 p. 109), *Thruswelker* 1200s (Stallingborough: *Coucher Book of Selby* 2 p. 197), *Thyrstpit* 1372 (Usselby: 3 p. 171), Thirspitts 1601 (Waltham: 4 p. 192)

troll. *Trolleheudland* 1309 (Goxhill: 2 p. 134)

Middlesex. Uncredited references from *PN Midd*

gobelin. Goblin Oake 1680 (p. 195)
pūca. *Pukwelle* 1436 (p. 204)

Norfolk. Uncredited references from *PN Norfolk* and Norfolk Record Office

ælf. *Alvenelond* 1318 (Downham Market: The National Archives E 326/1316), *Elueshyll* c.1300 (Edgefield: 3 p. 123), *Elvernedele* 1316 (Holme by the Sea: MR 251, 242X2), *Alvehoghe* c.1250 (Little Ryburgh: BL/MD 8), *Elfringhe* 1347 (South Creake: MC 550/1, 774X5), *Alfrith* 1367 (Stow Bardolph: HARE 2958, 201X2)

bugge. *Bugeham* 1267/8 (Chatgrave: Blomefield, *Norfolk* 10 p. 122), *Buggiscroft* 1316 (Taverham: DCN 44/108/21)

nicor. *Nikeresmer* c.1300 (Edgefield: 3 p. 123), *Nikeresfleet* 1390 (Kings Lynn: KL/C 50/362)

pūca. *Pokesty* 1338 (South Creake: BL/MD 25/7/20), *Pokedych* 1250 (Terrington: HARE 3555, 206X6)

þyrs. *Thirspol* 1305 (Cringleford: NCR 25a/7/80), *Thyrspyt* 1343 (Fincham: HARE 1385, 191X4), *Thrysmer* 1484/5 (Gimingham: 3 p. 18), *Turesfort* 1086 (Thursford: Ekwall, *Dictionary of PNs* p. 472)

Northamptonshire. Uncredited references from *PN Northants* and Northamptonshire Archives

bugge. *Buggenb'h* 1277 (Pottlebury: Forward, 'PN Whittlewood' p. 145) *gobelin.* Goblin Furlong 1775 (Crick: Hall & Harding, 'Crick' p. 29)

nicor. *Nikerespol* 1200s (Passenham: Forward, 'PN Whittlewood' p. 66)

pūca. *Pokepyt* 1300s (p. 268: two instances), Puckwell 1712 (Aynho: Morton, *Northampton* p. 282), *Pokeho* 1216x72 (Boughton: The National Archives C 146/2005), *Puckwelle feilde* 1563 (Glapthorn: Map/2991), *Pocabroc* 1076 (Polebrook: p. 215), *Pukefurlong* 1288/9 Silverstone: Forward, 'PN Whittlewood' p. 107), *Le Poukeput* c.1300 (Welton: The National Archives E 40/7602), *Pocheslei* 1086 (Passenham: p. 102)

skratti. Scratchers Hearne 1667 (Cosgrove: A(F)/13/004/5), *Scrathawe* 1400 (Dogsthorpe: p. 264)

scucca. *Shuckeburgh* 1333 (Hollowell: A(F)/13/004/5)

þyrs. *Thursput* 1280 (p. 268, five instances), *Thirsqueche* 1292 (p. 268), *Thirspitt* 1393 (Ailsworth: Kilby, 'Encountering the Environment'), Thurspit 1849 (Nether Heyford: p. 282), *Thruspittemor* c.1250 (Welton: E 40/7602)

Northumberland. Uncredited references from Mawer, *PN Northumberland & Durham*

ælf. Elpha Green 1859 (Allendale: OS at NY 845 487), Elf Kirk 1862 (Falstone: OS at NY 695 860), Elf-hills 1827 (Wallington Demesne: Hodgson, *Northumberland* 2i p. 323)

screawa. *Scravenwod* 1242 (Scrainwood: Ekwall, *Dictionary of PNs* p. 408)

þyrs. *Therspettes* 1256 (Dinnington: Page, *Assize Rolls* pp. 409–10), *Thrusheland* 1170s (Holy Island: Crossman, 'Cuthbert's island')

troll. Trollop 1352 (Heathpool: p. 200), Trowupburn 1860 (Kirknewton: OS at NT 875 265)

Nottinghamshire. Uncredited references from *PN Notts* and Nottinghamshire Archives

ælf. *Elflandes* 1200s (Eakring: p. 298)

bugge. *Buggewant* 1154x89 (Kelham: p. 316), Bugg-Holes 1694 (Nottingham: M/1770), Bug Whong 1831 (Ruddington: C/QA/H/31/6)

pūca. Puck Lane 1801 (Nottingham: Steedman, *Everyday Life* p. 19)

skratti. Scratta 1700s (East Retford: DD/HO/16/9), Scratmoor 1786 (Grassthorpe: DD/TB/8/4/3), *Scrathawe* 1256 (Weston: p. 197), Skratta 1539 (Worksop: p. 108)

þyrs. Thruspitts 1734 (Averham: DD/MN/2/2), *Thrussepittes* 1520 (Eakring: p. 298), *Thirsepol* c.1275 (Hoveringham: p. 312)

Oxfordshire. Uncredited references from *PN Oxon*

ælf. Elfwelle c.1240 (Garsington: 1 p. 175), *Ulvenden* c.1240 (Goring: 1 p. 52; cf. Cole, 'Two Chiltern place-names' pp. 65–67)

bugge. Buglande 1551 (Caversham: Kift, 'Field names' p. 32)

gobelin. The Goblins' Bank 1679 (Middleton Stoney: 1 p. 5)

pūca. Poukepitsclade 1348/9 (Banbury: Fellows-Jensen, 'Place-names and word geography' pp. 219–20), *Poukwelleforlong* 1325 (Bicester: 1 p. 200), *Poukputte* 1435/6 (Burford: 2 p. 312), *Pokemedyforlang* 1422 (Deddington: 2 p. 258), *Poukebrugge* 1406 (Eynsham: 2 pp. 259, 263), *Pukkespytte* 1470x80 (Newington: 1 p. 133), *Pucheput* 1148x55 (Stoke Talmage: 1 p. 93), Puck Lane 1829 (Witney: 2 p. 333)

scucca. Succhelauefurlong 1210 (Steeple Barton: 2 p. 250; cf. *Cartulary of Oseney Abbey* 4 p. 170)

þyrs. Therslande 1207 (Cowley: 1 p. 30; cf. Salter, *Feet of Fines* p. 37)

Rutland. Uncredited references from *PN Rutland*

scucca. Scucheved 1216x72 (Little Casterton: p. 137), Shockmore Balk 1843 (South Luffenham: p. 272)

þyrs. Thyrspit c.1275 (Barrowden: p. 238), *Thyrspyth* c.1265 (Empingham: p. 147), *Thirspit* 1300s (Glaston: p. 256)

Shropshire. Uncredited references from *PN Shropshire*

ælf. Elve Leasow 1839 (Worfield: Foxall, *Shropshire Field Names* p. 67)

bugge. Bugebruche 1461 (Condover: 2 p. 127)

fēond. Fendeshok 1301 (Barrow: 3 p. 102)

gobelin. Goblins Yard 1841 (Arleston: 3 p. 57), Goblin Dale 1841 (Eastwick: 5 pp. 41, 66), Goblin Hole 1700 (Myddle: 5 p. 95; cf. Gough, *Myddle* p. 32), Goblin Styles 1842 (Newnham: 2 p. 45), Goblin Meadow 1839 (Northwood: 5 p. 56), Goblin's Piece 1838 (Prees: Foxall, *Shropshire Field Names* p. 67), Goblin Meadow 1840 (Shifnal: Foxall, *Shropshire Field Names* p. 67), Goblin's Yard 1840 (Wellington: Foxall, *Shropshire Field Names* p. 67), Goblin's Lane 1796 (Whixall: 5 p. 286)

pokere. Pokers Hole 1844 (Winsley: 2 p. 74)

pūca. The Powke Acre 1622 (Broadstone: 3 p. 179), Poulk Pool 1845 (Cardington: 3 p. 119), Pow Croft 1840 (Claverley: Foxall, *Shropshire Field Names* p. 67), Powke Field 1842 (Culmington: Foxall, *Shropshire Field Names*

p. 67), *Pokemore* 1232 (Ditton Priors: 3 p. 131), Powckpitts Hedge 1592 (Farley: 3 p. 259), Powks Pit 1840 (Kemberton: Foxall, *Shropshire Field Names* p. 67), Powk Pool 1788 (Minton: 3 p. 236), Powke Lane 1754 (Much Wenlock: 3 p. 261), Puppets Orchard 1844 (Winsley: 2 p. 74), Powkhole 1839 (Worfield: Foxall, *Shropshire Field Names* p. 67), Powkewall 1650 (Wrockwardine: 3 p. 85)

pūcel. Pokelshull 1305 (Worthen: The National Archives C 241/83/67)

þyrs. Thursbache 1569/70 (Highley: 7 p. 201), *Thrissecroft c.*1228 (Shrewsbury: 4 p. 90)

Somerset. Uncredited references from Somerset Heritage Centre

ælf. Alve Crofte 1322 (Milverton: DD/SF/2/39/4)

bugge. Buggs Moor 1813 (Buckland St Mary: DD/WY/2/11/2), *Bugebur* 1400x1450 (Chard: T/PH/rop/1), Bug Hole 1600s (Langford Budville: Swainson, 'Langford Budville' p. 246), *Bugewde c.*1250 (Stogumber: DD/WY/2/58/1)

gobelin. Goblin Combe 1883 (Cleeve: OS at ST 469 654)

pokere. Puckers Wood 1837 (Puckington: Ellerington, 'Puckington' p. 76)

pūca. Pukeputte 1216x*c.*1250 (Batten, *Two Cartularies* p. 168), Pockeridge 1808 (Ashbrittle: Devon Heritage Centre 4618M/L/1), *Pokelane* 1455 (Axbridge: D/B/AX/9/1/222), Puckpittes 1563 (Babcary: DD/SF/12/9/2), Poke Piece 1742 (Bath: Quinn, *Holy Wells* p. 56), *Ponkeput* 1310 (Batheaston: Dobbie, *Rural Community* p. 151), Pux Pit 1843 (Bleadon: TM), *Pukecrofte* 1200s (Bruton: Batten, *Two Cartularies* p. 8), Pookemore 1705 (Curry Rivel: DD/CM/210), Puckpits 1838 (Ditcheat: TM), Pucks Pitts 1705 (Drayton: DD/CTV/305), *Poukewalle* 1299/1300 (East Luccombe: Hancock, *Minehead* p. 457), Puxpitt 1746 (Flax Bourton: Quinn, *Holy Wells* p. 179), Pookmore 1683 (Goathurst: A/CGS/14), Puckwell Field 1571 (Ilminster: Ellerington, 'Puckington' p. 76), Pook Hole 1718 (Meare: DD/AH/46/3/6), *Poukestrete* 1482 (Milborne Port: DD/MP/5), Puckthorne Yeate 1574 (Milverton: DD/SF/2/39/4), Pokewodde 1530 (Nettlecombe: DD/WO/12/2/2), Pook Fields 1840 (Nunney: TM), Puckham Meade 1571 (Puckington: Ellerington, 'Puckington' p. 76), Puck's Well 1840s (Rode: A/DAS/1/333/2), Pokes Mill 1687 (Spaxton: A/CWY/2/1), Puckpitt 1548 (Watchet: DD/WY/2/56/85), *Pukehaye* 1436 (Wellington: A/CTP/3/5/2), *pucan wylle* 946 (Weston: S 508), Pookmore 1839 (Yeovil: DD/ED/1839/114)

pūcel. Pucklewell 1816 (Somerton: DD/S/BT/26/12/3)

skratti. Scratch Close 1851 (Oake: DD/CH/119/3)

scucca. Shuck Lake 1755 (Porlock: G165/350/1)

Staffordshire. Uncredited references from Horovitz, *PN Staffs* and Staffordshire Record Office

ælf. Elfelders 1647 (Kings Bromley: D615/D/265)

bugge. Buggestrete 1394 (Burton: D603/A/Add/587), Bug Pit 1845 (Bushbury: TM), *Buglawe* 1478/9 (Darlaston: p. 158), Bugs Pit 1843 (Essington: TM), Bughouse Lane 1849 (Tipton: TM), Bugg Lane Field 1883 (Whittington: D5510/A/1/20)

gobelin. Goblin's Lane 1847 (Abbots Bromley: TM), Goblinhole 1882 (Church Eaton: OS at SJ 846 155), Goblins Mills 1719 (Stone: D1798/685/416), Goblins Pit 1775 (Walsall: p. 319), Goblins Hole 1841 (Willenhall: TM), Goblin's Croft 1841 (Yoxall: TM)

niht-mare. Naughmarethorn 1290 (Cannock: p. 172)

pokere. Poker's Acre 1757 (Uttoxeter: D1194/10/10)

pūca. Powkemore Hills 1769 (Amblecote: Enville Hall Archive estate map), Poukehill 1661 (Bentley: p. 444), *Pochefelde* 1461 (Broad Oak: D239/M369), Pokeyard 1616 (Huntington: D260/M/T/6/33), Pook Head 1879 (Ipstones: D3359/52/3/1), Powk Lane 1647 (Rowley Regis: DE/1/6/255), Pouk Piece 1838 (Shenstone: TM), Powgh Lane 1536 (Walsall: p. 444), Powkcroft 1653 (Yoxall: TM)

pūcel. Pucklesitch 1726 (Castle Church: D856/1)

scucca. Shokeburew 1285 (Colwich: p. 493), Shuckbarrow Field 1670 (Hamstead: p. 493), Shagdale 1850 (Upper Elkstone: TM)

þyrs. Thurse-house 1686 (Alton: Plot, *Natural History* p. 172), Thrustintake 1819 (Armitage: D802/8), Thurse-house 1686 (Frittenden: p. 535), Thurse-house 1686 (Wetton: Plot, *Natural History* p. 172), Thorswood 1639 (Wootton: p. 535)

Suffolk. Uncredited references from Briggs & Kilpatrick, *Suffolk PNs* and Suffolk Record Office

ælf. Eluedena 1086 (Elveden p. 49)

bugge. Buggs Wood 1647 (Badley: HA1/D/A/1/8/8), Bughouse Close 1804 (Mettingham: 2249/3/9)

nicor. Nickersmarsh 1687 (Kirton: HA1/E/A/6/7)

pūca. Pokecroft 1200x33 (Edwardstone: Cavill, *New Dictionary* p. 336), Puck Field 1838 (Hasketon & Boulge: Arnott, *PN Deben Valley* p. xiii), *Puchedole* 1419 (Walton: Arnott, *PN Deben Valley* p. xiii)

skratti. Scratchford 1674 (Layham: HD1108/2)

screawa. Screwsmere 1828 (Shottisham: Arnott, *PN Deben Valley* p. 68)

Surrey. Uncredited references from *PN Surrey* and Surrey History Centre

ælf. Elvis Field 1843 (Send: TM)

bugge. Bugs Pasture 1839 (Capel: TM), Bug Hill 1842 (Chelsham: Leveson-Gower, 'Surrey etymologies II' p. 215), Bughawe 1688 (Nutfield: 3089/6/22), Bugs Hill 1842 (Warlingham: TM)

pokere. Pokers Hole 1842 (Ash: TM), Pokerscroft 1506 (Crowhurst: Leveson-Gower, 'Surrey etymologies I' p. 103), Pokers Plat 1838 (Dorking: TM), Pokerhills 1845 (Hambledon: TM)

pūca. Poukelane 1350 (p. 363, two instances), Pokelane 1545 (Albury: 1322/7/2), Pokes Pit 1843 (Banstead: TM), Puckmires 1704 (Bletchingley: p. 397), *Pokeneghe* 1315 (Charlwood: p. 288), *Pokeford* 1199 (Chiddingfold: p. 191), Pook Lane 1622 (Chiddingfold: p. 193), Puckeridge 1703 (Compton: LM/355/2), *Pokacre* c.1250 (Coulsdon: Rumble, 'Coulsdon' p. 35), Pokeham 1842 (Cranleigh: TM), *Poukhacche* 1400 (Crowhurst: Leveson-Gower, 'Surrey etymologies I' p. 102), *Puckmede* 1493 (Croydon: p. 374), *Poukelane* 1384 (Dorking: p. 270), Pucklands 1772 (Eashing: 1739/box 1), *Le Puchschroneaker* 1326 (Effingham: Suffolk Record Office C/6/6/3/1), *Pokeputte* 1408 (Ewell: Deedes, *Register* p. 113), Puckfield 1840 (Ewhurst: p. 393), *Poukesham* 1341 (Godalming: G105/1/93), Puckham 1764 (Godstone: Lambert, *Godstone* p. 180), *Poke Lane* 1382 (Guildford: G70/4/2), Pockewell 1663 (Hambledon: G106/4/5), Poke Field 1840 (Hascombe: TM), *Pukesudde* 1320 (Haslemere: p. 206; cf. G105/1/50), *Poukeneye* 1332 (Horley: p. 396), Puckmire 1841 (Horne: Leveson-Gower, 'Surrey etymologies I' p. 88), Poke Hatch Gate 1642 (Lingfield: 326/22), *Pokemede* 1240 (Malden: Ross, *Malden* p. 9), Puckmires 1839 (Newdigate: p. 288), Puckhawe 1577 (Nutfield: 3089/4/36/1), Pucknees 1841 (Ockley: TM), *Powkebroke* 1474/5 (Oxted: Leveson-Gower, 'Surrey etymologies II' p. 147), Puklane 1537 (Ripley: G86/23/6), Puckridge Bottom 1871 (Seale and Sands: OS at SU 886 452), Pugswell 1843 (Thames Ditton: TM), Pucknells 1672 (Windlesham: 1201/37), *Pokenlands* 1400 (Witley: p. 391),

Puckshill 1669 (Woking: 1209/13/1/1 to 7), Puck Street 1676 (Woodmansterne: Lambert, *Woodmansterne* p. 23), Pook Field 1839 (Wotton: p. 395)

pūcel. The Pucklers 1842 (Reigate: TM)

skratti. Scratches Meadow 1841 (Alfold: TM), Scratch Wood 1843 (Banstead:
TM)

scucca. *Shuchenhulle* 1200s (Artington: LM/344/47)

þyrs. *Thurstrehacche* 1250x99 (Chiddingfold: G105/1/8)

Sussex. Uncredited references from *PN Sussex*

dweorg. Dwarfe Gate 1771 (Dallington: East Sussex Record Office SAS-RF/8/9)

nicor. *Nikerpoll* 1263 (2 p. 562)

pokere. *Pokerle* 1327 (Henfield: 1 p. 218)

pūca. *Poghemill* 1324 (2 p. 562), *Pokerithe* 1457 (2 p. 562), *Pokeryde* 1484 (2 p. 562),
Poukehale 1379 (2 p. 562), *Poukehol* 1357 (2 p. 560), *Poukestrete* 1400 (2 p. 562),
Poukham 1418 (2 p. 562), *Powkehagh* 1428 (2 p. 562), *Powkeland* 1399 (2 p. 562),
Pukehole 1327 (2 p. 562), *Pukewisse* 1200s (2 p. 562), *Puklane* 1455 (2 p. 562),
Pookehill 1648 (2 p. 562), Pugh Dean Bottom 1850 (Arundel: Arundel
Castle MS. HI/48), *Puchehole* 1176 (Battle: *Chronicle of Battel* pp. 14–15),
pucan wylle 772 (Bexhill: 2 pp. 493, 562; cf. S 108), Pugshole 1873 (Burwash:
OS at TQ 653 227), *Poukelane* 1250x99 (Chichester: 1 p. 11), *Pukeputte* 1296
(Clapham: Hudson, *Subsidies* p. 64), *Poukerithe* 1327 (Cuckfield: 2 p. 265),
Pookchurch Pit 1874 (Cuckfield Rural: OS at TQ 285 248), Puck Lane 1633
(Eartham: West Sussex Record Office Papers of Homes, Campbell & Co.),
Pukeneghe 1332 (Ewhurst: Hudson, *Subsidies* p. 281), Pook Hole Shaw 1872
(Fairlight: OS at TQ 866 127), Pock Hill 1873 (Forest Row: OS at TQ
437 364), Pookhole 1852 (Hailsham: Cooper, 'Abbey of Otteham' p. 174),
Pookchurch 1879 (Handcross: OS at TQ 270 295), *Pukestie* 1287 (Hartfield: 2
p. 368), *Poukeput* 1350 (Harting: 1 p. 37), Pookes 1696 (Heathfield: Macleod,
'Heathfield PNs' p. 103), Puckeridge Stream 1874 (Herstmonceux: OS at
TQ 620 105), Pook Bourne 1875 (Hurstpierpoint: OS at TQ 278 199), Pook
Lane 1875 (Lavant: OS at SU 858 081), Powcrofts 1614 (Rusper: 1 p. 233),
Poukehale 1350 (Selmeston: 2 p. 415), Puckney 1629 (Shermanbury: Attree,
Post-Mortems in Sussex p. 566), Puck Street 1876 (Sutton: OS at SU 965 140),
Pook Pit 1706 (Wadhurst: Kent History Centre U840/T129), Pookread
1877 (Waldron: OS at TQ 575 207), Puck Lane 1762 (Warburton: West
Sussex RO Add MSS 8525 & 6)

pūcel. *Pokeleserse* 1176 (Brightling: 2 p. 472), Buckle Church 1872 (Seaford: OS
at TV 450 975), Pochelers 1561 (Selsey: 2 p. 472)

Warwickshire. Uncredited references from *PN Warks* and Warwickshire County Record Office

Alfhames Wellesiche 1200s (Merston: L0001/15)

bugge. Buggenfeld 1433 (Coventry: The National Archives C 1/12/109)

dweorg. Dwarfeholys 1490 (Aston: *PN Yorks NR* p. xlv), *Dwarewmere* 1200s (Fenny Compton: L0001/12)

pokere. Pokers Close *c.*1750 (Aston Cantlow: DR0259/3)

pūca. Poukelone 1272x1307 (p. 330), Puck Lane 1776 (Aston Cantlow: *VCH Warks* 3 p. 34), *Pouke Land* 1349 (Lapworth: p. 290), Puckwell Hill 1824 (Little Compton: DDHE/74/1), Pug Bit 1847 (Rowington: p. 370), Powke Lane 1591 (Solihull: pp. 68, 71), *Pukkelane* 1479 (Warwick: p. 260; cf. DR0115/29), Pouke Ditch 1572 (Wootton Wawen: p. 373)

skratti. Scratslade 1200s (Churchover: p. xxii)

scucca. Shukmore 1200s (Coventry: p. 363; cf. DR0115/29), *succan pyt* 969 (Kineton: p. 282; cf. S 773), *Socheberge* 1086 (Shuckburgh: p. 143)

þyrs. Thurstput 1200x90 (Whitnash: CR4141/2/115a)

Westmorland. Uncredited references from *PN Westm*

ælf. Ellfaw Foot 1841 (Firbank: 1 p. 35), Elfhowes 1687 (Hartley: 2 p. 5), Elpha Knott 1836 (New Hutton: 1 p. 133), Elfhow 1694 (Over Staveley: 1 p. 175), Elvrigg 1836 (Scalthwaiterigg: 1 p. 136)

bugge. Bug Garth 1843 (Asby: 2 p. 59), Bug Mire 1838 (Beetham: 1 p. 74)

gram. Gramskeugh 1721 (Hartley: 2 p. 4), Gramshaw Head 1842 (Nateby: 2 p. 23)

pūca. le Poke Miln 1473 (Yanwath: 2 p. 206)

skratti. Scratchmill Scar 1856 (Lazonby: OS at NY 514 381)

skyrsi. Skirsgill Hill 1859 (Askham: 2 p. 202)

þyrs. Thursb'ht 1256 (Appleby: 2 p. 96), Thurgill 1838 (Askham: 2 p. 204), Thrushgill 1839 (Bampton: 2 p. 199), Thirst Gate 1769 (Kaber: 2 p. 8), Thrushgill 1859 (Milburn: 2 p. 123), *Thrusgyll* 1170x84 (Whinfell: 1 p. 143), *le Thursmyre* 1256 (Windermere: 1 p. 198)

troll. Trollgilleghes 1366 (Cliburn: 2 p. 137)

Isle of Wight. Uncredited references from Mills, *PN Wight*

bugge. Bugberie 1607 (Newport: Hampshire Archives 1607AD/12)

pūca. Puckes Mead 1653 (Binstead: p. 84), Puckpool 1672 (Newchurch: Hampshire Archives 1672A/076), Pooklane 1541 (Newport: Kökeritz, *PN Wight* p. 177), *Pokewell* 1461 (Niton: Kökeritz, *PN Wight* p. 184), Puckester 1608 (Niton: Kökeritz, *PN Wight* p. 183)

skratti. Scratchell's Bay 1736 (Yarmouth: p. 93)

Wiltshire. Uncredited references from *PN Wilts* and Wiltshire and Swindon History Centre

ælf. Elves Tyning 1841 (Castle Combe: p. 466)

bugge. Bugmore 1563 (Salisbury: p. 23), *Buggelega* 1236 (Warminster: p. 158)

dweorg. Dwarfs Brake 1842 (Ramsbury: p. 290)

gobelin. Goblin's Pit 1773 (Corsham: Dodgson & Khaliq, 'Addenda' p. 51), Goblihearne Copice 1606 (Corsley: Somerset Heritage Centre DD/SE/17/6)

nicor. Nikerpole 1272 (Mildenhall: p. 499)

pūca. Pokepulle 1528 (p. 444), *Pukeputte* 1200s (p. 445), *Puckshepene* 1303 (Beechingstoke: p. 319), *Pukpole* 1232 (Bishopstrow: p. 480), Puck Hay 1841 (Crudwell: p. 462), Puckpits 1661 (Landford: p. 387), Pugpits 1842 (Milton Lilborne: p. 506), *Pokcombe* 1496 (Ogbourne St Andrew: p. 304), *Pokkeput* 1398 (Purton: p. 39), *Poukeryche c.*1300 (Sherston: p. 472), Pook Croft 1839 (Upton Scudamore: TM), Puckwell 1804 (West Knoyle: p. 177; cf. 383/889)

pūcel. Pucklechurch 1604 (Keevil: 1976/4/32), Pucklewood 1841 (Limpley Stoke: TM), Poculchurchmede 1529 (Lyneham: p. 495; cf. *PN Cumb* p. lxxv), Pockle church 1570 (Winterborne Bassett: p. 495)

skratti. Scratchburie 1609 (Norton Bavant: p. 154)

Worcestershire. Uncredited references from *PN Worcs*

bugge. Bug Hole 1861 (Dudley: Census)

pūca. Poukeput 1408 (p. 391), Puck Piece 1846 (Ab Lench: Allies, *Ignis Fatuus* p. 12), Puck Pit 1846 (Abberton: Allies, *Ignis Fatuus* p. 12), Puck Hill 1846 (Acton Beauchamp: Allies, *Ignis Fatuus* p. 12), Puck Dole 1846 (Berrow: Allies, *Ignis Fatuus* p. 12), Puck Croft 1846 (Bradley: Allies, *Ignis Fatuus* p. 12), Pug's Hole 1846 (Bromsgrove: Allies, *Ignis Fatuus* p. 12), Puckpitt Farm 1632 (Claines: Warwickshire County Record Office CR0611/316), *Pukemulle* 1255 (Dodderhill: p. 391), Puckall 1846 (Elmley Lovatt: Allies, *Ignis Fatuus* p. 12), Puck Close 1846 (Feckenham: Allies, *Ignis Fatuus* p. 12),

Puck Piece 1846 (Fladbury: Allies, *Ignis Fatuus* p. 12), Powke Putte 1540
(Great Malvern: Smith, *Malvern* p. 171), Puck Meadow 1846 (Hallow: Allies,
Ignis Fatuus p. 12), Puck Hall Field 1846 (Hartlebury: Allies, *Ignis Fatuus*
p. 12), Puck Hill 1846 (Himbleton: Allies, *Ignis Fatuus* p. 12), Puck Meadow
1846 (Oldbury: Allies, *Ignis Fatuus* p. 12), Puck Croft 1846 (Powick: Allies,
Ignis Fatuus p. 12), Puck Croft 1846 (Stock: Allies, *Ignis Fatuus* p. 12), Puck
Lane 1846 (Stoke Prior: Allies, *Ignis Fatuus* p. 12)

pūcel. Pokeleston 1553 (Kidderminster: p. 252)

screawa. Schrewenhulle *c.*1330 (Badsey: p. 261)

þyrs. *þyrspit* 883x911 (Cleeve Prior: p. 391; cf. S 222), *þyrspytt* 900x50 (Honey-
bourne: S 1591a)

Yorkshire (East Riding). Uncredited references from *PN Yorks (ER)* and East Riding Archives

ælf. Elf Howe 1877 (Folkton: Greenwell, *British Barrows* p. 173), *Elvelaye* 1372
(Rowley: Hampshire Archives DC/P5/2)

bugge. Bugdale 1752 (Fangfoss: DDGR/42/2/82), *Buggryfftt* 1409 (Scarborough:
DDCC/130/84), Buggend Close 1690 (York: DDCR/2/12/1/8)

skratti. Scratters 1826 (Burnby: DDAN/163), *Scrathou* 1200s (Hayton: p. 233)

þyrs. *Thursmare* 1227 (p. 328), *Thirshowe* 1292 (Barmston: p. 84), Thrusmire
1640 (Eastoft: DDBE/26/2), *Thurspole c.*1295 (Heslington: Crossley, *Miscellanea* 4 p. 24), Thrusome Closes 1678 (Kilnwick: DDKI/5/77), *Thursegayle*
1191x1210 (York: p. 299)

Yorkshire (North Riding). Uncredited references from *PN Yorks (NR)* and North Yorkshire County Record Office

ælf. Elfahall 1544 (East Witton: East Riding Archives DDHU/9/11), *Elvescarebrec* 1300x25 (Marton in Cleveland: *Cartularium Gyseburne* 2 p. 16)

skratti. Scrathowe 1388 (Thimbleby: p. 215)

scucca. Scugdale 1856 (Bulmer: OS at SE 703 671), *Scuggedale c.*1190
(Guisborough: p. 152), *Schugedale* 1228 (Whorlton: p. 177)

skyrsi. Skirsegill 1612 (Giggleswick: ZXF 1/6/76)

þyrs. Thrushwood 1567 (Kirkleatham: ZK), *Thuresgylle c.*1540 (Startforth:
Leland, *Itinerary* 1 p. 77), *Thrusbrige* 1272x1307 (Whitby: *Cartularium de
Whiteby* 1 p. 340)

troll. *Trollesers* 1335 (Lockton: p. 324)

Yorkshire (West Riding). Uncredited references from *PN Yorks (WR)*

ælf. Alvedel c.1200 (Bramhope: Nottinghamshire Archives DD/A/51/2), *Elfonenghouses* 1308 (Dacre: 5 p. 142), *Alueridinges* 1200s (Farnley: 5 p. 59), Elf Holme 1842 (Hawkswick: 6 p. 125), *Elvene Tres* c.1200 (Hook: East Riding Archives DDSE(3)/4), *Elfknolle* 1310 (Rawdon: 4 p. 154), *Alfhov* 1216x72 (Rimington: 6 p. 180), *Elueshov* 1200s (Ripon: 5 p. 168), *Alphenstone* 1468 (Saddleworth: 2 p. 312), Elfhole 1753 (Selby: 4 p. 34), Awfe Hole 1773 (Soyland: 3 p. 66), Elve Wood 1840 (St Mary Bishopshill Junior: 4 p. 227), Elfe Ynge 1583 (Swinton: 1 p. 117)

cangun. Congon Park 1843 (Gargrave: 6 p. 54)

dēofol. Dewelfeld 1487 (Sowerby Bridge: 3 p. 141), *Dowelloynhed* 1492 (Soyland: 3 p. 63)

dweorg. Dueridene 1272x1307 (Bradfield: 1 p. 223), Dwarfe-banks 1729 (Carlton: 4 p. 5)

fēond. Finsdale Nab 1845 (Bowland Forest Higher: 6 p. 213

gram. Gram'skebanch 1225 (Hebden: 6 p. 101)

pūca. Puknalfriht 1387 (Aston: 1 p. 161), Pockley Garth 1840 (Long Drax: 4 p. 13), *Pokerrid* 1366 (Mettley: 2 p. 135), *Pukenhale* 1310 (Sandal Magna: 2 p. 108), Netherpookroyde 1555 (Skircoat: 3 p. 113), Puck Close 1840 (St Mary Bishopshill Junior: 4 p. 228)

scinna. Scinclif 1200s (East & West Marton: 6 p. 41)

skratti. Scratt Brow 1847 (Cowling: 6 p. 15), Serates 1847 (Cridling Stubbs: 2 p. 62), Scrat Lane 1849 (Gomersal: County Poll 1848 p. 36), Scrathewed 1579 (Ingleton: Lancashire Archives WRW/L/R589C/24), Scrat Haigh 1891 (Kexbrough: 1 p. 319)

scucca. Shugdenhall 1488 (Queensbury: 3 p. 87), *Shokeforth-brooke* 1412 (Soyland: 3 p. 71)

skyrsi. Skirsgill 1690 (Horton in Ribblesdale: 6 p. 225), *Skircegayre* 1100s (Rylstone: 6 p. 95), Skirskell 1580 (Settle: 6 p. 153)

þyrs. le Þuspitte 1100s (Bramham: 4 p. 86), Thursemyer 1553 (Broughton: 6 p. 44), Thruskills 1773 (Carlton: East Riding Archives DDX324/26), Thruswell 1500s (Eccleshall: 1 p. 202; cf. Addy, *Glossary of Sheffield* p. 258), Thrush Gill 1846 (Garsdale: 6 p. 263), *Thursdene* 1271x81 (Grantley: 5 p. 197), Ruskall Springe 1579 (Hebden: 6 p. 102), Thirstwell 1591 (Hipperholme: 3 p. 82), Thurskgill 1859 (Horton in Ribblesdale: 6 p. 223), *Thurskeld* 1200s (Long Drax: 4 p. 13), *Thirslande* 1268 (Marr: 1 p. 76), *Thirskerr* 1382 (Methley: 2 p. 132), *Thursegilmos* 1220x50 (Sedbergh: 6 p. 270), Hursthous

1709 (Soyland: 3 p. 69), *Thursefen* 1200x1250 (Stainburn: 5 p. 48), Thirsley Holme 1596 (Todmorden: 3 p. 188), *Thirswelleflat* 1345 (Whiston: 1 p. 171), *Thrusmyre* 1400s (Wighill: 4 p. 244)

troll. Trollers Gill 1805 (Appletreewick: 6 p. 80), Trow Gill 1893 (Clapham cum Newby: OS at SD 755 717)

Notes

Chapter 1: Strange Meetings

1. Walsingham, *Historia Anglicana* 1 p. 199 and *Chronicon Angliae* pp. 15–16, discussed in Wade, 'Abduction, surgery, madness'. I identify the young man *qui fuerat in familia Domini J. Baronis de Grastok* with William Wynfeld, having for his patron Sir Ralph, baron of Greystoke, who was appointed by exchange of benefices to the rectory of Thorpe Bassett in 1377: Register 12 of the Archbishops of York, 1374–88, f. 55v, calendared at https://archbishopsregisters.york.ac.uk/home_page/index. Walsingham had just begin writing at this date.
2. *Cerneret siliginem in modum aequoris fluctuare*; *siligo* is 'winter wheat' in the dictionaries but you wouldn't have wheat as far north as Cumberland.
3. M. Margaret pp. 100–5.
4. M. Thomas (Benedict) 2 pp. 129–30.
5. *Nuntium de morte materna.* I think this means the uncles' mother, Richard's grandmother, though it could be their sister, Richard's mother.
6. Green, *Elf Queens* has demonstrated the hardening of medieval learned thought on the fairies—boarding up the way to fair Elfland, and diverting traffic down the braid, braid road. But this does not exclude a complementary, bottom-up process.
7. M. Thomas Cantilupe p. 676. Christina's father had a Psalter (presumably structured for lay reading) but this is definitely a Book of Hours: *libellum, in quo matutine et cetere Hore, que de B. Maria dicuntur communiter, erant scripte.*
8. M. John of Beverley pp. 293–94 (trans. pp. 189–90).
9. Green, *Elf Queens* pp. 42–47, deals with fairies in aristocratic experience. 'There was nothing "popular" abut these beliefs, except in the sense that they were widespread', says Bartlett in his section on 'Beings Neither Angelic, Human, nor Animal', *Norman and Angevin England* p. 692.
10. M. Henry VI (1935) pp. 125–27.
11. M. Margaret pp. 126–27.
12. M. Edmund p. 97.
13. M. Æthelthryth p. 307 *natalibus generosa* (trans. p. 375), p. 307 *illustris viri* (trans. p. 376), p. 309 shared bedroom (trans. 379), p. 311 costs of trip paid for by elder

brother (trans. 383), and p. 311 *rei familiaris angustia nobilitatis nomen in suos non fuscaret* (trans. 384).

14. M. Swithun pp. 274–75, *civis*; pp. 434–35, *vir quidam locuples*.

15. Byland p. 415 (trans. p. 365).

16. *Lanercost* pp. 155–56 (trans. pp. 104–5).

17. M. Wulfstan p. 129. He is a *puer*, and his parents are worried about him; 'boy' can be a marker of status rather than age but evidently he was young.

18. M. Wulfstan p. 132 and CD p. 143 (trans. p. 182).

19. M. Cuthbert (Durham) p. 250 (trans. pp. 218–19) and *Register of John Morton* 3 pp. 215–16.

20. M. Æbbe p. 33 and *Descriptio Insularum Orchadium* in Macfarlane, *Geographical Collections* 3 p. 304.

21. *Register of John Stafford* 2 pp. 225–27.

22. M. John of Beverley p. 362 (trans. p. 223). The 'school of Goxhill' would be the school of fourteen boys kept at the almonry of the neighbouring Thornton Abbey (*VCH Lincolnshire* 2 p. 164), though as he was discovered by his mother lying on the floor, he must have lived in the village. His healing vision, including 'the Lord Jesus Christ bearing the cross with bloodstained hands', is more clerically orthodox than most: he must have been an attentive pupil.

23. M. Thomas (William) 1 pp. 203–4.

24. M. Hand of James p. 9 (translation). The detail about the fire, though presented simply as a proof of madness, may be linked to the dangers of looking on a fire after seeing an apparition, as in Byland p. 418 (trans. p. 369). Watkins, *The Undiscovered Country* p. 29, finds a parallel in Caesarius of Heisterbach.

25. M. Bartholomew pp. 41–44 (translation).

26. M. William pp. 79–85; Yarrow, *Saints and their Communities* pp. 156–9 discusses the clerical networking behind William's miracles.

27. M. Thomas Cantilupe p. 676, *per quinquennium fuerat sollicita*.

28. Thus one hagiographic narrative 'offers footholds for women to resist being traded or to trade themselves': Wogan-Browne, *Saints' Lives* p. 102.

29. CD pp. 122–23 (trans. p. 159).

30. M. Æthelthryth pp. 309, 310 (trans. pp. 379, 381).

31. M. Bartholomew p. 42 (translation).

32. M. Ive (Goscelin) p. lxxvi. Christina in her trance state heard wonderful singing, M. Margaret pp. 102–5; the elf-maidens overheard by Edric Wilde sang a delicate, solemn harmony that he could not understand, Map pp. 154–6.

33. M. Thomas (William) 1 pp. 263–64: *non est illusio phantastica; non somniorum sed veris visionibus ad statum pristinum redacta sum*.

34. M. Henry VI (1923) pp. 128–29.

35. *Lanercost* p. 237 (trans. p. 223). The longest account of John's confession, this has been recast as a standard political witchcraft accusation: Childs, 'Welcome, my brother' pp. 152–56.

36. Bannister, 'Visitation' p. 287, using 'curate' as the nearest equivalent for a *capellanus* appointed to a parish.

37. Discussed (chapter 4, 'The Lady of the Night') in Hutton, *Queens of the Wild* pp. 110–42.

38. *IC* pp. 57–61 (trans. pp. 116–20).

39. Byland p. 417 (trans. p. 369).

40. Bromyard, *Summa* 2 p. 369b, 371b: *dicunt se de die, vel de nocte a quodam pulchro populo rapi, vel cum eis loqui, vel volare, seu quisquam societatis habere ... dicunt se rapi a quodam populo, et duci ad loca quaedam pulchra, & ignota.* We are in the Welsh border country, as he was based in Hereford, collecting his material in the 1320s and 30s: Holland, 'John Bromyard'.

41. The Welsh term is first attested in late C15 (Rudiger, 'Y *Tylwyth Teg*' pp. 177–8) and the Scots in 1513 (*Dictionary of the Older Scots Tongue*, https://dsl.ac.uk/entry/dost/dost00062839).

42. *Register of John Morton* 3 pp. 215–16.

43. M. Cuthbert (Durham) pp. 32–37. The events took place in the episcopate of Geoffrey Rufus of Durham, 1133–1140, and Walter was still alive when Reginald was writing in 1165.

44. M. Thomas (Benedict) 2 pp. 44–45.

45. The demon as discarded lover of the convert was a hagiographical trope (Ruys, *Demons* pp. 22–3) but evidently also accessible to ordinary people trying to articulate their relations with a spirit.

46. M. Cuthbert (Farne) pp. 14–16 (trans. pp. 101–3).

47. M. Cuthbert (Durham) p. 37. It is standard in *exempla* that demons are aware of secret sins, until confession wipes the slate clean. Malekin the Suffolk spirit enlivened her conversation by *aliorum occultos actus detegens*: *CA* p. 121 (trans. pp. 118–19).

48. Hall, 'Elves on the brain' pp. 235–43.

Chapter 2: Tales of Wonder, Tales of Sorrow

1. Bromyard, *Summa* 2 pp. 372–372a.

2. Ostling's introduction to *Small Gods* pp. 1–53 is the best account of the cognitive marginality of fairies.

3. Blakiston, 'Ghost stories'.

4. Lipson makes this point in 'Supernatural Visitation' p. 7: 'if one wishes to examine the many supernatural persons who pervasively populate medieval literature, one must ... contend with ... diverse appellations and often overlapping categories'.

5. Luke 8: 26–29 closely follows Mark; Matthew 8: 28–34 abbreviates the story but gives us two demoniacs in place of one. It is Matthew who locates the story at

Gadara (hence 'Gadarene swine'), the other evangelists naming Gerasa. Neither place is on the Sea of Galilee, something which has kept the commentators busy.

6. Madness is the fourth most frequent affliction listed by Salter, *Saints, Cure-Seekers* pp. 64–65; but even so it was not common, accounting for 21 out of 260 healings, one in 13.

7. M. Dunstan p. 149.

8. In the vernacular, *elfe y-take* and *elve-inome* are similarly ambiguous: Fraaije, 'Wicked dreams' p. 35.

9. L. Godric pp. 428–31, 472–73, 424–27, 446–49 (taking *corticum ilicis* as 'holly bark' rather than the translator's 'bark of a holm-oak').

10. Koopmans, *Wonderful to Relate* p. 111.

11. Finucane, *Miracles and Pilgrims* p. 72, had already suspected that stories of sudden illness outdoors 'may originally have contained further information, perhaps that during sleep the victim was accosted by field or forest spirits'. M. Æbbe and M. Margaret, which were not available when he wrote, bear this out perfectly.

12. Koopmans, *Wonderful to Relate* pp. 6–8, has a timeline for the production of *miracula*.

13. Finucane is fond—e.g. *Miracles and Pilgrims* pp. 59–82—of reconstructing what really happened, a near-impossible process for which he relies on cherry-picked examples, concepts such as 'psychogenic illness' which are just as culture-bound as 'miraculous', and a generally disdainful attitude to twelfth-century life. He went much further than any current historian will go and Katajala-Peltomaa, *Companion to Medieval Miracles* gently corrects his attitude: p. 5, 'explaining away cures as vitamin deficiency or remissive illness is not always a helpful way to understand medieval beliefs'.

14. M. Swithun pp. 276–77; M. Wulfstan p. 129; M. Aebbe pp. 32–33; M. Godric pp. 742–45.

15. Wilson, 'Writing miracle collections' pp. 15–35 discusses the process of transmission.

16. *Longe lateque circumspiciens neminem videre potuit, cum nec homuncio illum latere posset, etiam in quinto vel sexto milliario constitutus*, M. Thomas (Benedict) 2 p. 130.

17. Though shrines liked to present themselves as never-failing conduits of the divine mercy, in real life lower-class supplicants could get a brush-off if they turned up at inconvenient times: Salter, *Saints, Cure-Seekers* pp. 189–92. Reinburgis is pulling rank here.

18. M. Æthelthryth p. 311 (trans. p. 384). Evidently she knew about the canonical injunction against letting blood fall on the floor of a church.

19. Lapidge, *Cult of St Swithun* pp. 182–83. Eadsige had a complicated past: a former canon of the Old Minster, he had initially refused to become a monk in the reformed establishment. He got away with it because he was a kinsman of Æthelwold, the bishop who later joined him in promoting Swithun's cult.

20. M. Swithun pp. 274–85. Wulfstan adds details—the man's wealthy status, the location of his pastures, his return through the east gate—which are not in Lantfred (Lapidge, *Cult of St Swithun* pp. 434–35, 438–39); he does the same for other miracles, including a place-name (*petram regis/kinges stan*) which can be corroborated by charters, so evidently these stories were still circulating.

21. Whatever they were. Jones. 'Furies', thought the women were *hægtessan*; Lacey, 'Water meadows', *wælcyrian*. Of course, the townsman may not have named them at all; supernatural stories often confront the listener with an unnamed 'something'.

22. I have used this archaic spelling of Ethiopian for medieval texts, to make it clear that we are talking about a literary trope, not visitors from Addis Ababa. The trope of the demon as a Black man is dicussed in Ruys, *Demons* p. 16, from the Lives of the Fathers. It is present in Insular Latin, Irish and Old English texts from the eighth century: Wright, 'Three Utterances'.

23. Jones, 'Furies' pp. 414–19 finds many Virgilian echoes but none of them are explicit enough to make the reader think aha, it's a parody of the death of Turnus! When medieval writers really do want us to notice something, they are not subtle.

24. M. Æthelthryth p. 308 (trans. p. 377). The visitants do not claim any connection with Æthelthyth until the second week's visions. Finally, p. 310 (trans. p. 382), they describe Ely as the place *quem cum domina nostra pariter incolimus et corporum nostrorum presentia decoramus*, as if they were Seaxburh and Wihtburh, but this looks very much like a rationalization.

25. M. Margaret pp. 101–3.

26. M. Margaret pp. 83–85.

27. As claimed in Harilla, 'Politics and Sainthood' p. 203. But Mutinus was not tempted, and he had not sinned: he was a sleeping five-year-old.

28. M. Margaret pp. 130–31. At once you think of Snow White's apple—also lodged in her mouth, also bringing healing when dislodged; but the Grimms' version of this tale-type has set a misleading standard. The object that causes seeming death is more usually a comb in the hair or a thorn in the flesh—something that sticks into the body rather than being caught in the throat.

29. M. Thomas (Benedict) 2 pp. 153–55, 263.

30. M. Henry VI is the only collection to have a reject list as well as fully recorded miracles: usually material was dropped because the witnesses were too few or too hard to find, not because their stories were unlikely.

31. Mutinus worked for years (unpaid, presumably) in the building yard; another dumb man had a similar job at Wilton in the 1060s, Hollis, *Writing the Wilton Women* pp. 91–93. William Paternoster was given to Beverley Abbey by his father as a thank-you for being cured: M. John of Beverley p. 294 (trans. p. 190). Alice worked as Reading Abbey's laundress after her cure, until she walked out and married a blacksmith, M. Hand of James p. 10 (translation).

32. Koopmans, *Wonderful to Relate* pp. 40–43.

33. M. Gilbert pp. 325–27.

34. M. Osmund pp. 69–70. Her message to Osmund is '*Domina tua te salutavit*' which would make sense if she was the Virgin, but this is not stated or implied anywhere in the text.

35. Hermann and Guibert are compared by Yarrow, *Saints and their Communities* pp. 74–75.

36. M. Margaret pp. 124–27.

37. L. Hugh pp. 269–73. The story was afterwards used as an exemplum: Herbert, *Catalogue* p. 527.

38. Kittredge, *Witchcraft* pp. 119–21. This is a subtype of the tale-type ML 6000 'Tricking the Fairy Suitor'.

39. Number 1 in Child, *Ballads*.

40. L. Bartholomew p. 298. *Kambeyn*, the name of the *malignum spiritum*, is apparently an ON loanword from Irish *cammán*, found as the byname of Grímr Kamban.

41. L. Bartholomew p. 314.

42. M. Cuthbert (Farne) p. 102. The tale-type is generally known as The Friend Among the Fairies, although the detail of the dead friend who gives advice is missing from this version.

43. Lapidge, *Cult of St Swithun* pp. 434–49, 651, 756–57.

44. LE p. 13 (trans. pp. 39–40).

45. Herbert, *Catalogue* pp. 632–3.

46. CD pp. 120–1 (trans. pp. 156–7).

47. Herbert, *Catalogue* p. 672; Owst, *Literature and Pulpit* p. 166; Herbert, *Catalogue* p. 620; Herbert, *Catalogue* p. 676.

48. LE pp. 51–3 (trans. pp. 79–80).

49. Herbert, *Catalogue* p. 661. Mother and son may be equally mythical: the story sounds like a very reworked version of the Witch of Berkeley.

50. Herbert, *Catalogue* pp. 642, 647, 644.

51. Wright, *Latin Stories* p. 17; the demon is Gillebochat in a second version (p. 43) of what was evidently a much-travelled story. For other clairvoyant demoniacs, see Tubach, *Index Exemplorum* p. 124.

52. As Barnes says, 'Haunting Matters' p. 103 'some demonic spirits demonstrated varying degrees of moral correctness and turpitude'.

53. M. Margaret pp. 120–21, rendering *in rubo* as 'bramble patch' rather than the translator's 'thorn-bush'. Cf. the 'strange writings' which old women taught 'should be carried round the neck or in the purse, or fastened or stitched into the cap or on the clothing': Owst, '*Sortilegium*' p. 291.

54. Byland pp. 416, 418 (trans. pp. 367, 369).

55. Wordsworth, 'Two Yorkshire charms' p. 402, reading *uos* for *nos*. This charm (now University of Leeds Special Collections YAS/MS393) is early thirteenth century; the Byland MS was written shortly after 1400.

56. Examples are given in Fraaije, 'Wicked dreams' and Simek, 'Tangible religion'. A Southern English origin seems likely since the key word is consistently *elphes* or *ellves* with an *e*, even in dialects and other languages where the corresponding local word was *alf* or *alp*.

57. M. Thomas (Benedict) 2 pp. 102–3.

58. Pettit, *Lacnunga* 1 pp. 72–75. Gay, 'Against a Dwarf' reviews the earlier literature on this charm. After some false starts in interpretation, it is generally agreed that the *dweorh*, *spiderwiht* and *deor* in the charm are one and the same, and this is the figure that rides the sufferer.

59. Hall, *Anglo-Saxon Elves* pp. 1, 110–122 argues for both *stice* and *scot* as intense localised stabbing pain. In the *miracula*, this kind of pain is not an ailment in itself but the onset of one. Reinburgis has a nail thrust in her head, M. Æthelthryth p. 310 (trans. pp. 381–82); a girl walking in the garden is suddenly attacked by the Enemy and struck in the head by a dart that sends her mad, M. Æbbe pp. 60–1 (taking *pila* as 'dart' and not the translator's 'ball'); Matilda Roper of Salisbury got out of bed at midnight and suddenly felt as if someone had jabbed a knife into her right thigh, leaving her with a contracted leg, M. Osmund pp. 76–7. If these analogies have value, then it is useless to ask what *fǣrstice* was: it was whatever you suffered from after the initial stabbing pain.

60. Bromyard, *Summa* 2 p. 372b. *A morsu* in the original must mean 'against the sting or cut' not literally 'bite'.

61. Histories and curiosity literature taken together constitute less than 20% of the encounters which I have been able to identify but they are fuller and, because they focus on the elfin rather than the demonic, more attractive.

62. The suit was in 1266: *VCH Lincolnshire* 2 p. 174.

63. *Lanercost* pp. 125–26 (trans. pp. 56–58). The 1201–1297 portion of the chronicle was written by a Franciscan, Richard of Durham (Gransden, *Historical Writing to c.1307*, p. 495).

64. *Chronica de Mailros* p. 80.

65. *ASC* 7 p. 129 (trans. p. 194).

66. *WC* pp. 119–20: Warkworth was the owner not the author of this chronicle.

67. Kaufman, 'Portents and wonders' p. 62 attempts various interpretations and is unconvinced by any of them.

68. Partner, *Serious Entertainments* p. 222: 'Between an author's vaguest prefatory remarks about the didactic purposes of written history, and his particular catalogue of demons, ponds of blood, and comets, there is usually a rather empty middle distance containing little that connects the movements of the empyrean with life in Berkshire'.

69. *HA* 2 pp. 314–15. John of Tynemouth's *Historia aurea* was used for a post-1327 continuation of Walter of Guisborough/Hemingburgh by the compilers of a text in MS Cotton Nero D II, hence its appearance under Walter's name.

70. For Freeman, 'Wonders, prodigies and marvels', these stories are about heretical 'transgressions of bodily form': but she never clarifies whether Ralph thought 'I know what this chronicle needs right now, a good punchy section on transgressions of form', or whether it was an unconscious concern that bubbled up just when he was trying to tell a good story. It's an important distinction, and we may 'fail to be convinced', with Staunton in his level-headed discussion of symbol-hunting, that medieval historians had such modern preoccupations: *Historians of Angevin England* pp. 124–27.

71. *CA* pp. 120–1 (trans. pp. 118–19). 'Malekin' may have been a name chosen by the de Bradwells, as -kin fornations were an Anglo-French affectation at this date: McClure, 'Kinship of Jack' p. 99.

72. Young, *Suffolk Fairylore* pp. 48–51.

73. *ARH* p. 196. 'O cursed mother, hell is deep/And there thou'll enter step by step' says the child-ghost in *The Cruel Mother* (number 20 in Child, *Ballads*) under similar circumstances: I don't know if there's any connection.

74. Poltergeists are discussed in Barnes, 'Haunting Matters' pp. 123–63.

75. Given-Wilson, *Chronicles* pp. 11–14 discusses witness testimony. As Partner notes—*Serious Entertainments* p. 187—historians who relied almost exclusively on eye-witnesses for mundane events could hardly disregard them when they reported supernatural ones.

76. The primary sources are *CA* pp. 118–20 (trans. pp. 122–23) and *HRA* (1–2) 1 pp. 114–17. Like everyone who has written on the Green Children, I am indebted to John Clark, whose study at https://www.academia.edu/10089626/The_Green_Children_of_Woolpit has long been essential reading, and is now to be published by University of Exeter Press.

77. For the chronology of the *Chronicon*, see Carpenter, 'Abbot Ralph' p. 1228 and Staunton, *Historians* pp. 118–20.

78. Partner, *Serious Entertainments* p. 55.

79. As observed by Purkiss, *Troublesome Things* p. 63, the story is told 'in reverse-angle shot'. A similar thought experiment—what are *we* like to *them?*—is implied by Gervase's story of the aerial ship which snagged her anchor on a sepulchre in a churchyard, and whose mariner drowned in our atmosphere, *Otia Imperialia* pp. 80–81; originally an Irish story, Ross, 'Anchors in a three-decker world' pp. 63–64. The anchor was kept as testimony to the physicality of the encounter, like William's fairy cup.

80. *CA* pp. 117–18 (trans. p. 124) and pp. 134–35.

81. Partner devotes a chapter of *Serious Entertainments*—pp. 114–40—to William's intellectual struggle over the anomalous.

82. *HRA* (1–2) 1 pp. 114–15.

83. Thorpe, 'A public reading'.

84. Gervase, *Otia Imperialia* pp. 558–59. For a historian's taxonomy of marvellousness, see Le Goff, *Medieval Imagination* pp. 27–44.

85. *HRA* (1–2) 1 pp. 118–21. The best fit for his description—a hill a few furlongs from the village at the head of the Gypsey Race—is Duggleby Howe, but Willy Howe, halfway along the Race, has been the conventional scene ever since a version of the story was recorded there in 1861 (Wright, *Archaeological Subjects* 1 p. 35). However, this may derive from William's history, which had been available in English since 1850, in Keightley, *Fairy Mythology* pp. 283–84. Perhaps significantly, though Keightley says the hill is near the Gipse, he omits the words specifying it is at the source.

86. Similarly Walter Map is impressed, not that a man should see his dead wife in a fairy ring, but that he should pull her out and later have children by her: *De Nugis* pp. 344–45. You can't get more substantial than that.

87. For the record, the barrow encounter in Firth, *Fairies and Merfolk* pp. 16–17 is not an independent medieval text: it's William of Newburgh artfully transposed to the latitude of Whitby. I'm grateful to the author for fessing up on this one.

88. *HRA* (3–5) 2 pp. 474–82 (trans. 4ii pp. 656–61), discussed in Gordon, *Supernatural Encounters* pp. 75–101.

89. *IC* p. 61 (trans. p. 120).

90. *IC* pp. 73–8 (trans. pp. 133–36).

91. It may be significant that Gerald tells the tale anonymously—*adductus est puer … solebat puer ad nostrum hemispherium ascendere*—after opening *sibi contigisse presbyter Eliodorus constantissime referebat*; he seems not to have been entirely convinced by this attribution.

92. Loomis, 'Arthur and the Antipodes'.

93. Gervase, *Otia Imperialia* pp. 642–44.

94. Later, pp. 96–97 (trans. p. 154), Gerald tells us of a demon servant who never went to church. Subconsciously, he may have felt that demons like this were closer to the little people than he admits in his text, for the servant's master, who was apparently Eustace of Stackpole, appears in the text as *Elidyr* of Stackpole.

95. Gervase, unlike his contemporaries, records the lore of ordinary people. The follets inhabit *domos simplicium rusticorum*, the *portuni* take advantage of *simplicitatem fortunatorum colonorum*, the grant appears to *cumvicaneis*: *Otia Imperialia* pp. 98–99, 676–77.

96. A hypothetical **puiton* would match the OE plural *pūcan* but there is no evidence for early ME *pouke* retaining a strong plural.

97. Gervase, *Otia Imperialia* pp. 674–77.

98. *HRA* (1–2) 2 pp. 86–91.

99. Gervase, *Otia Imperialia* pp. 674–75, rendering *effigies* as 'apparitions' rather than the translator's 'ghosts'.

100. Newman, 'The good, the bad, and the unholy' discusses the origins of third way pneumatology.

101. Gervase, *Otia Imperialia* pp. 730–31.

102. Map, *De Nugis* pp. 350–65 and pp. 315–41. Eudo shares a name with Eon de l'Étoile, who also consorted with demons of a very fairy cast, sacked towns and churches, and died expiating his crimes in the marketplace: I do not know if there is any connection. See *HRA* (1–2) 1 pp. 86–93.

103. Watkins, 'Fascination and anxiety', takes a quite opposite view of Map: 'he made the novelty of his material work for archly conservative moral and theological ends'. For him, the moral frame reveals how we should read the apparently subversive content: for me, disturbing content mocks the routine pieties which top and tail it.

104. Gervase, *Otia Imperialia* pp. 668–73. The setting is important: Wandlebury, unlike most ancient earthworks, looks just like a circular level jousting-ground with tiered seating.

105. M. Margaret pp. 126–27; Herbert, *Catalogue* p. 637; Pettit, *Lacnunga* 1 pp. 90–95.

106. 1183, when Gervase left England for the last time, is the latest date at which he could have heard the story; the 1130s, when Osbert first appears as a charter witness, are the earliest time when he was likely to have been on business outside the home region of the West Midlands where he was active together with his mother, Eustacia de Say. Though Gervase got the story *ab incolis et indigenis*, he must have been seeking confirmation of what he had heard previously, as people in Cambridge would not have known about the wound subsequently opening each year, or the knight leaving for a Crusade. Even taking the chronological gap at its widest, there could be witnesses—the squire, for instance—who were present when the events happened and still alive to tell them to Gervase.

107. Goetink, for instance, treats Osbert's experience as ancient Celtic myth ('Wandlebury legend'); Wade wonders whether William Wynfeld's account 'developed out of folk legend' ('Abduction, surgery, madness' p. 15); Kevin Crossley-Holland says of the Green Children 'for hundreds of years before that, it was passed by word of mouth from grandfather to father to son' (*Green Children* p. 38). The category of legend is so normative for these writers that, faced with historical texts describing personal experience, they seem incapable of recognizing them for what they are.

108. *HRA* (1–2) 1 pp. 120–21.

Chapter 3: Inconstant Shapes

1. M. Thomas (Benedict) 2 pp. 129–30; M. Henry VI (1935) pp. 125–27; M. Wulfstan pp. 129–30; M. Swithun pp. 274–85.

2. There were three Furies, as Lantfred was well aware. His words may be more than classical window-dressing, since later we hear of a woman in Durham *a demonibus, quos Eumenides vocant, ita seducta at pergravata*: M. Godric pp. 660–61.

This appears in a very matter-of-fact *miracula*, as if the *Eumenides* were commonly understood to be demons who caused madness, perhaps specifically a trio of them.

3.   M. Margaret pp. 82–85.

4.   M. Æthelthryth pp. 307–11 (trans. pp. 375–85).

5.   L. Hugh pp. 269–73.

6.   Pettit, *Lacnunga* 1 pp. 72–75 and commentary at 2 pp. 172–96. The crux of the poem lies in its third and fourth lines: after a fairly clear opening in which the *dweorg* prepares to ride 'you', the patient, the viewpoint shifts to 'they' who leave the land. Presumably one of the 'they' was the *dweorg*, but who was the other?

7.   Robbins, *Lyrics of the XIVth and XVth Centuries* p. 61.

8.   *King Lear* III.iv.117–21; relations with '*Seynt Iorge, our lady knygth*' are discussed in Simpson, 'Nightmare charm'.

9.   L. Samson pp. 20–1 (trans. pp. 30–33), discussed in Marzella, '*Hirsuta*'.

10. *Beowulf* line 1519 (*mere-wīf mihtig*); Pettit, *Lacnunga* 1 pp. 90–95 and commentary, especially 2 pp. 238–39. Hall, *Anglo-Saxon Elves* pp. 85–6 provides a semantic diagram of 'the extensive lexicon of monstrous, dangerous and/or martial supernatural females available to Anglo-Saxons'.

11. M. Cuthbert (Durham) p. 250 (trans. pp. 217–18).

12. M. Margaret pp. 82–85. But the white lady in M. Swithun pp. 276–77 also speaks of her victim as *homuncionem*, and he is an adult. Perhaps all mortals are little and contemptible to the other crowd.

13. M. John of Beverley p. 362 (trans. p. 223).

14. M. Æbbe pp. 65–67.

15. M. Mildthryth pp. 179–80.

16. M. Osmund pp. 69–70; M. Margaret pp. 100–5; L. Godric pp. 75–79.

17. *Demon* and *diabolus* are both masculine, and if a demon is given an individual name, it will be male: *Robinetus* and *Gillebochat* in Wright, *Latin Stories* pp. 38, 43, *Pokerellus* in Bromyard, *Summa* 1 p. 152b.

18. *ARH* p. 360—apparently the original text, as the annalist had a fondness for Bedford affairs, but also found in Walsingham, *Historia Anglicana* 2 p. 254, and in Capgrave, *Chronicle* p. 281.

19. M. Gilbert pp. 324–27.

20. LE pp. 85–6 (trans. pp. 113–14).

21. *HA* 2 p. 298–300.

22. Walsingham, *Historia Anglicana* 1 p. 295; *Chronicon Angliae* p. 49.

23. There is one in Cambridgeshire *s.a.* 1400 in *ARH* p. 332.

24. Map, *De Nugis* pp. 30–31, 370–71.

25. The original word was French and seems from the forms in Lecouteux, *Phantom Armies* pp. 120–1, 180–3 to have been Herlequin; Herlething is a folk-etymology. Map apparently understood *þing* as 'troop' rather than 'assembly', and invented an eponymous King Herla.

26. Gervase, *Otia Imperialia* pp. 336–37. Evidently he had been told this happened in *Britannia*, but is undecided whether Britain or Brittany was meant: probably the former, royal forests being rare in Brittany.

27. M. Cuthbert (Farne) pp. 14–15 (trans. p. 101).

28. M. Margaret pp. 126–27.

29. Gobi, *Scala Coeli* pp. 267–68.

30. *ASC* 7 p. 129 (trans. p. 194).

31. *IC* p. 58 (trans. p. 117); Byland p. 416 (trans. p. 366). The demon impersonating the *forestarius* boyfriend of Joan of Kingsley would also have been dressed as a hunter, like the devil in the Friar's Tale.

32. M. Ithamar pp. 432–3. His *mulierculae* could be 'girls', 'old women' or conceivably 'dwarf women'.

33. L. Godric pp. 474–75.

34. L. Godric pp. 342–43, 472–73.

35. L. Bartholomew p. 314.

36. Pliny says that otherwise the cranes would overcome them: *Natural History* 7.26. The original motif of the crane-combat has been worked up into an imaginary ethnography—well, if they were really at risk from cranes, they'd fight them, wouldn't they, with cavalry to scale.

37. Map, *De Nugis* pp. 26–27.

38. *IC* p. 75 (trans. pp. 133–34).

39. Gervase, *Otia Imperialia* pp. 676–77.

40. *Register of John Morton* 3 p. 215.

41. *Lanercost* pp. 127–28 (trans. pp. 60–1).

42. *IC* p. 58 (trans. p. 117).

43. M. Æbbe pp. 44–45.

44. Walsingham, *Historia Anglicana* 1 p. 199.

45. *CA* p. 121 (trans. p. 118).

46. M. Oswine pp. 29–30.

47. Pettit, *Lacnunga* 2 pp. 186–89; for wider views on the spirit-insect connection see Scott, 'Devil and his imps' and the two articles by Allen, 'Superstition on Vocabulary'.

48. M. Thomas (Benedict) 2 p. 45. However, Stephen is shown afflicted by three full-sized demons in the Canterbury miracle windows, recently restored and discussed by Rachel Koopmans as 'Demons and discoveries in a miracle window of Canterbury Cathedral' in the online journal *Vidimus*, https://www.vidimus.org/issues/issue-123/feature/. One of them is floating, more or less, but that doesn't seem sufficient grounds to edit the *nanus* of Benedict's text to *avis*.

49. M. Thomas Cantilupe p. 662.

50. L. Godric pp. 342–43, 474–75 (possibly the same story, told on two occasions); cf. pp. 424–25.

51. M. Godric pp. 718–21.

52. L. Godric pp. 372–73; cf. the tallness of the digging demon, pp. 446–47.

53. *Lanercost* pp. 136–37 (trans. p. 76).

54. CD p. 126 (trans. p. 163).

55. Map, *De Nugis* pp. 154–55.

56. Byland p. 417 (trans. p. 368).

57. M. Hand of James p. 9 (translation).

58. L. Godric pp. 446–49.

59. 'I conjure you, elf', says a German charm, 'who has … a back like a kneading trough': Lecouteux, *Elves and Dwarfs* p. 138.

60. *WC* pp. 119–20.

61. Higden, *Polychronicon* 2 pp. 42–3.

62. *DA* pp. 264–65; cf. the man transported by *spiritibus immundis* into a stable in C12 Northumberland, although in this case they were acting under permission from a saint, M. Henry of Coquet p. 426.

63. Byland p. 415 (trans. p. 365).

64. M. Thomas (William) 1 pp. 263–64; M. Henry VI (1923) pp. 128–29.

65. Herbert, *Catalogue* pp. 599, 624, 644, 659.

66. M. Margaret pp. 124–27.

67. M. Margaret pp. 132–35.

68. LE p. 13 (trans. pp. 39–40).

69. Gervase, *Otia Imperialia* pp. 692–93; *caniculam grandem* should surely grammatically be a bitch, although the translator says 'huge dog'.

70. M. Modwenna pp. 194–95.

71. I have not found any literature on early bear-keeping, but the Derbyshire place-name Bearwardcote suggests an OE etymon for ME *bereward*. Norwich's annual rent-charge in Domesday of a bear and six baiting dogs is evidence for regular imports. The earliest depiction of a performing bear comes from the 1120s, in Cambridge: Trinity College Library MS 0.4.7 f. 75.

72. L. Godric pp. 622–25. See Tubach, *Index Exemplorum* p. 126, for demon bears.

73. Herbert, *Catalogue* pp. 260–61.

74. Wright, *Latin Stories* p. 75.

75. *HRA* (1–2) 2 pp. 90–91.

76. Herbert, *Catalogue* pp. 632–33.

77. M. Simon de Montfort p. 90. Philip was *capellano de Brenteles*, evidently in Herefordshire but not easily identified, like many other place-names in these *miracula*. There is another fall from a horse caused by a spirit in Byland p. 415 (trans. p. 365).

78. *In ipso coitu infelix illa, quod dictum horrendum est, fluxum seminis per os … evomeret*: M. Ive (John) 2 p. 89.

79. Gervase, *Otia Imperialia* pp. 676–79. Some MSS have *gyant* not *grant*: Oman, 'Folklore of Gervase'. But given that Gervase—or his copyist—was capable

of setting down *Wichium* (Droitwich) as *Ibichun*, attempting to reconstruct his original forms is a mug's game.

80. *HRA* (3–5) 2 pp. 476, 480 (trans. 4ii p. 657, 660).

81. Pentangelo, 'The grant, the hare' notes the similarity with modern beliefs that a hare running through the village presages fire, but goes too far in assuming that the grant *is* a hare and not a spirit. It takes the form of a bipedal horse, as other spirits do; it is followed by dogs, as other spectral things are; and it presages disaster, as supernatural manifestations often did.

82. Byland p. 414 (trans. p. 364).

83. Byland p. 419 (trans. p. 372).

84. CD pp. 123 (trans. pp. 159–60).

85. M. Margaret pp. 126–27; *Chronica de Mailros* p. 80; Gervase, *Otia Imperialia* pp. 672–73. For the theme in *exempla*, see Tubach, *Index Exemplorum* pp. 133–5.

86. The (literary) afterlife of the Witch, from her first appearance in William of Malmesbury to a hack-work by Monk Lewis, is traced in Gordon, *Supernatural Encounters* pp. 28–74.

87. Gobi, *Scala Coeli* p. 204; LE p. 45 (trans. p. 72); Herbert, *Catalogue* pp. 592, 637.

88. M. Margaret pp. 134–35.

89. M. Æbbe p. 46–49 (crows), 32–33, 62–63 (doves).

90. LE 83 (trans. p. 111), a sinner picked up and dropped to his death by crows; Herbert, *Catalogue* p. 284, a crow flies out of a confessing woman's mouth—embodying the metaphor also found in manuscript illumination.

91. Gobi, *Scala Coeli* p. 267.

92. M. Swithun pp. 274–77. Medieval Latin used *corvus* for both species, though they were distinguished in the vernacular.

93. Lacey, 'Water meadows' pp. 206–7 has examples of *valkyrjas* (and by implication *wælcyriges*) as raven-like.

94. Byland p. 415 (trans. p. 36).

95. L. Godric pp. 422–29.

96. L. Godric pp. 574–75. Later in this servant's dealings with spirits (though earlier in the *Life*) he saw a demon crow in the oratory: pp. 427–9.

97. M. Cuthbert (Farne) pp. 14–16 (trans. pp. 101–3).

98. *Gawain* lines 150, 151, 175.

99. Pastoureau, *Green* p. 165. Millett, 'How green?' shoots down the idea that the Green Knight is representative of nature, for his colour is compared as readily to enamel as to grass, lines 235–36.

100. Maxwell-Stuart, *Satan* p. 139; Friar's Tale lines 1380–2, 1447–8, in Chaucer, *Works* pp. 90–1.

101. L. Godric pp. 446–49, 600–1. Robertson, 'Devil wears green', thinks he does because hunters, who wear green professionally, stand typologically for devils: but these demons are nothing like hunters.

102. Map, *De Nugis* pp. 26–27; cf. pp. 164–65.

103. Walsingham, *Historia Anglicana* 1 p. 199.

104. Bromyard, *Summa* 1 p. 273a and (a better text) in Wright, *Latin Stories* pp. 108–9.

105. L. Samson, if that's the correct translation of the obscure *bribetham*; Julian, *Revelation of Love* p. 27.

106. *IC* pp. 96–97 (trans. pp. 154–55). There is no criticism of Simon in this story, demon though he is—but then Gerald was of mixed race himself, which was why he was so good at ethnography: Bartlett, *Gerald of Wales* pp. 211–12. Otter, *Inventiones* p. 146 sees Elidyr's story, with its lost Welsh(ish) land of ease and its present reconciliation to clerical advancement, as paradigmatic of life for Gerald 'and indeed in any occupied country at any time'. This would be more convincing if Latin had been a language exclusive to the conquerors, and if Gerald's first language had been that of the conquered.

107. *HA* 2 pp. 314–15.

108. *Lanercost* pp. 80–81, assuming that *Rivelle* is a poor form for Ryal. Seven times is not necessarily a tribute to demon potency for it also features, with the sexes reversed, in Thomas of Erceldoune's encounter with the fairy queen: Child, *Ballads* 2 p. 327.

109. Herbert, *Catalogue* p. 394; a marginal note compares a story *consimilis*—but how?—from Banham in Norfolk.

110. *IC* p. 57 (trans. p. 116).

111. M. John of Beverley pp. 293–4 (trans. pp. 189–90).

112. Walsingham, *Historia Anglicana* 2 p. 254; *vel fatalis* is his own addition to the source text, *ARH* p. 360. The same usage appears in Map, *De Nugis* p. 167 (Achilles, as the son of a nymph, has *fatalitas*) and p. 332 (*fatalitas* is the quality of the self-identifying good demon/fairy Olga).

113. M. Margaret pp. 108–9.

114. M. Modwenna pp. 194–95.

115. *CRH* 4 p. 123 (trans. 1 p. 486), reading *bufones* for *buffones*.

116. Byland pp. 415–8 (trans. pp. 365–69); p. 414 (trans. p. 364).

117. L. Godric pp. 428–31 and 340–45.

Chapter 4: Haunted Landscapes

1.   Dorothy Whitelock was the first to collate this kind of evidence nationally, in *Audience of 'Beowulf'* pp. 72–5. The post-War volumes of the Survey of English Place-Names have routinely reported on supernatural qualifiers in their introductions: much of this was collected in 1999 by Edward Smith for his list at http:// Germanic.eu/Heathen-and-mythological-elements-in-English-place-names. htm, accessed Jan 2019. The most recent discussion, in Semple, *Perceptions of the Prehistoric*, places the names in archaeological context.

2.   Atkinson, *Forty Years* p. 51.

3. Beare, 'Particular description' p. 392.

4. Fayraye Gill 1606 in Sedbergh (*PN Yorks WR* 6 p. 267) and Fayrye Hole 1641 in Hexton (*PN Herts* p. 112).

5. As Pascual points out, 'Material monsters' pp. 205–6, 209, the characters in *Beowulf* use a different vocabulary for monsters from the poet himself: they see monsters, where he from an authorial Christian perspective sees devils.

6. Orme, *Going to Church* p. 108.

7. Terms from the supernatural lexicon whose attestation in place-names is not convincing include *cradden* 'changeling', *PN Yorks WR* 2 pp. 228, 283, 287; *fifel* 'monster', *PN Yorks ER* p. 110; *flagð* 'she-troll', Ekwall, *Dictionary of English Place-Names* p. 181; *gāst* 'ghost', *PN Glos* 2 p. 39; and *lob* 'goblin' *PN Herts* p. 126. Ghost-words include **boia* 'goblin', *PN Rutland* p. 313; **flecg* 'giant', Semple, *Perceptions of the Prehistoric* p. 263 (misunderstanding *PN Berks* p. 534); **gregge* 'dwarf', *PN Cheshire* 5:1i p. 200; **hobbin* 'little goblin', *PN Dorset* 1 p. 101; **malkin* 'female spectre', *PN Yorks WR* 4 p. 202; **pēac*, 'goblin', *PN Derbs* 1 p. 56; and **þūma*, 'dwarf', *PN Oxon* 1 pp. 11, 189–90.

8. The problems of these names were first identified in *PN Worcs* p. 126. The best discussion is by Insley, 'Addenda' p. 43, referencing volumes of the English Place-Names Survey up to that date.

9. *PN Leics* 6 p. 315, Goblin Pit 1601 and Hobgoblyn Pitt 1606 in Twycross; Owen 'Two Lincolnshire names' p. 56, Hobthurste Hill 1602 in Croft.

10. Bower, 'PN Lindsey' p. 345, Tom Thrush Lane in Winteringham 1824; Wise, *New Forest* pp. 276/7 (map), Tom Pook's Hill in Minstead at SU 260 127.

11. Dickins, 'Yorkshire hobs' p. 19.

12. *PN Derbs* 1 pp. 43, 65, 67, 104, 127, 146, 158, 2 pp. 207, 225, 245, 263, 266, 289, 307, 311, 316, 329, 334, 350, 355, 356, 377, 382, 413, 416, 423, 440, 442, 506, 514, 3 pp. 517, 521, 528, 562, 564, 565, 572, 584, 586, 608, 651; *PN Yorks WR* 1 pp. 34, 51, 82, 152, 174, 178, 191, 199, 255, 300, 325, 2 pp. 42, 110, 130, 140, 147, 192, 216, 222, 250, 275, 318, 3 pp. 55, 67, 165, 270, 272, 4 pp. 27, 112, 148, 160, 169, 199, 201, 228, 243, 259, 5 pp. 57, 62, 63, 161, 182, 6 pp. 9, 24, 133, 268.

13. Hudson, *Subsidies* pp. 17, 64, 94, 145 (and 266), 248, 251, 254, 264, 266, 288, topographical names; 16, 18, 71, 82, 103, 256, 259, 281, 291, descriptive names.

14. Young, *The Boggart* is strong on the relationship between place-names and traditions.

15. The list of names is from Briggs, *Dictionary of Fairies*.

16. The last reference in living tradition seems to be the Poake in Allies, *Ignis Fatuus* pp. 7–8.

17. Forby, *Vocabulary of East Anglia* 2 p. 238 (Shuck); Oates & Wood, *Coven of Scholars* p. 59 (Shucky); Cranworth, 'East Anglian superstitions' pp. 170–71 (Skeff); Payne, *Ghost Hunter* p. 134 (Shaggy). Newton, *Origins of Beowulf* pp. 143–44 thinks he has found Black Shuck the *scucca* a.k.a. Grendel surviving in East

Anglian tradition. How easy it is to find things in folklore, if you're not a folklorist.

18. *PN Yorks ER* p. 299.

19. *PN Leics* 5 p. 144; *PN Shropshire* 7 p. 201.

20. I suspect that *Gobelins* 1457 at North Petherton in Somerset (National Archives E 40/9690) belongs here rather than with the personal names. Otherwise I have kept clear of orphan simplexes—those place-names where, e.g., Goblins is deemed to stand for Goblins Field.

21. S 108, a charter for Barnhorne in Bexhill.

22. *PN Dorset* 3p225; *PN Yorks WR* 4 p. 154, 5 p. 168.

23. *PN Warks* pp. 68, 71.

24. 'There can be no doubt that the men who created names like Shugborough and Drakelow believed in the objective reality of spectres and dragons ... In the eighth century the supernatural had not yet been subdued to the purposes of literary decoration': Stenton, 'Anglo-Saxon Heathenism' in *Preparatory to Anglo-Saxon England* p. 285.

25. Burne, 'Scraps of folklore' p. 162; Buckle Church on the OS, Puck Church Parlour in Heath, *The English Peasant* p. 174. *Pūcel* often reduces to *pūca*.

26. *PN Glos* 3 p. 64. Hough, 'Ælfric, Pucklechurch' pp. 113–16, derives the name instead from **pohhel*, the diminutive of **pohha* 'fallow deer'; neither word is universally accepted as a vocabulary item. The suggestion that 'a reference to a goblin would be ... incongruous in combination with the generic element' would surprise anyone living near an Elf Kirk or Trollkyrkja.

27. Gelling, 'Smith's *Elements*' p. 42.

28. Hobthust Church at Mansfield Woodhouse in Nottinghamshire was 'a large rock ... which has been there time out of mind', Harrod, *History of Mansfield* pt 2 p. 42. Elf Kirk at Falstone, NY 695 860, is a stone platform overlooking a valley, now Kielder Water. There is another Elf Kirk at Banff, NJ 680 646 on the 1867 OS, a coastal rock shelf. The Green Chapel in *Gawain* belongs to this group, if it was indeed a real location: Hawker-Yates, 'Barrows' pp. 174–201.

29. The popularity of these names is shown by Trollkyrkja, found in Norway for mountains in Sogndal and Rogaland, hills in Ålesund, Dombås and on an island west of Landro, and a cave complex near Elnesvågen. The name-type is likely to have come from England, where it was already current and made sense as a metaphor in the tenth century, while there were no stone churches in Scandinavia until the twelfth.

30. Gollancz, 'Gringolet': the text can be reconstructed as *Summe sende ylues &summe sende nadderes,/Sumne sende nikeres the bi ðe wates wunien/Nis þer man nenne bute ildebrand onne*. We cannot reconstruct an epic from three lines, but it seems that Hildebrand is in some situation where he is the only human in a company of supernatural creatures. The phrasing is traditional: the *niker* (*iker* by false analysis) that *woneth in water* is in *King Alisaunder* line 6172, and as for spirits,

an early fifteenth-century sermon says that *summe ben elues and summe gobelynes* (Hudson & Gradon, *Wycliffite* 1 p. 686).

31. Hall, *Anglo-Saxon Elves* pp. 103–4, reads *sende* as 'they sent', not as a variant spelling of *sind* 'they are'. This doesn't make much sense.

32. I have a paper forthcoming in *Nomina*, 'The Devil you know', that deals with these post-medieval names.

33. M. Æbbe pp. 40–5.

34. M. Wulfstan pp. 131, 146, 132–33. The boy from Clun is said to have also been epileptic, but this sounds like the conflation of two separate miracles.

35. M. Cuthbert (Farne) pp. 16–17 (trans. p. 103). The miraculist says *pedem* not *crurem* but I assume he means 'leg': having one foot disproportionately long wouldn't prevent you from walking.

36. M. Æbbe pp. 65–67.

37. M. Margaret pp. 83–85.

38. More reports of this kind can be found in M. Thomas (Benedict) 2 p. 80; M. Hand of St James p. 14 (translation); M. Gilbert p. 265; M. Simon de Montfort p. 87. In M. Nectan p. 413 (trans. 77) the young man is afflicted, not after sleeping outdoors, but because he has decorated his bed with greenery—unless this is the miraculist's misunderstanding.

39. M. Godric pp. 742–43.

40. M. Thomas Cantilupe pp. 684–85: in the printed text, Richard comes from *Brunburst* near *Wembeburis*, but the Bollandists made such a dog's dinner of transcribing place-names that Wombridge seems the best guess.

41. M. Swithun pp. 274–77, with geographical notes by Lapidge. The timing—in July, with the 2nd (Swithun's death-day) *appropinquante*—is compatible with St John's Day, the medieval Midsummer, 10 Kal Iul by Latin reckoning. Lantfred's *mannos*, literally 'mules', must have been packhorses: mules don't come in herds.

42. Lantfred (M. Swithun pp. 274–75) says the man was *fatigatus ex itinere* but this does not mean he had walked a long way: in these stories, tiredness is sent down at the will of the spirits. The man from Wombridge collapsed *ex abrupto* (M. Thomas Cantilupe p. 684) and there is a good description of this state in L. Godric pp. 566–77, where the great weariness comes not from demons but St John the Baptist, who has a dream-message to impart.

43. Lacey, 'Water meadows' pp. 196–201.

44. M. Hand of St James p. 9 (translation); M. Æbbe pp. 62–63.

45. Naming the Devil 'Old Scrat, Old Scratch' is often seen as a survival of ME *scrat* (*English Dialect Dictionary* accessed at https://eddonline-proj.uibk.ac.at/edd/index.jsp). But there are no early forms, and it might be a nineteenth-century borrowing from German. I am not altogether happy treating field-names in Scratch- as part of this series, since occasional forms like Scratchy Lane suggest they were places overgrown by thorns and brambles. If you take a rigorous line

on this (and that means contradicting *PN Wilts* p. 154 and Mills, *London PNs* p. 204) then there are no southern English names in *scratta* at all: the only reliable attestations are for *skratti*, from the Danelaw.

46. Walsingham, *Historia Anglicana* 1 p. 199 and *Chronicon Angliae* pp. 15–16.

47. Map, *De Nugis* pp. 148–51. Map skips some of the story; he has the lake ladies say to one another *Si hoc fecisset, unam de nobis cepisset*, but had obviously forgotten what *hoc* was.

48. *Elven* could in theory be the analogical ME weak genitive plural, as in the *South East Legendary* line 255, or even the OE female *ælfen*, which however Hall, *Anglo-Saxon Elves* pp. 78–81, assumes to be a glossator's nonce-word. But analogy with *buggen* suggests it is meant to be adjectival. I suspect that the qualifier in *Powkenlane* 1449 at Windsor, a later form of *Pokelane* 1310 (*PN Berks* 1 p. 35), is also adjectival rather than a surviving genitive.

49. The plural *lands* is also found with *ælf* in two Dorset names, at Chideock and Buckland Newton. Evidently *land* in place-names, singular or plural, means a particular place in the fields, not the generalised *eluenlond* used in *Fasciculus Morum* pp. 579–80 for the realm of Faerie or Elfhame.

50. *VEPN* 2 p. 164. This is only one of many formal traps lying in wait for the onomast: a hopeful *eluenacres*, for instance, can be 'eleven acres' or 'the acres of Elwin'. I can only say that in each case I have considered the alternatives and excluded a name from the corpus unless there was a reasonable possibility that it was supernatural.

51. Assuming that the -r- in *Elvernedele* is inorganic. Names in *deill* can be pasture or meadow as well as arable: Gardiner, 'Dales'.

52. Taking Beds, Berks, Bucks, Herts, Midd (with London) and Oxon as the Home Counties (67 names in 3676 square miles) against Yorkshire (81 names in 6071 square miles).

53. LE pp. 51–53 (trans. pp. 79–80).

54. Gervase, *Otia Imperialia* pp. 676–77; Briggs, *Dictionary* p. 343. Cf. the demon that screeches *hach hach hach* in L. Godric pp. 446–47, the goat that *ter circa ivit circulum dicendo a.a.a.* in one Byland story p. 417 (trans. p. 368) and the spirit that cries *how how how* in another, p. 419 (trans. p. 372). The demon brother calls *heu heu heu* in M. Margaret pp. 100–1. Triple repetition is evidently a marker for the eerie, as in the *bowes, bowes, bowes* of the Dunsmore phantom.

55. Owst, *Literature and Pulpit* p. 113.

56. *Fasciculus* pp. 696–9. The remedy of turning your cloak, ubiquitous in modern accounts of pixy-leading, was evidently known *c.*1410, since Adam of Usk uses it as a metaphor for getting out of uncertainties: Given-Wilson, *Chronicles* p. 151.

57. Gloucester SO 833 189, Eynsham SP 435 094 (Puck Lane 1615 is perhaps to be associated with *Poukebrugge* 1406, but there is no obvious river crossing), and Much Wenlock SO 621 999.

58. Guildford SU 997 494 and Witney SP 355 102.

59. However, Puck Street at Sutton in Sussex is not in a settlement at all: the path runs past Glatting Farm up onto common land (SU 965 140). Cf. the interchange of generics in *Pukestie* 1287, *Poukestrete* 1337, surviving in Puckstye Fam at Hartfield in Sussex: *PN Sussex* 2 p. 368, Mawer and Stenton 'Corrigenda VIII' p. 213. The *stīg/strǣt* heads eastwards up a hill onto grazing land, TQ 461 383.

60. M. Henry VI (1935) p. 104.

61. M. Frideswide p. 582.

62. Pucklewood at ST 780 611; M. Wulfstan p. 129.

63. Hayman, *Trees* pp. 52–53.

64. *Liber Luciani* pp. 63–64: *quem de latibulis insidiantium recte dicunt Vallem Demonum.*

65. M. Swithun pp. 276–77; *PN Oxon* 2 p. 267.

66. The case for this recurrent *gram skógr* as an elfin name is very weak. I assume that Smith (*PN Yorks WR* 6 p. 101) proposed it because 'angry wood' doesn't make much sense either.

67. Or be sent away: the walking dead of Drakelow were finally laid at a place called *Dodefreseford* or *Dodescrossefora*, M. Modwenna pp. 196–97. Unfortunately the forms are bad and the place cannot be identified. The additive generic cannot, as suggested in Blair, 'Dangerous dead' p. 558, be *fȳr* as that is not a productive element in place-names.

68. Bridges also appear in secondary names, such as Thirsley Hebley 1596 at Todmorden (*hebley* is Yorkshire dialect for 'bridge').

69. For sunset and twilight, see *ARH* p. 196, M. Modwenna pp. 194–95, M. Margaret pp. 126–27, M. Henry VI (1935) p. 125. For the hour before dawn (Old English *uht*), M. Hand of James p. 9 (translation), M. Thomas (Benedict) 2 p. 129, M. Cuthbert (Farne) p. 14 (trans. p. 101).

70. Noon, *meridies*, is the time of apparition in two tales from *Lanercost*, pp. 80–81 and p. 126 (trans. p. 57); see also Map, *De Nugis* pp. 370–71, and Gervase, *Otia Imperialia* pp. 336–37. The grant, in Gervase pp. 676–77, appears either at noon or sunset. Dawn and twilight appear more often in *miracula*, noon in histories, *mirabilia* and fiction: Friedman, 'Noon-Day Demon'.

71. *Coniuncros* 1216x72 at Derby is the only example, and a *cangun* is not quite a spirit. Most standing crosses marked crossroads, but not all, and *cros* was not used for the junction itself before Modern English.

72. M. Hugh p. 71.

73. Certainly they did in Scotland: Henderson and Cowan, *Scottish Fairy Belief* pp. 37, 38, 49, 128. But in England the motif had died out by early modern times.

74. Blakiston, 'Ghost stories'.

75. Versions in Herbert, *Catalogue* pp. 394 and 525 have the motif of the golden hairs but not the meeting at the cross.

76. The first cry was *super montem*, on Noddle Hill; the crossroads must have been the one at SE 565 788.

77. Byland p. 419 (trans. p. 372).

78. National Archives SC 8/230/11481.

79. *Maxims* II lines 42–43 in Dobbie, *Anglo-Saxon Minor Poems* p. 56.

80. Formally, one might expect names with -*u*- to derive from ON *þurs* and those in
-*i*- from OE *þyrs*. But both vowels are found mixed in every county. Smith gives
þyrs as the etymon for all names in vols 1 to 3 of *PN Yorks WR*, and *þurs* for all
those in vols 4 to 6, which does not inspire confidence.

81. *Elvenfen* in *EPNE* 1 p. 149; I omitted it from the corpus as Smith gives no date
for the form.

82. Jacobsson, *Wells, Meres and Pools* pp. 21–3, 208–18 discusses the semantic range
of *mere*. Keith Briggs has found four examples of *Thersmere* in his as yet unpublished corpus of Suffolk place-names: English Place-Name List (jiscmail.ac.uk)
3 January 2018.

83. *Pukemere* was the capital messuage of a manor, emparked in 1321 and afterwards
renamed Foxleighs: *VCH Berkshire* 3 p. 101. It was at SU 884 769.

84. 'This extraordinary combination of inland and seashore, of marsh and mountain,
of fresh water and salt water': Lawrence, 'Haunted mere' p. 221.

85. S 416. The *grendel* charters are collected in Chambers, *Beowulf* pp. 42–44,
304–11.

86. *PN Devon* 1 p. 6 and 2 p. 586 (S 669); *PN Cambs* p. 319 (suggested as a compound
in *dell*); Suffolk Assize Rolls in Zachrisson, 'Grendel' p. 43; the National Archives
E 40/6389 and E 40/6375; Tymms, *Wills of Bury* p. 31; PN *Leics* 4 pp. 115, 225
and 5 p. 78; *PN Rutland* pp. 59, 67, 96.

87. Zachrisson, 'Grendel in *Beowulf*'. As early as 1894 Thomas Miller, 'Grendel', had
realized that the element referred to rivers, not monsters.

88. *PN Cambs* p. 339; *PN Derbs* 1 pp. 94–95; *PN Yorks WR* 6 pp. 195–96; *PN Devon*
2 p. 489; Hertfordshire Archives DE/Bw/28416; Plymouth Archives 308/90.

89. Tengstrand, *Genitival Composition*——a work which traces its genesis (p. xiv) to the
test-case of *grendlesmere*.

90. S 78 (with photo in Hooke, 'Rivers, wells and springs' p. 116); *PN Devon* 2 p. 489
(S 255); *PN Wilts* p. 441 (S 416) and Buchanan-Dunlop, *Ham* pp. 24–5; Horovitz,
PN Staffs p. 285 (S 579); S 645; S 786; *PN Midd* p. 57 (S 1450); *PN Essex* p. 422;
PN Leics 7 p. 259; Somerset Heritage Centre DD\WHb/1022; *PN Devon* 2 p. 489;
PN Leics 5 p. 153.

91. Turner, *Christian Landscape* p. 123 describes the Crediton *grendeles pyt* as
'indicative of the learned context of the boundary clause's composition': but
boundaries were not 'composed', they were transcribed from the capacious local
memory of old illiterate men. Scholars forget that the past was not as bookish
as themselves.

92. Bored? Well, they certainly weren't interested in what the poem said,
transcribing it in a mechanical auto-correct mode which frequently made
nonsense of the text: Neidorf, *Transmission of Beowulf* pp. 103–5.

93. As argued by Lapidge in his paper '*Beowulf*, Aldhelm, the *Liber Monstrorum* and Wessex', accessible as pp. 272–311 of *Anglo-Latin Literature 600–899*. He argues (pp. 299–302) that this tradition came from Aldhelm's home area, since Abbots Moreton, Alfrick, Battersea, Crediton, Ham, Hendon and Oldswinford centre on Malmesbury—rather a large circle, and as good a match for Old English charters in general as for those containing the word *grendel*.

94. After drafting this section, I heard Richard Dance deliver his paper to the centenary conference of the English Place-Name Society (9 September 2023) and found that we had independently come to the same conclusion, from very similar evidence. I am grateful to him for allowing me priority of publication.

95. Byland p. 418 (trans. p. 370). Cold Kirby was a chapelry of Easingwold, so Tankerlay may have been rector there.

96. CD p. 143 (trans. p. 182); Herbert, *Catalogue* p. 619.

97. M. Aldhelm pp. 118–19. The demon subtext, though not stated in the original, was obvious to contemporaries, and in his retelling William of Malmesbury has the other fishermen argue whether it was a chance gust of wind that blinded their friend, or something diabolical: *Gesta Pontificum* pp. 630–1.

98. Gervase, *Otia Imperialia* pp. 718–21.

99. It cannot be coincidence that we have a wain-man called Wayneman. By the date of the Byland MS, 1399x1420, surnames were semantically arbitrary; either we are dealing with a memory going back three or four generations to the days of occupational bynames, or this is a family legend: 'You wonder why we're called Wayneman? Well, it's because of our ancestor Roger…'.

100. M. Edmund pp. 11, 145. The witch of Berkeley was also sewn up in a deerskin; sewing in hide was, amongst other things, a way of ensuring that bodies stayed where they were put.

101. L. Kenelm pp. 72–73.

102. For other examples, see Blair, 'The dangerous dead' pp. 549–51.

103. Brown, *Fate of the Dead* pp. 24–34.

104. Westwood & Simpson, *Lore of the Land* pp. 155, 179, 317, 568; for other exorcisms into water, see pp. 20, 421, 540, 568, 765, 810.

105. Bromyard, *Summa* 2 p. 359b and (a better text) in Wright, *Latin Stories* p. 107.

106. Dickins, 'Gerard as a goblin name'. This seems to originate in a misremembered story of Caesarius, *Miracles* 2 pp. 61–63, where Gerard is the name of the knight who is served, not the fiend that serves him. Attempts to find him in place-names (*PN Cumb* 1 p. 174) are misguided. Tubach, *Index Exemplorum* p. 128, has demon servant stories.

107. Owst, *Literature and Pulpit* p. 270.

108. L. Godric pp. 196–201. Even in the seventeenth century, Milton's 'drudging Goblin' with 'hairy strength' (*L'Allegro* lines 105–14) still has something undomesticated about him.

109. Briggs, *Dictionary of Fairies* pp. 46–49.

110. *EPNE* 2 p. 50, a name otherwise unrecorded and with no date, so I have excluded it from the corpus.

111. Although Cavill, *New Dictionary of Field-Names* pp. 297–98, is confident that modern names in Nicco- represent *nicor-*, I cannot see how they can be distinguished from the personal name Nichol, adopted in dialect as a word for 'goldfinch'. Spellings in Nicker- are not conclusive when they come from periods where -er- is used orthographically for ə, and confining ourselves to names with watery generics like Nicker Meadow (399 on the 1847 Tintwistle TA) and Nickersitch (622, 623 on the 1848 Butterton TA) is open to the same criticism we had earlier for names in *hob-* and *grim-*: it cherry-picks the evidence.

112. The Mildenhall name survives as Nickamoor Field on the TM at SU 214 694 (thanks to Katy Jordan for this); the Sutton one is located by *PN Cheshire* 2 p. 258 at SJ 672 630; for Lincoln, see Hill, *Medieval Lincoln* p. 34.

113. *Lanercost* pp. 155–56 (trans. pp. 104–5). That detail of the horse's hoof recalls the *each uisge* of later tradition, who—like the *nicor/nykere*—could be both a monstrous water-creature and a seductive stranger in human form.

114. Michael of Northgate, *Ayenbite of Inwyt* p. 61.

115. Harrod, *Records of Colchester* p. 13. Probably the Nikerhole 1603 at Radcliffe in Lancashire was a hole in this sense, a pool in the Irwell rather than a cave or hollow.

116. Forby, *Vocabulary of East Anglia* 2 p. 387.

117. Norfolk Record Office HARE 5084, 219X1.

118. Norfolk Record Office HARE 3555, 206X6; National Archives E 40/3156. The old and new Pokedyche appear in *Letters & Papers of Henry VIII* 1 p. 608.

119. Gelling, *Signposts to the Past* p. 150 drawing on *PN Warks* p. 246, 373 (Wootten Wawen). The causeway runs past Hobditch Copse at SP 133 687.

120. The -o- in *Thorsdyche* is unexpected and may reflect influence from a Scandinavian name in *þór-*; evidently the word *þyrs* was no longer easily recognized in southern England by 1327.

121. There has been some uncertainty as to whether this last group of names derive from *ric* 'stream' or *hrycg* 'ridge' but personal names derived from the Standon settlement which end in -*ich* put it beyond doubt: National Archives TNA C 241/27/167 and Hertfordshire Archives 44975. Even the latest of the group, Pockeridge 1808 in Ashbrittle, seems to match with the unlocated form *Pukewelleriche* in Scherr, 'Springs in Somerset' p. 83. S 1559 is *pokerythe* in the Electronic Sawyer but -*ryche* in Austen and Hill, 'Boundaries of Itchen', a more careful transcription.

122. Pascual, 'Material monsters' pp. 210, 217. He cites glossary entries identifying *scocha* with words for 'inciter, enticement', as if dialogue were part of its nature.

123. M. Cuthbert (Farne) p. 14 (trans. p. 101); M. Margaret pp. 126–27.

124. Byland p. 415 (trans. p. 365). The *torrente* that Snowball crosses is the Holbeck, probably at SE 589 770.

125. Denham, *Tracts* 2 p. 355; W.H.H., 'Devil's Hole' and Dugdale, *Mysterious North Lakeland* p. 8.

126. Assuming that the *Elfringemad* of the Chamberlayne family papers (Hadley, *Hollow Places* p. 307), which otherwise relate to Brent Pelham, is the Elfaring Croft of the Little Hadham court rolls 1632–75 (Hertfordshire Archives DE/Sr/T12).

127. Hunt, *Plant Names* p. 87. The transcriber of S 877 in *c.*1400 read *Alfryng* for *ælfrucge* (Wallenberg, *Kentish PNs* p. 265), an error but one which shows what he thought was possible as a name.

128. Chaucer, *Works* p. 84.

129. Map, *De Nugis* pp. 148–61.

130. *South English Legendary* 2 p. 410, reading *Men sieþ* for the *Me sicþ* of the published text.

131. *Fasciculus Morum* pp. 579–80.

132. Rutter, 'Away with the fairies'.

133. Smith (*PN Yorks WR* 5 p. 142) was happy to derive *Elfon-* from *Elfen-*, but this would be an irregular development of the vowel. Could it be the plant-name *ælfðone*, 'woody nightshade'?

134. Latham, 'West Sussex superstitions' p. 27; found in Puckstool 1748 at the Gloucester hamlet of Wotton (Gloucester Archives GDR/Q3/51, a marriage license allegation) and in Puckstool Wood at Shackleford in Surrey, 1870 OS at SU 923 455.

135. There is also Scugdale, a house in Hartoft (SE 747 932) on the 1893 OS. But the 1854 edition names the same property as Spires House, so we seem to be dealing with a transferred house-name.

136. *PN Yorks NR* p. 152. For the analogous name, see Cox, 'Dimmingsdale': ironically, this is often analogically reformed to *Demons*, and as early as *c.*1460 Dimmin Dale at Taddington in Derbyshire appears as a *valey … ubi spiritus sunt tormentati*.

137. Shucdale 1655 at Haxey in Lincolnshire looks formally like *dalr* 'valley' but must be *deill* 'share of land': there's nothing deeper than a wheel-rut in the Isle of Axholme.

138. Gelling and Cole, *Landscape of Place-Names* pp. 113–14.

139. First recorded as *Fendesfeld* (*PN Cumb* 1 p. 243), but it is clear from the series that this is a bad form for *-fell*. There was another Fiendsfell, 'a deadfull Rock', above Glenkirk: p. 152 of 'Description of Tweddale' *c.*1680 in Macfarlane, *Geographical Collections* 3 pp. 140–54.

140. Rowling, *Folklore of the Lake District* p. 22; cf. Robinson, *Westmorland and Cumberland* pp. 39–40.

141. Skirsgill at Dacre is Christkeld al. Skurgill 1619 (*PN Cumb* 1 p. 189) but I don't think this is an intended exorcism, simply a parallel place-name for the same farm.

142. Gelling, *PN Oxon* 1 p. 52, thought that Elvendon was from *dūn* but Cole, 'Two Chiltern place-names' pp. 65–67, 74, corrects the *c.*1240 form from *Ulvendon'* to *Ulvenden'*.

143. M. Wihtburh p. 211. I don't think that *demon* ever appears directly in place-names: it was proposed in *PN Oxon* 1 p. 250 for *Demnesweye c.*1215 at Steeple Barton but a metathesised *demeynes* is also possible. Gelling thought that the presence of *Succhelaue c.*1210 in the same parish argued for derivation from *demon*, but supernatural names don't cluster in theme parks.

144. *Liber Luciani* pp. 63–64. As far as we can make out from Lucian's wordplay, three roads divide east of the town at SJ 419 664, of which the lefthand one *venitur ad locum quem de latibulis insidiantium recte dicunt Vallem Demonum*. This must be Watling Street: I don't think he is punning on Hoole/Hell, which is on a different road.

145. The valley at Rainow is the eponym of Alan Garner's novel *Thursbitch*.

146. Gatty, *Life at One Living* pp. 205–6. We have to take his word for it, since the valley is now flooded for the Broomhead reservoir.

147. Bradley, 'English place-names' p. 30.

148. Gambier-Parry, *Goring Charters* 1 p. xxix.

149. Chibnall, *Sherington* p. 11.

150. Although a C7 text glosses *Echo* as *wudumær*: Hall, *Anglo-Saxon Elves* p. 85. This may just match Echo, a nymph, with the *mær*, a female spirit; but it may imply that *wudumærs* were responsible for the sound of echoes.

151. Watson, *Halifax* p. 27.

152. Duignan, *Warwickshire PN* p. 99; *PN Yorks NR* p. xlv.

153. Dwarf Holes is also the name of a disused mine at West Dean in Gloucestershire, but only on the 1920 OS (SO 635 092). In earlier editions it is 'Old Shaft'.

154. Hough, 'Carolside and *Carelholpit*' pp. 82–84; OS for Warcop NY 757 187, Harwich TM 250 314, Melkridge NY 728 670 and Dartford TQ 604 728, a small selection from a treasure-trove of names collected and generously shared by Simon Young.

155. *Coucher Book of Whalley* 2 p. 397. Geoffrey son of Adam de Dutton, who made the grant, died *c.*1248; it was witnessed by Roger, Prior of Norton, who was in office 1249–1261. After the first Geoffrey's death it seems to have been renewed by Geoffrey son of Hugh de Dutton.

156. Battles, 'Dwarfs' discusses traditional materials behind the idea of the dwarf.

157. It is this that leaves me undecided about the theorizing in Lecouteux, *Elves and Dwarfs*: he writes as if the lore had 'originally' (in the first century? in proto-Indo-European?) made systematic sense, as it certainly does not in the surviving sources. I don't think folklore was ever more coherent than it is today: probably less.

158. MS Lansdowne 1033, cited by Allies, *Folk-Lore of Worcestershire* p. 44.

159. Plot, *Natural History of Stafford-shire* p. 172.

160. Witcutt, 'Staffordshire folklore'.

161. Bede, *Ecclesiastical History* pp. 434–39.

162. The words *ad alteram insulam modicum, quae Thrusheland vocatur* are in a text of Gerald's *Topographica Hibernica* printed in Crossman, 'St Cuthbert's island'. The destination is only *ad alteram insulam* in the text edited by James Dimock, p. 82.

163. L. Cuthbert p. 64 (lines 2177–80).

164. *WB* 1 p. 284. Modern translations are much duller and replace the uncanny menagerie with goats and owls.

165. The classical *empusae* had equine feet, as did the C16 Sicilian *donna di fuore*: Warner, *Beast to Blonde* p. 121.

166. Gough, *History of Myddle* p. 32.

167. Puckes 1653 at Binstead in the Isle of Wight is Puckhouse on the 1862 OS, and *pūca hūs* rather than a genitive *pokeres* might also be the true derivation for names like Puckers Field (Herefs) and Puckers Wood (Somerset).

168. Hough, 'Dwerryhouse' felt that supernatural being + *hūs* was an unlikely compound (forgetting the *nicor-hūsa fela* of *Beowulf* line 1411) and suggested a sense 'hospital' from the secondary meaning of *dweorg* as 'fever'. This seems unnecessary.

169. This cannot be put down to a fondness for finding *cangun* names on the part of Reaney and Cameron, respectively. I have read all the complete EPNS county surveys and if there had been other instances of the element, I'd have noticed them.

170. Schmitt, *Holy Greyhound* pp. 71–72.

171. Henderson & Cowan, *Scottish Fairy Belief* pp. 97–98.

172. *Congeonshole* survives as Quindal Hole on the Tithe Map of 1839 and Quanguins Oak lay in Pound Field, mapped in Darby, *Place and Field Names* p. 73.

173. Green, *Elf Queens* pp. 110–18 is perhaps too schematic on this point.

174. *IC* p. 75 (trans. pp. 133–35).

175. *CA* pp. 118 (trans. p. 122) and *HRA* (1–2) 1 pp. 114–15.

176. CD p. 122 (trans. pp. 158–59). Henry was bishop 1227–1235, and the Cambridge Dominican was assembling stories from the 1240s onwards. I don't know why a spoon: they don't seem to have been used in magic at the time, and ordinary homage never required the vassal to present gifts to the lord.

177. Gervase, *Otia Imperialia* pp. 334–37: if Gervase picked this up in Italy in the 1190s, he could have told it to Ralph when they were both back in England *c.*1200. The Sicilians were not shy about retelling this story and two other versions are discussed in Green, *Elf Queens* pp. 179–80.

178. Map, *De Nugis* pp. 26–29.

179. Gervase, *Otia Imperialia* pp. 642–45: this episode, happening *c.*1115–1153, when William Peveril was Lord of the Honour of Peveril, was known to Robert, a local man (*exinde oriundo*) who afterwards moved south, became prior of Kenilworth in 1160 and presumably passed the story on to Gervase before he left England

in 1183. The story therefore reached our writer sixty to thirty years after the event, possibly with only one intervening witness. Oman, 'Folklore of Gervase' p. 12, is inclined to think the swineherd made it up, 'sleeping off a debauch': an ungenerous hermeneutic.

180. *Specus, siue subterraneus meatus (honorem prafabor) Diaboli Podex dictus*: Camden, *Britannia* p. 314.

181. *PN Derbs* 1 p. 56.

182. Whitaker, *History of Craven* p. 377.

183. In other words, a literal compound with a metaphorical generic, not an integral figurative construction, as noted by Dodgson in *PN Cheshire* 2 p. 197. There is also an unrelated *ersc* 'ploughland away from other fields', definitely the generic in Pokershe 1540 at Cheselbourne in Dorset, probably at Pokeleserse 1176 at Brightling and Pochelers 1561 at Selsey, both in Sussex; that matches the regional distribution of this term, discussed in Cole, '*Ersc*'.

184. Jacobsson, *Wells, Meres and Pools* pp. 219–29. The use of *wella* for a stream, usually the stream as it runs from the source, is so rare—6% of charter bounds, 2.6% of major settlement names—that it can be disregarded.

185. Jacobsson, *Wells, Meres and Pools* pp. 26–27.

186. M. Wulfstan p. 13.

187. The exceptions are *Biggputtlane* 1462 at Holnest in Dorset, Poker Pittes 1603x25 at Matlock Bath, *succan pyt* 969 in S 773, and *Schokepet* 1431 somewhere in Cambridgeshire.

188. Cavill, *New Dictionary of Field-Names* p. 201.

189. The generic cannot be the *hlēda* of Finberg, *Charters of the West Midlands* p. 80 (followed by *PN Glos* 3 p. 147); as Hall points out, 'Are there elves' pp. 64–66, the fifteenth-century manuscript must be mangling an OE strong masculine plural on X-*as*, *of* X-*um*. He proposes *elfet lædas* or *elm falodas*: but *elm* is no more (or less) probable than *ælf*. Here, in miniature, is the difference between Hall's approach and mine: he requires names that certainly, indisputably contain *ælf*, where I have assembled a corpus in which this and other supernatural qualifiers are a reasonably plausible interpretation.

190. Addy, *Glossary of Sheffield* p. 258.

191. Page, *Early Assize Rolls* pp. 409–10.

192. Assuming the identity of these medieval forms with Puck Pit at SO 806 242 and Pug Pit at SY 841 862 on the modern map. You might expect confusion with the trade term *pug pit* for a pit where clay is mixed for brickmaking, but none of these pits are on clay subsoil.

193. Discussed at https://www.heritagegateway.org.uk/Gateway/Results_Single. aspx?uid=MBL4906&resourceID=1025.

194. Dugdale, *Monasticon* 6i p. 430.

195. Hancock, *Minehead* p. 145; Stevens, 'Somerset coroner's roll' p. 457.

196. Morton, *Northampton-shire* p. 282; Brown, *'Capability' Brown* p. 145; Thompson, 'Peculiarities of waters: X' p. 67.

197. The later series shows that the 1579 form is a wrong analysis, understanding Thrus as Th' Rus, in the same way that Hobthurst was sometimes rationalized as Hob o' th' Hurst: Edwards, *Hobgoblin and Sweet Puck* p. 135.

198. *GH* 1 pp. 385–86 (trans. p. 654). A variant textual tradition was incorporated into the *Liber Eliensis* (as referenced under M. Æthelthryth) p. 183 (trans. p. 217, but the translation is unreliable).

199. In the *GH*, the two women converse, and both go to the well; in the *Liber Eliensis* Hereward hears the witch talking to herself, and she goes alone. It looks as if two stories have been superimposed: one where he overhears Normans talking to each other about the campaign, another where he listens to the witch talking at the well.

200. *In orientem affluentes iuxta hortum* (*GH*); *in parte orientali … decurrunt* (*Liber Eliensis*). I prefer to read, with *GH*, 'flowing eastwards next to the garden', not 'flowing on the east side of the garden', but then I'm influenced by later folkloric parallels. East-running springs were already being used for cures in Anglo-Saxon times: Jolly, *Popular Religion* p. 117.

201. The *GH* is inconsistent in its description of the witch: she is a French-speaking outsider, *adducta* by the Normans, but she seems to know her way around Brandon and to be familiar with the shrine in its grounds, a wicked parody of the conventional hermit's cell and holy well.

202. *Wilweorðunga and licwiglunga and hwata and galdra*: discussed in Meaney, 'Wulfstan and heathenism' pp. 477–78. She looks at evidence for cult at wells (p. 489), trees (pp. 490–1) and stones (p. 492). The idea of divination through dialogue with a spirit of natural places underlies the satirical cante-fable *Say me, wight in the brom*: Gray, *Simple Forms* p. 229.

203. Ælfric, *Lives of the Saints* 2 pp. 126–28 (*De Auguriis*).

204. Hough, 'Place-name Fritwell' and 'Name-type Fritwell' gives sources; Chetton now appears in *PN Shropshire* 7 p. 180 but with no earlier forms. Of the two names credited to *PN Yorks WR*, Fraight Lane can be found at 1 p. 84 and Fretwell Close at 4 p. 79.

205. Baines, 'Chicheley' pp. 8–9; *PN Yorks WR* 3 p. 7; Rattue, *Holy Wells of Kent* p. 36.

206. We find *frihtrung* and *wammfreht* (Serjeantson, 'Vocabulary' p. 54) which suggests an English origin.

207. II Cnut 5.1 in Whitelock, *English Historical Documents* p. 475.

208. Hooke, 'Rivers, wells and springs' p. 116. However, some forms may instead represent *hǣlu* 'health', and in any case *hǣl* may have meant 'bestowing good fortune' rather than 'telling your fortune'. The proposal that *hlot*, which survives in our 'casting lots', appears in Ladbrooke in Warwickshire (*hlodbroc* 998) is not convincing: the *h-*, which looks as if it should clinch the etymology, is in fact an inorganic spelling, *PN Warks* pp. 135–36.

209. *PN Essex* p. 265; Bower, 'PN Lindsey' p. 566; *PN Yorks WR* 1 p. 116. Rumwell in Bishop's Hull is *Runwille* 1327 (*Kirby's Quest for Somerset*) but this hamlet is named after a spring feeding the Fideoak stream, *hrumwyll* 1033 (S 972), which must be from *hruna* 'stump'.

210. 'Counsel' not 'council' as it appears in several reference works. As an element, *rūn* has an entry in *EPNE*, although Gelling (*PN Berks* 2 p. 531, 3 p. 757) pointed out that it could not yield the *-es* genitive found in *ofer runesforda* in a charter of *c.*895, now Runsford Hole in Streatley. Either we must accept a second element *run*, also something to do with water, or there is something wrong with the charter, or there is something wrong with the standard etymology of Runwell.

211. *South English Legendary* 2 pp. 409–10 (lines 243–50, 255–56).

212. *EPNE* 2 p. 114. The wood is at SU 519 355, but I have excluded it from the corpus as there are no dated forms.

213. The sixteenth-century redactor of the text read that Collen met the king of Annwn, and knew or thought he knew that Annwn was Avalon: Tristan Gray Hulse, 'Note on S. Collen' in Bord, *Fairy Sites* pp. 255–58. Glastonbury Abbey, avid as it was for Celtic saints, knew nothing of him.

214. Baring-Gould and Fisher, *British Saints* 2 pp. 158–59.

215. Cockin, *Staffordshire Encyclopaedia* pp. 464–65. In this name, *pūca* may simply stand for 'anomalous', as *Devil* often does in later names. Dorset has an Agglestone, thrown by the Devil at Corfe Castle, and near to it a Puckstone, Puketon 1585, possibly reflecting an earlier form of the legend.

216. M. Swithun pp. 276–77.

217. Gervase, *Otia Imperialia* pp. 672–75. Gervase had also seen the horn given by Simeon the patron saint of the knight of Penrith, and recognized it as coming from an aurochs (probably an Eastern European import), pp. 692–5. As Hawker-Yates, notes, 'Barrows' pp. 158–61, horns were linked to mounds by associations with assembly and tenure as well as feasting. The green riders also hand round a horn: M. Cuthbert (Farne) pp. 14–16 (trans. pp. 101–3).

218. Hall, 'Are there elves' pp. 67–68 calls this etymology into question because it compounds an OE qualifier with an ON generic. As there are fifteen other examples of the same combination, it seems captious to disallow this one—allowing that it is not a hybrid of two languages, but a monolingual compound in the Middle English of Yorkshire. Gillian Fellows Jensen felt (in Hall & Whyman. 'Ripon' p. 65) 'it is rather odd to have a genitive singular', but there are parallels for this sort of thing: *Puckysbarry* 1451 in Dorset, *Pokelshull* 1305 in Shropshire, and *Elueshyll c.*1300 in Norfolk.

219. Assuming that the last is a bad form for Scratthowe. Bowers, 'PN Lindsey' p. 406, proposes a derivation from ON *skatt*, the cognate of OE *sceot*, but this has never been encountered elsewhere.

220. Unpublished excavations in 1982 found two burials, one with an Anglo-Saxon brooch, although it is not clear whether these were from the mound itself:

MHU12058, generously discovered for me in the Historic Environment Record by Neil Holbrook.

221. Hall & Whyman, 'Ripon' pp. 65–124.

222. Horovitz, *PN Staffs* p. 493 derives Shugborough from *byrig*, dative of *burh*, but the forms are ambiguous. Analogy with the other names supports *beorg*, although that is a rare element in Staffordshire. If we discount Scratchbury Hill in Wiltshire as ModE *scratch* not OE *scratta*, the only remaining name in *burh* is Skinburness in Cumberland: an odd location, where the *næss* lies between the Solway Firth and the Great Gutter, as flat as you can get, with no obvious place for a fortification.

223. 'Unlocated' in Horovitz, *PN Staffs* p. 158, but the source—Wrottesley, 'Plea Rolls' p. 115—tells us that Hugh Yardeley of Buglawe stole goods at Darlaston, and there is a Bug Hole 1775 at Darlaston Green, apparently a shift-name from the original form.

224. The plural Elf-hills in Northumberland suggests small mounds, but the name only survives transferred to a farm (NZ 012 857), so we don't know where they were.

225. A surprising number of these hills have been quarried, in some cases almost to destruction: Ailcy, Eldon, Shucknall, Shugborough, Pouke Hill, Elva Hill in Setmurphy, and Elfa Hill in Uldale. I don't have an explanation for this, unless old quarries like pits were haunted places. Near the summit of Eldon Hill is Eldon Hole, a 180-foot pothole, good for entry to another world.

226. Baines, 'Winslow charter' p. 14.

227. Grinsell, *Dorset Barrows* p. 89.

228. 'Fearful places, housing other-worldly and evil creatures': Semple, 'Perceptions of place' p. 146.

229. Chadwick, 'Norse ghosts' has all the primary sources.

230. Hreinsson, *Complete Sagas* 1 p. 217.

231. The closest parallel is the theft from fairies of the Luck of Edenhall (Westwood & Simpson, *Lore of the Land* pp. 131–2); this is first recorded in a literary ballad of 1791, perhaps imitated from the Manx or Danish versions of the story which were already in print.

232. Webster, *Displaying of Witchcraft* pp. 300–2.

233. Macculloch, 'Mingling of fairy and witch'; Henderson & Cowan, *Scottish Fairy Belief* p. 41.

Afterword

1.   *IC* p. 93 (trans. p. 151).

Sources

Abbreviations

ARH

Annales Ricardi Secundi et Henrici Quarti in Henry Thomas Riley (ed.) *Johannis de Trokelowe, et Henrici de Blaneforde, monachorum S. Albani, necnon quorundam anonymorum, chronica et annales* (Rolls Series 28.3, 1866): 155–422.

ASC

The Anglo-Saxon Chronicle, ed. David Dumville and Simon Keynes (Cambridge: D.S. Brewer, 1983–2004) with translation in *The Anglo-Saxon Chronicle*, tr. Dorothy Whitelock, David Douglas and Susie Tucker (London: Eyre & Spottiswoode, 1961).

Byland

Montague Rhodes James, 'Twelve mediaeval ghost-stories', *English Historical Review* 37 (1922): 413–22, with translation in Arthur James Grant, 'Twelve medieval ghost stories', *Yorkshire Archaeological J.* 27 (1923): 363–79.

CA

Stevenson, Joseph, ed., *Radulphi de Coggeshall Chronicon anglicanum, De expugnatione Terræ Sanctæ libellus, Thomas Agnellus De morte et sepultura Henrici regis Angliæ junioris, Gesta Fulconis filii Warini, excerpta ex Otiis imperialibus Gervasii Tileburiensis* (Rolls Series 66, 1875) with partial translation in Francis Young, *Suffolk Fairylore* (Norwich: Lasse, 2019): 118–24.

CD

Stephen Forte, 'A Cambridge Dominican collector of Exempla in the thirteenth century', *Archivum Fratrum Praedicatorum* 1st ser 28 (1958): 115–48 with partial translation in David Jones, *Friars' Tales: Thirteenth-Century* Exempla *from the British Isles* (Manchester University Press, 2011): 154–88.

CRH   *Chronica magistri Rogeri de Houedene*, ed. William
               Stubbs (Rolls Series 51, 1868–71) with translation in
               The Annals of Roger de Hoveden, tr. Henry Thomas Riley
               (London: Bohn, 1853).

DA   Alexander of Canterbury, *Liber ex dictis Beati Anselmi* in
               Southern, Richard William, and Franciscus Salesius
               Schmitt, *Memorials of St Anselm* (Oxford University
               Press, 1969): 105–270.

EPNE   Albert Hugh Smith, *English Place-Name Elements*
               (English Place-Name Soc. 25–26, 1956)

Gawain   *Sir Gawain and the Green Knight* in *Pearl, Cleanness,*
               Patience, Sir Gawain and the Green Knight, ed. A.C.
               Cawley and J.J. Anderson (London: Dent, 1962):
               159–254.

GH   *Gesta Herwardi* in Geoffrey Gaimar, *Lestorie des*
               Engles, ed. Thomas Duffus Hardy and Charles Trice
               Martin (Rolls Series 91, 1888–89): 1.339–404 with
               translation in Michael Swanton, Stephen Knight and
               Thomas Ohlgren (eds) *Robin Hood and Other Outlaw*
               Tales (Western Michigan University Press, 1997):
               633–37

HA   John of Tynemouth, *Historia aurea* in *Chronicon domini*
               Walteri de Hemingburgh de gestis regum Angliae, ed. Hans
               Claude Hamilton (English Historical Soc., 1848–9)
               2.297–426.

HRA (1–2)   William of Newburgh books 1 and 2, *The History*
               of English Affairs, ed., tr. Peter Walsh and Michael
               Kennedy (Warminster: Aris & Phillips, 1988–2007).

HRA (3–5)   William of Newburgh books 3 to 5 in Richard
               Howlett, ed., *Chronicles of the Reigns of Stephen, Henry II*
               and Richard I (Rolls Series 82, 1884–9) 1.203–408,
               2.415–500 with translation in Joseph Stevenson,
               The Church Historians of England (London: Seeleys,
               1853–8): 4:2.656–61.

IC   Gerald of Wales, *Itinerarium Cambrie* in *Itinerarium*
               Kambriae et Descriptio Kambriae, ed. James Dimock
               (Rolls Series 21:6, 1868): 3–152 with translation in
               The Journey Through Wales and the Description of Wales,
               tr. Lewis Thorpe (Harmondsworth: Penguin, 1978):
               63–209.

L. Bartholomew   *Vita S. Bartholomaei* in Simeon of Durham, *Symeonis monachi opera omnia*, ed. Thomas Arnold (Rolls Series 75, 1882): 1.295–325.

L. Cuthbert   *The Life of St. Cuthbert in English Verse, c.1450*, ed. Joseph Thomas Fowler (Surtees Soc. 87, 1891).

L. Godric   Reginald of Durham, *The Life and Miracles of Saint Godric, Hermit of Finchale*, ed., tr. Margaret Coombe (Oxford University Press, 2022).

L Hugh   Adam of Eynsham, *Magna vita S. Hugonis episcopi Lincolniensis*, ed. James F. Dimock (Rolls Series 37, 1864).

L. Kenelm   Goscelin, *Vita et Miracula S. Kenelmi* in Rosalind Love, *Three Eleventh-Century Anglo-Latin Saints' Lives* (Oxford: Clarendon, 1996): 49–89.

L. Samson   *La très ancienne vie inedite de S. Samson, premier évêque de Dol en Bretagne*, ed. François Plaine (Paris: Bray & Retaux, 1998) with translation in *The Life of St Samson of Dol*, tr. Thomas Taylor (Soc. for Promoting Christian Knowledge, 1925).

LE   *Liber exemplorum ad usum praedicantium*, ed. Andrew George Little (Aberdeen University Press, 1908) with translation in David Jones, *Friars' Tales: Thirteenth-Century* Exempla *from the British Isles* (Manchester University Press, 2011): 27–153.

Lanercost   *Chronicon de Lanercost*, ed. Joseph Stevenson (Maitland Club, 1839) with partial translation in *The Chronicle of Lanercost*, tr. Herbert Maxwell (Glasgow: James Maclehose, 1913).

M. Æbbe   Bartlett, Robert (ed., tr.), *The Miracles of Saint Æbbe of Coldingham and Saint Margaret of Scotland* (Oxford: Clarendon, 2003).

M. Æthelthryth   Book of Miracles incorporated into *Liber Eliensis* ed. Ernest Oscar Blake (Royal Historical Society, Camden 3rd Series 92, 1962) with translation in *Liber Eliensis: A History of the Isle of Ely from the Seventh Century to the Twelfth*, tr. Janet Fairweather (Woodbridge: Boydell, 2005).

M. Aldhelm   Winterbottom, Michael, 'An edition of Faricius, *Vita S. Aldhelmi*', *J. of Medieval Latin* 15 (2005): 93–147.

M. Bartholomew   *Liber fundacionis ecclesie Sancti Bartholomei Londoniarum,*

<table>
<tr><td></td><td>London, British Library MS Vespasian B. IX, unedited with translation in Edward A. Webb, The Book of the Foundation of the Church of St. Bartholomew the Apostle (Oxford University Press, 1923).</td></tr>
<tr><td>M. Cuthbert (Durham)</td><td>Reginald of Durham, Libellus de admirandis beati Cuthberti virtutibus, ed. James Raine (Surtees Soc. 1, 1835) with partial translation in Haki Antonsson, Sally Crumplin, and Aidan Conti, 'A Norwegian in Durham: an anatomy of a miracle in Reginald of Durham's Libellus de admirandis Beati Cuthberti', 195–226 of Smith, Taylor and Williams, West over Sea (2007).</td></tr>
<tr><td>M. Cuthbert (Farne)</td><td>Edmund Craster, 'The miracles of St Cuthbert at Farne', Analecta Bollandiana 70 (1952): 5–19 with translation in Edmund Craster, 'The miracles of Farne', Archaeologia Aeliana 4th ser 29 (1951): 93–107.</td></tr>
<tr><td>M. Dunstan</td><td>Osbern, Liber miraculorum beatissimi patris nostri Dunstani in William Stubbs, ed., Memorials of Saint Dunstan, Archbishop of Canterbury (Rolls Series 63, 1874): 129–61.</td></tr>
<tr><td>M. Edmund</td><td>Herman the Archdeacon and Goscelin of Saint-Bertin, Miracles of St Edmund, ed., tr. Tom Licence (Oxford: Clarendon, 2014).</td></tr>
<tr><td>M. Frideswide</td><td>Acta Sanctorum: Octobris VIII (Paris: Victor Palmé, 1863–70): 569–89.</td></tr>
<tr><td>M. Gilbert</td><td>The Book of St Gilbert, ed., tr. Raymond Foreville and Gillian Keir (Oxford: Clarendon, 1987).</td></tr>
<tr><td>M. Godric</td><td>Reginald of Durham, The Life and Miracles of Saint Godric, Hermit of Finchale, ed., tr. Margaret Coombe (Oxford University Press, 2022).</td></tr>
<tr><td>M. Hand of James</td><td>Miracles in Gloucester, Dean and Chapter, MS 1 fols 171v–75v, unedited with translation in Brian Kemp, 'The miracles of the hand of St James', Berkshire Archaeological J. 65 (1970): 1–19.</td></tr>
<tr><td>M. Henry of Coquet</td><td>Acta Sanctorum: Januarii II (Paris: Victor Palmé, 1863–70): 424–6.</td></tr>
<tr><td>M. Henry VI</td><td>The Miracles of King Henry VI, ed., tr. Ronald Knox and Shane Leslie (Cambridge University Press, 1923) and Henrici VI Angliae regis miracula postuma, ed. Paul Grosjean (Société des Bollandistes, 1935).</td></tr>
</table>

M. Hugh   Gerald of Wales, *The Life of St Hugh of Avalon, Bishop of Lincoln 1186–1200*, ed., tr. Richard Morgan Loomis (New York: Garland, 1985).

M. Ithamar   Denis, Bethell, 'The miracles of St Ithamar', *Analecta Bollandiana* 89 (1971): 421–37.

M. Ive (Goscelin)   Goscelin, *Miracula S. Ivonis* in *Chronicon abbatiae Rameseiensis*, ed. W. Dunn Macray (Rolls Series 83, 1886): lix–lxxxiv.

M. Ive (John)   *De sancto Yvone episcopo et confessore* in *Nova Legenda Anglie, as Collected by John of Tynemouth, John Capgrave, and Others*, ed. Carl Horstmann (Oxford: Clarendon, 1901): 2.86–90.

M. John of Beverley   *Alia Miracula* in Susan Wilson, 'The Cult of St John of Beverley', PhD thesis, University of Southampton, 2000, with translation in Susan Wilson, *The Life and After-Life of St John of Beverley: The Evolution of the Cult of an Anglo-Saxon Saint* (Aldershot: Ashgate, 2006).

M. Margaret   Bartlett, Robert (ed., tr.), *The Miracles of Saint Æbbe of Coldingham and Saint Margaret of Scotland* (Oxford: Clarendon, 2003).

M. Mildthryth   Rollason, David, 'Goscelin of Canterbury's account of the translation and miracles of St Mildrith', *Mediaeval Studies* 48 (1986): 139–210.

M. Modwenna   Geoffrey of Burton, *Life and Miracles of St Modwenna*, ed., tr. Robert Bartlett (Oxford: Clarendon, 2002).

M. Nectan   Paul Grosjean, 'Vie de S. Rumon; vie, invention et miracles de S. Nectan', *Analecta Bollandiana* 71 (1953): 359–414 at 405–14 with translation in Gilbert H. Doble, *The Saints of Cornwall V: Saints of Mid-Cornwall* (Dean & Chapter of Truro, 1970): 65–78.

M. Osmund   Malden, Arthur Russell (ed.), *The Canonization of St Osmund* (Salisbury: Bennett Brothers, 1901).

M. Oswine   *Vita Oswini Regis* in James Raine, *Miscellanea Biographica* (Surtees Soc. 8, 1838): 1–59

M. Simon de Montfort   *Miracles of Simon de Montfort* in James Orchard Halliwell, ed., *The Chronicle of William de Rishanger of the Barons' Wars and the Miracles of Simon de Montfort* (Camden Soc. 1st ser 15, 1840): 67–110.

M. Swithun   Lantfred of Winchester, *Translatio et miracula*

| | *S. Swithuni* in Michael Lapidge, *The Cult of St Swithun* (Oxford: Clarendon, 2003): 217–334. |

M. Thomas (Benedict)   Benedict of Peterborough, *Miracula Sancti Thomae Cantuarensis* in Robertson, James Craigie, *Materials for the History of Thomas Becket* (Rolls Series 61, 1875–76): 2.21–281

M. Thomas (William)   William of Canterbury, *Vita et passio S. Thomae* in Robertson, James Craigie, *Materials for the History of Thomas Becket* (Rolls Series 61, 1875–76): 1.1–546

M. Thomas Cantilupe   *Acta Sanctorum: Octobris I* (Paris: Victor Palmé, 1863–70): 549–629.

M. Wihtburh   *Vita Sancte Witburge virginis* in Goscelin of Saint-Bertin, *The Hagiography of the Female Saints of Ely*, ed., tr. Rosalind Love (Oxford: Clarendon, 2004): 53–93.

M. William   Thomas of Monmouth, *The Life and Miracles of St William of Norwich*, ed. Augustus Jessopp and Montague Rhodes James (Cambridge University Press, 1896).

M. Wulfstan   William of Malmesbury, *Vita Wulfstani*, ed. Reginald Darlington (Royal Historical Soc. Camden Series 40, 1928).

OS   Ordnance Survey

PN Berks   Margaret Gelling, *The Place-Names of Berkshire* (English Place-Name Soc. 49–51, 1973–76).

PN Bucks   Allen Mawer and Frank Stenton, *The Place-Names of Buckinghamshire* (English Place-Name Soc. 2, 1925)

PN Cambs   Percy Reaney, *The Place-Names of Cambridgeshire* (English Place-Name Soc. 19, 1943).

PN Cheshire   John McNeill Dodgson, and Alexander Rumble, *The Place-Names of Cheshire* (English Place-Name Soc. 44–48, 54, 74, 1970–97).

PN Cumb   Aileen M. Armstrong *et al.*, *The Place-Names of Cumberland* (English Place-Name Soc. 20–22, 1950–52).

PN Derbs   Kenneth Cameron, *The Place-Names of Derbyshire* (English Place-Name Soc. 27–29, 1959).

PN Devon   John Gover, Allen Mawer and Frank Stenton, *The Place-Names of Devon* (English Place-Name Soc. 8–9, 1931–32).

PN Dorset   David Mills, *The Place-Names of Dorset* (English Place-Name Soc. 52–3, 59/60, 86/7, 94, 1977–2020).

PN Essex   Percy Reaney, *The Place-Names of Essex* (English Place-Name Soc. 12, 1935).

PN Glos   Albert Hugh Smith, *The Place-Names of Gloucestershire* (English Place-Name Soc. 38–41, 1964–65).

PN Herts   John Gover, Allen Mawer and Frank Stenton, *The Place-Names of Hertfordshire* (English Place-Name Soc. 15, 1938).

PN Leics   Barrie Cox, *The Place-Names of Leicestershire* (English Place-Name Soc. 75, 78, 81, 84, 85, 90, 91, 93, 1998–2019).

PN Lincs   Kenneth Cameron, *The Place-Names of Lincolnshire* (English Place-Name Soc. 58, 64/5, 66, 71, 73, 77, 1985–2001 and ongoing).

PN Midd   John Gover, Allen Mawer and Frank Stenton, *The Place-Names of Middlesex apart from the City of London* (English Place-Name Soc. 18, 1942).

PN Norfolk   Karl Inge Sandred and Bengt Lindström, *The Place-Names of Norfolk* (English Place-Name Soc. 61, 72, 79, 1989–2002 and ongoing).

PN Northants   John Gover, Allen Mawer and Frank Stenton, *The Place-Names of Northamptonshire* (English Place-Name Soc. 10, 1933).

PN Notts   John Gover, Allen Mawer and Frank Stenton, *The Place-Names of Nottinghamshire* (English Place-Name Soc. 17, 1940).

PN Oxon   Margaret Gelling, *The Place-Names of Oxfordshire* (English Place-Name Soc. 23–24, 1953).

PN Rutland   Barrie Cox, *The Place-Names of Rutland* (English Place-Name Soc. 67–69, 1989–92).

PN Shropshire   Margaret Gelling *et al.*, *The Place-Names of Shropshire* (English Place-Name Soc. 62/3, 70, 76, 80, 82, 89, 1990–2012 and ongoing).

PN Surrey   John Gover, Allen Mawer and Frank Stenton, *The Place-Names of Surrey* (English Place-Name Soc. 11, 1934).

PN Sussex   Allen Mawer and Frank Stenton, *The Place-Names of Sussex* (English Place-Name Soc. 6–7, 1929–30).

PN Warks   John Gover, Allen Mawer and Frank Stenton,

    The Place-Names of Warwickshire (English Place-Name Soc. 13, 1936).

PN Westm   Albert Hugh Smith, *The Place-Names of Westmorland* (English Place-Name Soc. 42–43, 1967).

PN Wilts   John Gover, Allen Mawer and Frank Stenton, *The Place-Names of Wiltshire* (English Place-Name Soc. 16, 1939).

PN Worcs   Allen Mawer and Frederick T.S. Houghton, *The Place-Names of Worcestershire* (English Place-Name Soc. 4, 1927).

PN Yorks ER   Albert Hugh Smith, *The Place-Names of the East Riding of Yorkshire and York* (English Place-Name Soc. 14, 1937).

PN Yorks NR   Albert Hugh Smith, *The Place-Names of the North Riding of Yorkshire* (English Place-Name Soc. 5, 1928).

PN Yorks WR   Albert Hugh Smith, *The Place-Names of the West Riding of Yorkshire* (English Place-Name Soc. 30–37, 1961–63).

S   Peter Sawyer, *Anglo-Saxon Charters: An Annotated List and Bibliography* (Royal Historical Soc., 1968) supplemented by https://esawyer.lib.cam.ac.uk.

TM   Tithe Map and Apportionment

TNA   The National Archives

VCH   *Victoria County History*, as detailed in https://www.history.ac.uk/research/victoria-county-history.

VEPN   David Parsons and Tania Styles, *The Vocabulary of English Place-Names* (Centre for English Name-Studies, 1997–2004 and ongoing).

WB   *The Holy Bible in the Earliest English Versions made from the Latin Vulgate by John Wycliffe and his Followers*, ed Josiah Forshall and Frederick Madden (Oxford University Press, 1850).

WC   *Warkworth's Chronicle* in Lister Matheson, ed., *Death and Dissent: The Dethe of the Kynge of Scotis and 'Warkworth's' Chronicle, the Chronicle Attributed to John Warkworth, Master of Peterborough, Cambridge* (Boydell, Cambridge, 1999): 93–124.

Bibliography

Addy, Sidney Oldall, *A Glossary of Words Used in the Neighbourhood of Sheffield* (English Dialect Soc., 1888).

Ælfric, *Old English Lives of Saints*, ed., tr. Mary Clayton and Juliet Mullins (Harvard University Press, 2019).

Allen, Hope Emily, 'Influence of superstition on vocabulary: two related examples I', *Publications of the Modern Language Association* 50 (1935): 1033–46. https://doi.org/10.2307/458106

Allen, Hope Emily, 'Influence of superstition on vocabulary: two related examples II', *Publications of the Modern Language Association* 51 (1936): 904–20. https://doi.org/10.2307/458074

Allies, Jabez, *On the Ignis Fatuus or Will-o'-the-Wisp and the Fairies* (London: Simpkin Marshall, 1846).

Allies, Jabez, *On the Ancient British, Roman and Saxon Antiquities and Folk-Lore of Worcestershire* (London: J.H. Parker, 1852).

Arnott, William George, *The Place-Names of the Deben Valley Parishes* (Ipswich: Norman Adlard, 1946).

Atkinson, John C., *Forty Years in a Moorland Parish: Reminiscences and Researches in Danby in Cleveland* (London: Macmillan, 1891).

Attree, Frederick William Town, *Notes of Post Mortem Inquisitions Taken in Sussex, 1 Henry VII to 1649* (Sussex Record Soc. 14, 1912).

Austen, David, and David Hill, 'The boundaries of Itchen and Crondall', *Proc. of the Hampshire Field Club and Archaeological Soc.* 27 (1972): 63–64.

Baines, Arnold, 'The Winslow charter of 792 and the boundaries of Granborough', *Records of Bucks* 22 (1980): 1–18.

Baines, Arnold, 'The furlong-names of Chicheley', *Records of Bucks* 39 (1997): 1–17.

Bannister, Arthur Thomas, *The Place-Names of Herefordshire* (Privately, 1916).

Bannister, Arthur Thomas, 'Visitation returns of the diocese of Hereford in 1397: I', *English Historical Review* 44 (1929): 279–89. https://doi.org/10.1093/ehr/XLIV.CLXXIV.279

Baring-Gould, Sabine, and John Fisher, *The Lives of the British Saints* (London: Charles Clark, 1907–13).

Barnes, Rex Delno, 'Haunting Matters: Demonic Infestation in Northern Europe, 1400–1600', PhD thesis, Columbia University, 2019.

Bartlett, Robert, *Gerald of Wales, 1146–1223* (Oxford: Clarendon, 1982).

Bartlett, Robert, *England under the Norman and Angevin Kings, 1075–1225* (Oxford: Clarendon, 2000). https://doi.org/10.1093/oso/9780198227410.001.0001

Bathurst, William Hiley, *Roman Antiquities at Lydney Park, Gloucestershire* (London: Longmans Green & Co., 1879).

Batten, John, *et al.* (eds), *Two Cartularies of the Augustinian Priory of Bruton and the Cluniac Priory of Montacute* (Somerset Record Soc. 8, 1894).

Battles, Paul, 'Dwarfs in Germanic literature: *Deutsche Mythologie* or Grimm's myths?', 29–82 of Shippey, *Shadow-Walkers* (2005).

Baxter, Stephen, *et al.* (eds), *Early Medieval Studies in Memory of Patrick Wormald* (Farnham: Ashgate, 2009).

Beare, Thomas, 'Particular description of a barrow lately explored', *Gentleman's Magazine* 1st ser 59 (1789): 392–93.

Bede, *Ecclesiastical History of the English People*, ed., tr. Bertram Colgrave and Roger Mynors (Oxford: Clarendon, 1969). https://doi.org/10.1093/oseo/instance.00258633

Beowulf, ed. Charles Leslie Wrenn and Whitney French Bolton, tr. Seamus Heaney (London: Faber & Faber, 2007).

Blair, John, 'The dangerous dead in early medieval England', 539–59 of Baxter *et al.*, *Early Medieval Studies* (2009).

Blakiston, Herbert, 'Two more medieval ghost stories', *English Historical Review* 38 (1923): 85–87. https://doi.org/10.1093/ehr/XXXVIII.CXLIX.85

Blomefield, Francis, *An Essay Towards a Topographical History of the County of Norfolk* (London: William Miller, 1805–10).

Bøgholm, Niels, Aage Brusendorff and Carl Adolf Bodelsen, eds, *A Grammatical Miscellany Offered to Otto Jesperson on his Seventieth Birthday* (London: George Allen & Unwin, 1930).

Bord, Janet, *The Traveller's Guide to Fairy Sites* (Glastonbury: Gothic Image, 2004).

Bower, Irene May, 'The Place-Names of Lindsey (North Lincolnshire)', PhD thesis, University of Leeds, 1940.

Bradley, Henry, 'English place-names', *Essays and Studies by Members of the English Association* 1 (1910): 7–41.

Briggs, Katharine M., *A Dictionary of Fairies* (London: Allen Lane, 1976).

Briggs, Keith, and Kelly Kilpatrick, *A Dictionary of Suffolk Place-Names* (English Place-Name Soc., Popular Series 6, 2016).

Bromyard, John, *Summa Praedicantium* (Venice: Dominico Nicolino, 1586).

Brown, Jane, *Lancelot 'Capability' Brown: The Omnipotent Magician 1716–1783* (London: Pimlico, 2012).

Brown, Theo, *The Fate of the Dead: A Study in Folk Eschatology in the West Country after the Reformation* (Folklore Soc., 1979).

Buchanan-Dunlop, Robert, *Ham: The Story of a Wiltshire Village* (Privately, 2011).

Buckinghamshire Sessions Records, ed. William Le Hardy and Geoffrey Reckitt (Buckinghamshire County Council, 1933–80).

Burne, Charlotte, 'Scraps of folklore collected by John Philipps Emslie', *Folklore* 26 (1915): 153–70. https://doi.org/10.1080/0015587X.1915.9718868

Caesarius of Heisterbach, *The Dialogue on Miracles*, tr. Henry von Essen Scott and C.C. Swinton Bland (New York Harcourt: Brace & Co, 1929).

Camden, William, *Britannia* (London: Ralph Newbury, 1586).

Capgrave, John, *The Chronicle of England*, ed. Francis Charles Hingeston (Rolls Series 1, 1858).

Carpenter, David, 'Abbot Ralph of Coggeshall's account of the last years of King Richard and the first years of King John', *English Historical Review* 113 (1998): 1210–30. https://doi.org/10.1093/ehr/113.454.1210

The Cartularies of Southwick Priory, ed. Katherine Hanna (Hampshire County Council, Hampshire Record Series 9–10, 1988–9).

Cartularium Abbathiae de Whiteby, ed. John Christopher Atkinson (Surtees Soc. 69, 72, 1879).

Cartularium Prioratus de Gyseburne, ed. William Brown (Surtees Soc. 86, 89, 1889–94).

The Cartulary of Alvingham Priory, ed. Jill Redford (Lincoln Record Soc., Kathleen Major Series 2, 2018).

Cartulary of Oseney Abbey, ed. H.E. Salter (Oxford Historical Soc. 89–91, 97–8, 101, 1929–36).

Cavill, Paul, *A New Dictionary of English Field-Names* (English Place-Name Soc., 2018).

Chadwick, Nora, 'Norse ghosts: a study in the *Draugr* and the *Haugbúi*', *Folklore* 57 (1946): 50–65. https://doi.org/10.1080/0015587X.1946.9717812

Chambers, Raymund Wilson, *Beowulf: An Introduction to the Study of the Poem* (Cambridge University Press, 1921).

Chartulary of Cockersand Abbey, ed. William Farrer (Chetham Soc. 2nd ser 38–40, 43, 56–7, 64, 1898–1909).

Chaucer, Geoffrey, *The Complete Works of Geoffrey Chaucer*, ed. Fred Norris Robinson (Oxford University Press, 1966).

Chibnall, Albert Charles, *Sherington: Fiefs and Fields of a Buckinghamshire Village* (Cambridge University Press, 1965).

Child, Francis James, *The English and Scottish Popular Ballads* (Boston MA: Houghton, Mifflin & Co, 1882–98).

Childs, Wendy, '"Welcome, my brother": Edward II, John of Powderham and the chronicles, 1318', 150–54 of Wood and Loud, *Church and Chronicle in the Middle Ages* (1991).

Chronica de Mailros, ed. Joseph Stevenson (Bannatyne Club, 1835).

The Chronicle of Battel Abbey, from 1066 to 1176, tr. Mark Antony Lower (London: John Russell Smith, 1851).

Coates, Richard, *Hampshire Place-Names* (Southampton: Ensign, 1989).

Cockin, Tim, *The Staffordshire Encyclopedia* (Barlaston: Malthouse Press, 2000).

Cole, Ann, '*Ersc*: distribution and use of this Old English place-name element', *Journal of the English Place-Name Soc.* 32 (1999–2000): 27–29.

Cole, Ann, 'Two Chiltern place-names reconsidered: Elvendon and Misbourne', *Journal of the English Place-Name Soc.* 50 (2018): 65–73.

Conti, Fabrizio (ed.), *Civilizations of the Supernatural: Witchcraft, Ritual, and Religious Experience in Late Antique, Medieval and Renaissance Traditions* (Budapest: Trivent, 2020). https://doi.org/10.22618/TP.HMWR.20201

Cooper, George Miles, 'Researches into the history of the Abbey of Otteham', *Sussex Archaeological Collections* 5 (1852): 155–75.

Coplestone-Crow, Bruce, *Herefordshire Place-Names* (BAR, British Series 214, 1989).

The Coucher Book of Selby, ed. J.T. Fowler (Yorkshire Archaeological Soc., Record Series 10, 1891).

The Coucher Book, or Chartulary, of Whalley Abbey, ed. William Adam Hulton (Chetham Soc. 10–11, 16, 20, 1847–9).

Cox, Barrie, 'Dimmingsdale', 350–51 of Padel and Parsons, *Commodity of Good Names* (2008).

Cranworth, Emily Francis, 'East Anglian superstitions: II', *Eastern Counties Magazine* 1 (1900–1): 169–75.

Crossley, Ely Wilkinson, *et al.* (eds) *Miscellanea* (Yorkshire Archaeological Soc., Record Series 61, 74, 80, 94 116, 118, 1920–53).

Crossley-Holland, Kevin, *The Green Children* (London: Macmillan, 1966).

Crossman, William, 'St Cuthbert's island', *Proc. of the Soc. of Antiquaries of Newcastle-upon-Tyne* 2nd ser 3 (1888): 408–10.

Darby, Stephen, *Place and Field Names, Cookham Parish, Berks* (Privately, 1899).

Davies, James Conway (ed.), *Studies Presented to Sir Hilary Jenkinson* (Oxford University Press, 1957).

Deedes, Cecil (ed.), *Register or Memorial of Ewell* (London: Mitchell Hughes & Clarke, 1913).

Denham, Michael Aislabie, *The Denham Tracts*, ed. James Hardy (Folklore Soc., 1892).

Dickins, Bruce, 'Gerard as a goblin name', *Times Literary Supplement* 1 Feb 1941: 55.

Dickins, Bruce, 'Yorkshire hobs', *Transactions of the Yorkshire Dialect Soc.* 7 (1942): 9–23.

Dobbie, Elliott Van Kirk (ed.), *The Anglo-Saxon Minor Poems* (Columbia University Press, 1942).

Dobbie, B.M. Willmott, *An English Rural Community: Batheaston with St. Catherine* (Bath University Press, 1969).

Dodgson, John McNeil, and Patsy Khaliq, 'Addenda and corrigenda to the Survey of English Place-Names: I', *Journal of the English Place-Name Soc.* 2 (1969–70): 18–74.

The Dorset Lay Subsidy Roll of 1327, ed. Alexander Rumble (Dorset Record Soc. 6, 1980).

Dugdale, Graham K., *Walks in Mysterious North Lakeland* (Wilmslow: Sigma, 1998).

Dugdale, William, *Monasticon Anglicanum: A History of the Abbies and Other Monasteries in England and Wales*, ed. John Caley, Henry Ellis & Bulkeley Bandinel (London: Longman, 1817–30).

Duignan, William Henry, *Warwickshire Place-Names* (London: Henry Frowde, 1912). https://doi.org/10.1093/nq/s11-V.126.413f

af Edholm, Klas Wikström, *et al.* (eds), *Myth, Materiality and Lived Religion in Merovingian and Viking Scandinavia* (Stockholm University Press, 2019).

Edwards, Gillian, *Hobgoblin and Sweet Puck* (London: Geoffrey Bles, 1974).

Ekwall, Eilert, *The Place-Names of Lancashire* (Manchester University Press, 1922).

Ekwall, Eilert, *The Concise Oxford Dictionary of English Place-Names* (Oxford: Clarendon, 4th edition, 1960).

Ellerington, Enoch, 'The derivation of the place-name Puckington', *Somerset & Dorset Notes & Queries* 34 (1996–2000): 75–8.

Fasciculus Morum: A Fourteenth-Century Preacher's Handbook, ed., tr. Siegfried Wenzel (Pennsylvania State University Press, 1989).

Fellows-Jensen, Gillian, 'Place-names and word geography: some words of warning' 215–24 of Laing & Williamson, *Speaking in Our Tongues* (1994).

Field, John, *English Field-Names: A Dictionary* (Newton Abbot: David & Charles, 1972).

Finberg, Herbert Patrick Reginald, *The Early Charters of the West Midlands* (Leicester University Press, 1972).

Finberg, Herbert Patrick Reginald, 'Some early Tavistock charters', *English Historical Review* 62 (1947): 352–77. https://doi.org/10.1093/ehr/LXII.CCXLIV.352

Finucane, Ronald, *Miracles and Pilgrims: Popular Beliefs in Medieval England* (London: J.M. Dent, 1977).

Firth, Chris, *The Fairies and Merfolk of North Yorkshire* (Whitby: Electraglade, 2020).

Forby, Robert, *The Vocabulary of East Anglia* (London: J.B. Nichols & Son, 1830).

Forward, Eleanor J., 'Place-names of the Whittlewood Area', PhD thesis, University of Nottingham, 2009.

Foxall, Hugh Denis George, *Shropshire Field-Names* (Shropshire Archaeological Soc., 1980).

Fraaije, Karel, 'Wicked dreams, teary eyes, and salty noses: elvish pathologies and folkloric exorcisms from medieval Germanic Europe', *Incantatio* 8 (2019): 29–58. https://doi.org/10.7592/Incantatio2019_8_Fraaije

Fraser, William, *Field-Names in South Derbyshire* (Ipswich: Norman Adlard, 1947).

Freeman, Elizabeth, 'Wonders, prodigies and marvels: unusual bodies and the fear of heresy in Ralph of Coggeshall's *Chronicon Anglicanum*', *J. of Medieval History* 26 (2000): 127–43. https://doi.org/10.1016/S0304-4181(99)00019-6

Friedman, John Block, 'Eurydice, Heurodis, and the Noon-Day Demon', *Speculum* 41 (1966): 22–29. https://doi.org/10.2307/2851843

Gambier-Parry, Thomas Robert (ed.), *A Collection of Charters Relating to Goring* (Oxfordshire Record Soc. 13–14, 1931–32).

Gardiner, Mark, 'Dales, long lands, and the medieval division of land in eastern England', *Agricultural Historical Review* 57.2 (2009): 1–14.

Gatty, Alfred, *A Life at One Living* (Worksop: Bell & Sons, 1884).

Gay, David E., 'Anglo-Saxon metrical charm 3 Against a Dwarf: a charm against witch-riding?', *Folklore* 99 (1988): 174–77. https://doi.org/10.1080/0015587X.1988.9716439

Gelling, Margaret, 'On looking into Smith's *Elements*', *Nomina* 5 (1981): 39–45.

Gelling, Margaret, *Signposts to the Past: Place-Names and the History of England* (London: J.M. Dent, 1978).

Gelling, Margaret, and Ann Cole, *The Landscape of Place-Names* (Stamford: Shaun Tyas, 2000).

Gerald of Wales, *Topographia Hibernica et Expugnatio Hibernica*, ed. James Dimock (Rolls Series 21:5, 1867).

Gervase of Tilbury, *Otia Imperialia: Recreation for an Emperor*, ed., tr. Shelagh Banks and James Binns (Oxford: Clarendon, 2002). https://doi.org/10.1093/actrade/9780198202882.book.1

Given-Wilson, Chris, *Chronicles: The Writing of History in Medieval England* (London: Hambledon & London, 2004).

Gobi, Jean, *La Scala Coeli*, ed. Marie-Anne Polo de Beaulieu (Centre National de la Recherche Scientifique, 1991).

Goetink, Glenys, 'The Wandlebury legend and Welsh romance', *Proc. of the Cambridge Antiq. Soc.* 77 (1988): 105–8.

Gollancz, Israel, 'Gringolet, Gawain's horse', *Saga Book of the Viking Club* 5 (1906): 104–9.

Gordon, Stephen, *Supernatural Encounters: Demons and the Restless Dead in Medieval England, c.1050–1450* (Abingdon: Routledge, 2020). https://doi.org/10.4324/9780429432491

Gough, Richard, *The History of Myddle*, ed. David Hey (Harmondsworth: Penguin, 1981).

Gransden, Antonia, *Historical Writing in England c.550 to c.1307* (London: Routledge & Kegan Paul, 1974).

Gray, Douglas, *Simple Forms: Essays in Medieval Popular English Literature* (Oxford University Press, 2015). https://doi.org/10.1093/acprof:oso/9780198706090.001.0001

Green, Richard Firth, *Elf Queens and Holy Friars: Fairy Beliefs and the Medieval Church* (University of Pennsylvania Press, 2016). https://doi.org/10.9783/9780812293166

Greenwell, William, *British Barrows: A Record of the Examination of Sepulchral Mounds in Various Parts of England* (Oxford: Clarendon, 1877). https://doi.org/10.5962/bhl.title.26823

Grinsell, Leslie V., *Dorset Barrows* (Dorset Natural History and Archaeological Soc., 1959).

Hadley, Christopher, *Hollow Places: An Unusual History of Land and Legend* (London: William Collins, 2019).

Hall, Alaric, 'Elves on the brain: Chaucer, Old English, and *elvish*', *Anglia* 124 (2006): 225–43. https://doi.org/10.1515/ANGL.2006.225

Hall, Alaric, 'Are there any elves in Anglo-Saxon place-names?', *Nomina* 29 (2006): 61–80. https://doi.org/10.1515/9781846155376

Hall, Alaric, *Elves in Anglo-Saxon England: Matters of Belief, Health, Gender and Identity* (Woodbridge: Boydell, 2007). https://doi.org/10.1515/9781846155376

Hall, David, and Ruth Harding 'Crick parish survey, SP 589723', *CBA Group 9 Newsletter: A Review of Archaeology in Bedfordshire, Buckinghamshire, Northamptonshire and Oxfordshire* 7 (1977): 29–31.

Hall, Richard, and Mark Whyman, 'Settlement and monasticism at Ripon, North Yorkshire, from the 7th to 11th centuries AD', *Medieval Archaeology* 40 (1996): 62–150. https://doi.org/10.1080/00766097.1996.11735599

Hancock, Frederick, *Minehead in the County of Somerset: A History of the Parish, the Manor, and the Port* (Taunton: Athenaeum, 1903).

Harilla, Claire Louise, 'Politics and Sainthood: Literary Representations of St Margaret of Scotland in England and Scotland', PhD thesis, University of Birmingham, 2017.

Harrod, Henry, *Report on the Records of the Borough of Colchester* (Borough of Colchester, 1865).

Harrod, William, *The History of Mansfield and its Environs* (Mansfield: W. Harrod, 1801).

Hawker-Yates, Lily Alice Gwendoline, 'Barrows in the Cultural Imagination of Later Medieval England', PhD thesis, Canterbury Christ Church University, 2019.

Hayman, Richard, *Trees: Woodlands and Western Civilization* (London: Hambledon & London, 2003).

Heath, Richard, *The English Peasant: Studies—Historical, Local, and Biographical* (London: T. Fisher Unwin, 1893).

Henderson, Lizanne, and Edward J. Cowan, *Scottish Fairy Belief: A History* (East Linton: Tuckwell, 2001).

Herbert, John Alexander, *Catalogue of Romances in the Department of Manuscripts: III* (British Museum, 1910).

Higden, Ralph, *Polychronicon Ranulphi Higden monachi Cestrensis*, tr. John Trevisa, ed. Churchill Babington and Joseph Rawson Lumby (Rolls Series 41, 1865–86).

Hill, James William Francis, *Medieval Lincoln* (Cambridge University Press, 1948).

Hodgson, John, *History of Northumberland* (Newcastle: Thomas and James Pigg, 1820–58).

Holland, Alexander William, 'John Bromyard's *Summa Praedicantium*: An Exploration of Late-Medieval Falsity through a Fourteenth-Century Preaching Handbook', PhD thesis, University of Kent, 2018.

Hollis, Stephanie, *Writing the Wilton Women: Goscelin's Life of Edith and* Liber confortatorius (Turnhout: Brepols, 2004).

Hooke, Della, 'Rivers, wells and springs in Anglo-Saxon England: water in sacred and mystical contexts', 107–35 of Hyer & Hooke, *Water and the Environment* (2017). https://doi.org/10.2307/j.ctt1ps31q2.11

Horovitz, David, *The Place-Names of Staffordshire* (Privately, 2005).

Hough, Carole, 'The place-name Fritwell', *Journal of the English Place-Name Soc.* 29 (1996): 65–69. https://doi.org/10.1080/00393279708588196

Hough, Carole, 'Carolside in Berwickshire and *Carelholpit* in Lincolnshire', *Nomina* 23 (2000): 79–86.

Hough, Carole, 'Dwerryhouse in Lancashire', *Notes & Queries* 248 (2003): 3–5. https://doi.org/10.1093/nq/50.1.3

Hough, Carole, 'The name-type Fritwell', *Journal of the English Place-Name Soc.* 42 (2010): 87–89.

Hough, Carole, 'Ælfric of Eynsham, Pucklechurch, and evidence for fallow deer in Anglo-Saxon England', *Nomina* 35 (2012): 103–30.

Hreinsson, Viðar (ed.), *The Complete Sagas of Icelanders* (Reykjavik: Leifur Eiríksson Publishing, 1997).

Hudson, Anne, and Pamela Gradon (eds), *English Wycliffite Sermons* (Oxford: Clarendon, 1983–96).

Hudson, William, *The Three Earliest Subsidies for the County of Sussex in the Years 1296, 1327, 1332* (Sussex Record Soc. 10, 1909).

Hunt, Tony, *Plant Names of Medieval England* (Woodbridge: D.S. Brewer, 1989).

Hutton, Ronald, *Queens of the Wild: Pagan Goddesses in Christian Europe—An Investigation* (Yale University Press, 2022). https://doi.org/10.12987/9780300265279

Hyer, Maren Clegg, and Della Hooke (eds), *Water and the Environment in the Anglo-Saxon World* (Liverpool University Press, 2017). https://doi.org/10.2307/j.ctt1ps31q2

Insley, John, 'Addenda to the Survey of English Place-Names: personal names in field and minor names', *Journal of the English Place-Name Soc.* 10 (1977–8): 41–72.

Jacobsson, Mattias, *Wells, Meres, and Pools: Hydronymic Terms in the Anglo-Saxon Landscape* (Uppsala University Press, 1997).

Jolly, Karen Louise, *Popular Religion in Late Saxon England: Elf Charms in Context* (University of North Carolina Press, 1996).

Jones, Christopher A., 'Furies, monks and folklore in the earliest Miracula of Saint Swithun', *Journal of English and Germanic Philology* 113 (2014): 407–42. https://doi.org/10.5406/jenglgermphil.113.4.0407

Julian of Norwich, *A Revelation of Love*, ed. Marion Glasscoe (University of Exeter Press, 1986).

Katajala-Peltomaa, Sari, Jenni Kuuliala and Iona McCleery (eds), *A Companion to Medieval Miracle Collections* (Leiden: Brill, 2021). https://doi.org/10.1163/9789004468498

Kaufman, Alexander, '"And many oþer diuerse tokens …": portents and wonders in "Warkworth's" *Chronicle*', 49–63 of Rajsic, Kooper and Hoche, *The Prose* Brut *and Other Late Medieval Chronicles* (2016).

Keightley, Thomas, *The Fairy Mythology* (London: H.G. Bohn, 1850).

Kift, Mary, 'Some Anglo-Saxon field names in the old parish of Caversham and their probable meanings', *South Oxfordshire Archaeological Group Bulletin* 49 (1993): 31–3.

Kilby, Susan, 'Encountering the Environment: Rural Communities in England, 1086–1348', PhD thesis, University of Leicester, 2013.

Kirby's Quest for Somerset, ed. Francis Henry Dickinson (Somerset Record Soc. 3, 1889).

Kittredge, George Lyman, *Witchcraft in Old and New England* (Harvard University Press, 1929). https://doi.org/10.4159/harvard.9780674182325

Kökeritz, Helge, *The Place-Names of the Isle of Wight* (Uppsala University Press, 1940).

Koopmans, Rachel, *Wonderful to Relate: Miracle Stories and Miracle Collecting in High Medieval England* (University of Philadelphia Press, 2011). https://doi.org/10.9783/9780812206999

Kristensson, Gillis, 'The place-name Scugger Ho (Cumberland)', *Notes & Queries* 231 (1986): 2–3.

Lacey, Eric, '*Wælcyrian* in the water meadows: Lantfred's Furies', 192–213 of Lavelle, Roffey and Weikert, *Early Medieval Winchester* (2021). https://doi.org/10.2307/j.ctv1wvndd9.16

Laing, Margaret, and Keith Williamson (eds), *Speaking in Our Tongues: Proceedings of a Colloquium on Medieval Dialectology and Related Disciplines* (Cambridge: Boydell & Brewer, 1994).

Lambert, Henry, *Woodmansterne: A Brief Historical Account* (Sutton: William Pile, 1931).

Lambert, Uvedale, *Godstone: A Parish History* (Privately, 1929).

Lapidge, Michael, *Anglo-Latin Literature 600–899* (London: Hambledon, 1996).

Lapidge, Michael, *The Cult of St Swithun* (Oxford: Clarendon, 2003).

Latham, Charlotte 'Some West Sussex superstitions lingering in 1868', *Folk-Lore Record* 1 (1878): 1–67. https://doi.org/10.1080/17441994.1878.10602542

Lavelle, Ryan, Simon Roffey and Katherine Weikert (eds), *Early Medieval Winchester: Communities, Authority and Power in an Urban Space, c.800–c.1200* (Oxford: Oxbow, 2021). https://doi.org/10.2307/j.ctv1wvndd9

Lawrence, William Witherie, 'The haunted mere in *Beowulf*', *Publications of the Modern Language Association of America* 27 (1912): 208–45. https://doi.org/10.1632/456778

Lecouteux, Claude, *Phantom Armies of the Night: The Wild Hunt and the Ghostly Processions of the Undead*, tr. Jon E. Graham (Rochester VT: Inner Traditions, 2011).

Lecouteux, Claude, *The Hidden History of Elves and Dwarfs: Avatars of Invisible Realms*, tr. Jon E. Graham (Rochester VT: Inner Traditions, 2013).

Le Goff, Jacques, *The Medieval Imagination*, tr. Arthur Goldhammer (University of Chicago Press, 1988).

Leland, John, *The Itinerary of John Leland in or about the Years 1535–1543*, ed. Lucy Toulmin Smith (London: George Bell, 1906–10).

Leveson-Gower, Granville, 'Surrey etymologies, Tandridge Hundred: I', *Surrey Archaeological Collections* 6 (1874): 78–108.

Leveson-Gower, Granville, 'Surrey etymologies, Tandridge Hundred: II', *Surrey Arch. Coll.* 6 (1874): 127–226.

Liber Luciani de Laude Cestrie, ed. Marjorie Venables Taylor (Lancashire and Cheshire Record Soc. 64, 1912).

Lipson, Joel Peter, 'Supernatural Visitation in Medieval Literature', PhD thesis, University of Cambridge, 2022.

Loomis, Roger Sherman, 'King Arthur and the Antipodes', *Modern Philology* 38 (1940–1): 289–304. https://doi.org/10.1086/388484

Macculloch, John Arnott, 'The mingling of fairy and witch beliefs in sixteenth and seventeenth century Scotland', *Folk-Lore* 32 (1921): 227–44. https://doi.org/10.1080/0015587X.1921.9719207

Macfarlane, Walter, *Geographical Collections Relating to Scotland*, ed. Arthur Mitchell and James Toshach Clark (Scottish History Soc. 51–3, 1906–8).

Macleod, Donald, 'Some Heathfield place-names: III', *Sussex Notes and Queries* 1 (1926–7): 102–5.

Map, Walter, *De nugis curialium*, ed., tr. Montague Rhodes James, Christopher Brooke, and Roger Mynors (Oxford: Clarendon, 1983).

Marzella, Francesco, '*Hirsuta et cornuta cum lancea trisulcata*: three stories of witchcraft and magic in twelfth-century Britain', 221–46 of Conti, *Civilizations* (2020).

Mawer, Allen, *The Place-Names of Northumberland and Durham* (Cambridge University Press, 1920).

Mawer, Allen, and Frank Stenton, '*The Place-Names of Sussex*: corrigenda and addenda VIII', *Sussex Notes and Queries* 4 (1933): 213–14.

Maxwell-Stuart, Peter, *Satan: A Biography* (Stroud: Amberley, 2008).

McClure, Peter, 'The kinship of Jack I: pet-forms of Middle English personal names with the suffixes *-kin*, *-ke*, *-man* and *-cot*', *Nomina* 26 (2003): 93–117.

Meaney, Audrey L., '*And we forbeodað eornostlice ælcne hæðenscipe*: Wulfstan and late Anglo-Saxon and Norse "heathenism"', 461–500 of Townend, *Wulfstan, Archbishop of York* (2004). https://doi.org/10.1484/M.SEM-EB.3.3720

Michael of Northgate, *Dan Mihel's Ayenbite of Inwyt*, ed. Richard Morris and Pamela Gradon (Early English Texts Soc. 1st ser 23, 1886/1965).

Miller, Thomas, 'Grendel', *The Academy* 45 (1894): 396.

Millett, Bella, 'How green is the Green Knight?', *Nottingham Medieval Studies* 37 (1994): 137–51. https://doi.org/10.1484/J.NMS.3.231

Mills, David, *The Place-Names of Lancashire* (London: Batsford, 1976).

Mills, David, *The Place-Names of the Isle of Wight* (Stamford: Paul Watkins, 1996).

Mills, David, *A Dictionary of London Place-Names* (Oxford University Press, 2001).

Morton, John, *The Natural History of Northampton-shire* (London: R. Knaplock, 1712).

Neidorf, Leonard (ed.), *The Dating of* Beowulf: *A Reassessment* (Cambridge: D.S. Brewer, 2014).

Neidorf, Leonard, *The Transmission of* Beowulf: *Language, Culture and Scribal Behaviour* (Cornell University Press, 2017). https://doi.org/10.7591/9781501708282

Newman, Coree, 'The good, the bad and the unholy: ambivalent angels in the Middle Ages', 103–22 of Ostling, *Small Gods* (2018). https://doi.org/10.1057/978-1-137-58520-2_4

Newton, Sam, *The Origins of* Beowulf *and the Pre-Viking Kingdom of East Anglia* (Cambridge: D.S. Brewer, 1993).

Oates, Caroline, and Juliette Wood, *A Coven of Scholars: Margaret Murray and her Working Methods* (Folklore Soc., 1998).

Oman, Charles, 'The English folklore of Gervase of Tilbury', *Folk-Lore* 55 (1944): 1–15. https://doi.org/10.1080/0015587X.1944.9717702

Orme, Nicholas, *Going to Church in Medieval England* (Yale University Press, 2022). https://doi.org/10.12987/9780300262612

Ostling, Michael (ed.), *Fairies, Demons and Nature Spirits: 'Small Gods' at the Margins of Christendom* (London: Palgrave Macmillan, 2018). https://doi.org/10.1057/978-1-137-58520-2

Otter, Monika, *Inventiones: Fiction and Referentiality in Twelfth-Century English Historical Writing* (University of North Carolina Press).

Owen, Arthur Ernest Bion, 'Two Lincolnshire coastal names', *Journal of the English Place-Name Soc.* 31 (1998–99): 55–62.

Owst, Gerald Robert, *Literature and Pulpit in Medieval England: A Neglected Chapter in the History of English Letters and of the English People* (Cambridge University Press, 1933).

Owst, Gerald Robert, 'Sortilegium in English homilectic literature of the fourteenth century', 272–303 of Davies, *Studies Presented to Hilary Jenkinson* (1957).

Padel, Oliver, and David Parsons (eds), *A Commodity of Good Names: Essays in Honour of Margaret Gelling* (Donnington: Shaun Tyas, 2008).

Page, Sophie (ed.), *The Unorthodox Imagination in Late Medieval Britain* (Manchester University Press, 2010).

Page, William (ed.), *Three Early Assize Rolls for the County of Northumberland* (Surtees Soc. 88, 1891).

Partner, Nancy, *Serious Entertainments: The Writing of History in Twelfth-Century England* (University of Chicago Press, 1977).

Pascual, Rafael, 'Material monsters and semantic shifts', 202–18 of Neidorf, *Dating of Beowulf* (2014). https://doi.org/10.1515/9781782043461-016

Pastoureau, Michel, *Green: The History of a Colour* (Princeton University Press, 2014). https://doi.org/10.1353/book.112587

Payne, Jessie K., *A Ghost Hunter's Guide to Essex* (Romford: Ian Henry, 1987).

Pentangelo, Joseph, 'The Grant, the hare, and the survival of a medieval folk belief', *Folklore* 130 (2019): 48–59. https://doi.org/10.1080/0015587X.2018.1515292

Pettit, Edward (ed., tr.), *Anglo-Saxon Remedies, Charms and Prayers from British Library MS Harley 585: The Lacnunga* (Lampeter: Edwin Mellen, 2001).

Plot, Robert, *The Natural History of Stafford-shire* (Oxford: At the Theatre, 1686).

Purkiss, Diane, *Troublesome Things: A History of Fairies and Fairy Stories* (London: Penguin, 2000).

Quinn, Phil, *The Holy Wells of Bath and Bristol Region* (Herefordshire: Logaston, 1999).

Rajsic, Jaclyn, Erik Kooper and Dominique Hoche (eds), *The Prose* Brut *and Other Late Medieval Chronicles—Books Have Their Histories: Essays in Honour of Lister M. Matheson* (York: York Medieval Press, 2016).

Rattue, James, *The Holy Wells of Kent* (Privately, 2003).

Reaney, Percy, *The Origin of English Place-Names* (London: Routledge & Kegan Paul, 1960).

The Register of John Morton, Archbishop of Canterbury 1486–1500, ed. Christopher Harper-Bill (Canterbury & York Soc. 75, 78, 89, 1987–2000).

The Register of John Stafford, Bishop of Bath and Wells, 1425–1443, ed Thomas Scott Holmes (Somerset Record Soc. 31–2, 1915).

Registrum Johannis Gilbert, Episcopi Herefordensis, A.D. MCCCLXXV–MCCCLXXXIX, ed. Joseph Henry Parry (Canterbury & York Soc. 18, 1915).

Registrum Johannis Trefnant, Episcopi Herefordensis, A.D. MCCCLXXXX–MCCCCIV, ed. William W. Capes (Canterbury & York Soc. 20, 1916).

Robbins, Rossell Hope, *Secular Lyrics of the XIVth and XVth Centuries* (Oxford: Clarendon, 1952).

Robertson, Durant Waite, 'Why the Devil wears green', *Modern Language Notes* 69 (1954): 470–72. https://doi.org/10.2307/3039609

Robinson, Thomas, *An Essay towards a Natural History of Westmorland and Cumberland* (London: J.L., 1709).

Roper, Jonathan (ed.), *Charms, Charmers and Charming: International Research on Verbal Magic* (Basingstoke: Palgrave Macmillan, 2009). https://doi.org/10.1057/9780230583535

Ross, Kenneth, *A History of Malden* (Privately, 1948).

Ross, Miceal, 'Anchors in a three-decker world', *Folklore* 109 (1998): 63–75. https://doi.org/10.1080/0015587X.1998.9715962

Rowe, Samuel, *A Perambulation of the Antient and Royal Forest of Dartmoor* (Plymouth: J.B. Rowe, 1848).

Rowling, Marjorie, *The Folklore of the Lake District* (London: Batsford, 1976).

Rudiger, Angelika, '*Y Tylwyth Teg*: An Analysis of a Literary Motif', PhD thesis, University of Bangor, 2022.

Rumble, Alexander, 'The medieval boundary of Coulsdon (Surrey)', *Journal of the English Place-Name Soc.* 4 (1971–2): 12–36.

Rutter, Gordon, 'Away with the fairies', *Fortean Times* 141 (2000): 34–38. https://doi.org/10.2307/1004367

Ruys, Juanita Feros, *Demons in the Middle Ages* (Kalamazoo MI: Arc Humanities Press, 2017). https://doi.org/10.1017/9781942401278

Salter, Herbert Edward (ed.), *The Feet of Fines for Oxfordshire, 1195–1291* (Oxfordshire Record Soc. 12, 1930).

Salter, Ruth, *Saints, Cure-Seekers and Miraculous Healing in Twelfth-Century England* (York: York Medieval Press, 2021). https://doi.org/10.1515/9781800101692

Scherr, Jennifer, 'Names of wells and springs in Somerset', *Nomina* 10 (1986): 79–91.

Schmitt, Jean-Claude, *The Holy Greyhound: Guinefort, Healer of Children since the Thirteenth Century*, tr. Martin Thom (Cambridge University Press, 1983).

Scott, Charles P.G., 'The Devil and his imps: an etymological inquisition', *Transactions of the American Philological Association* 26 (1895): 79–146. https://doi.org/10.2307/2935696

Semple, Sarah, *Perceptions of the Prehistoric in Anglo-Saxon England: Religion, Ritual, and Rulership in the Landscape* (Oxford University Press, 2013). https://doi.org/10.1093/acprof:oso/9780199683109.001.0001

Serjeantson, Mary S., 'The vocabulary of folklore in Old and Middle English', *Folk-Lore* 47 (1936): 42–73. https://doi.org/10.1080/0015587X.1936.9718626

Shippey, Tom (ed.), *The Shadow-Walkers: Jacob Grimm's Mythology of the Monstrous* (Arizona Center for Medieval and Renaissance Studies, 2005).

Simek, Rudolf, 'Tangible religion: amulets, illnesses, and the demonic seven sisters', 375–96 of af Edholm *et al.*, *Myth, Materiality and Lived Religion* (2019). https://doi.org/10.16993/bay.m

Simpson, Jacqueline, 'The nightmare charm in *King Lear*', 100–107 of Roper, *Charms, Charmers and Charming* (2009). https://doi.org/10.1057/9780230583535_8

Smith, Beverley Ballin, Simon Taylor and Gareth Williams (eds), *West over Sea: Studies in Scandinavian Sea-Borne Expansion and Settlement before 1300* (Leiden: Brill, 2007).

Smith, Brian S., *A History of Malvern* (Leicester University Press, 1964).

South English Legendary, ed. Charlotte d'Evelyn and Anna J. Mill (Early English Texts Soc. 1st ser 235–36, 244, 1956–59).

Staunton, Michael, *The Historians of Angevin England* (Oxford University Press, 2017). https://doi.org/10.1093/oso/9780198769965.001.0001

Steedman, Carolyn, *An Everyday Life of the English Working Class* (Cambridge University Press, 2013). https://doi.org/10.1017/CBO9781107055155

Stenton, Frank, *Preparatory to Anglo-Saxon England*, ed. Doris Mary Stenton (Oxford: Clarendon, 1970).

Stevens, Douglas, 'A Somerset coroner's roll, 1315–1321', *Somerset & Dorset Notes & Queries* 31 (1980–86): 451–72.

Swainson, Samuel James, 'Langford Budville revel (and devil)', *Somerset & Dorset Notes & Queries* 20 (1930–2): 245–6.

Tengstrand, Erik, *A Contribution to the Study of Genitival Composition in Old English Place-Names* (Uppsala: Almqvist & Wiksell, 1940).

Thompson, A. Hamilton (ed.), *A Calendar of Charters and Other Documents Belonging to the Hospital of William Wyggeston at Leicester* (City of Leicester, 1933).

Thompson, Beeby, 'Peculiarities of waters and wells: X', *Journal of the Northamptonshire Natural History Soc.* 18 (1915–16): 66–79.

Thorpe, Lewis, 'Gerald of Wales: a public reading in Oxford in 1188 or 1189', *Neophilologus* 62 (1978): 45–48. https://doi.org/10.1007/BF01511649

Townend, Matthew (ed.), *Wulfstan, Archbishop of York: The Proceedings of the Second Alcuin Conference* (Turnhout: Brepols, 2004). https://doi.org/10.1484/M.SEM-EB.6.09070802050003050202020401

Tubach, Frederic C., *Index Exemplorum: A Handbook of Medieval Religious Tales* (Folklore Fellows Communications 204, 1969).

Turner, Sam, *Making a Christian Landscape: The Countryside in Early Medieval Cornwall, Devon and Wessex* (University of Exeter Press, 2006).

Tymms, Samuel (ed.), *Wills and Inventories from the Registers of the Commissary of Bury St. Edmund's and the Archdeacon of Sudbury* (Camden Soc. 49, 1850). https://doi.org/10.1017/S2042169900012736

W.H.H., 'Devil's Hole, Kirby Stephen' *The Mirror of Literature, Amusement, and Instruction* 12 (1828): 36.

Wade, James, 'Abduction, surgery, madness: an account of a little red man in Thomas Walsingham's *Chronica majora*', *Medium Aevum* 77 (2008): 10–29. https://doi.org/10.2307/43630593

Wallenberg, Johannes Knut, *Kentish Place-Names* (Uppsala University Press, 1931).

Wallenberg, Johannes Knut, *The Place-Names of Kent* (Uppsala University Press, 1934).

Walsingham, Thomas, *Historia Anglicana*, ed. Henry Thomas Riley (Rolls Series 28:1, 1863–4).

Walsingham, Thomas, *Chronicon Angliae ab anno 1328 usque ad annum 1388*, ed. Edward Maunde Thompson (Rolls Series 64, 1874).

Warner, Marina, *From the Beast to the Blonde: On Fairy Tales and their Tellers* (London: Chatton & Windus, 1994).

Watkins, Carl, 'Fascination and anxiety in medieval wonder stories', 45–64 of Page, *Unorthodox Imagination* (2010).

Watkins, Carl, *The Undiscovered Country: Journeys among the Dead* (London: Bodley Head, 2013).

Watson, John, *The History and Antiquities of the Parish of Halifax, in Yorkshire* (London: T. Lounds, 1775).

Webster, John, *The Displaying of Supposed Witchcraft* (London: J.M., 1677).

Westwood, Jennifer, and Jacqueline Simpson, *The Lore of the Land: A Guide to England's Legends, from Spring-Heeled Jack to the Witches of Warboys* (London: Penguin, 2005).

Whitaker, Thomas Dunham, *The History and Antiquities of the Deanery of Craven in the County of York* (London: Nichols & Son, 1805).

Whitelock, Dorothy, *The Audience of 'Beowulf'* (Oxford: Clarendon, 1951).

Whitelock, Dorothy (ed.), *English Historical Documents c.500–1042* (London: Eyre & Spottiswoode, 1979).

William of Malmesbury, *Gesta Pontificum Anglorum: The History of the English Bishops*, ed., tr. Michael Winterbottom (Oxford: Clarendon, 2007). https://doi.org/10.1093/actrade/9780198207702.book.1

Wilson, Louise Elizabeth, 'Writing miracle collections', 15–35 of Katajala-Peltomaa, Kuuliala and McCleery, *A Companion to Medieval Miracle Collections* (2021). https://doi.org/10.1163/9789004468498_003

Wise, John R., *The New Forest: Its History and Scenery* (London: Smith Elder & Co., 1863). https://doi.org/10.5962/bhl.title.18484

Witcutt, William Purcell, 'Notes on Staffordshire folklore', *Folk-Lore* 52 (1941): 236–37. https://doi.org/10.1080/0015587X.1941.9718274

Wogan-Browne, Jocelyn, *Saints' Lives and Women's Literary Culture c.1150–1300: Virginity and its Authorizations* (Oxford University Press, 2001). https://doi.org/10.1093/acprof:oso/9780198112792.001.0001

Wood, Ian, and Graham Loud (eds), *Church and Chronicle in the Middle Ages: Essays Presented to John Taylor* (London: Hambledon, 1991).

Wordsworth, Christopher, 'Two Yorkshire charms or amulets: exorcisms and adjurations', *Yorkshire Archaeological J.* 17 (1893): 377–412.

Wright, Charles, 'More Latin sources for the Old English "Three Utterances" homilies', *Mediaeval Studies* 77 (2015): 45–80.

Wright, Thomas, *A Selection of Latin Stories* (Percy Soc., 1842).

Wright, Thomas, *Essays on Archaeological Subjects* (London: John Russell Smith, 1861).

Wrottesley, George, 'Extracts from the Plea Rolls, temp Edward IV, Edward V and Richard III', *Staffordshire Historical Collections* 2nd ser 6:1 (1903): 89–164.

Yarrow, Simon, *Saints and Their Communities: Miracle Stories in Twelfth Century England* (Oxford: Clarendon, 2006).

Young, Francis, *Suffolk Fairylore* (Norwich: Lasse, 2019).

Young, Simon, *The Boggart: Folklore, History, Place-Names and Dialect* (University of Exeter Press, 2022).

Zachrisson, Robert Eugen, 'Grendel in *Beowulf* and in local names', 39–44 of Bøgholm, Brusendorff and Bodelsen, *A Grammatical Miscellany* (1930).

Index

Entries such as 'elf', 'fairy' refer specifically to accounts where the spirit was identified as an elf, fairy etc. Entries default to naturalism, so that 'dogs' are flesh-and-blood dogs, while phantom examples appear as 'dogs, apparitions of'. Locations known only for having an elfin place-name are not indexed, as they can be found in the Appendix.

Adam of Eynsham   28
Adelais of Curridge   13
ælf as place-name element   75 *and passim*
      78–124
Æsir   36
Aethiopians, apparitions as   24, 47, 58
air, apparitions in the   55–6
Alice of Reading   11, 60, 85
altered states   12–13
Alton, Hants.   109
Ampleforth, Yorks. NR   63, 93–4
Anglo-Saxon Chronicle   38
animals, apparitions as   32–3. *See also*
      apes; bears; bulls; dogs; donkeys;
      dragons; goats; hares; horses;
      spiders; toads
Anselm of Bec   60
Antipodes   46
apes, apparitions as   62
apples   25, 51, 85
Appletreewick, Yorks. WR   114
arable land   86–9
Arkill the carpenter   58
attack, encounters involve   49, 51, 56
axes protect against spirits   33, 65
Aynho, Northants.   116
Ayrshire   59

backs, apparitions have no   60
Bardwell, Suffolk   41
Barker, Walter   8, 51

barrows   44, 50, 73, 121–4
Bartholomew the Englishman   91
Bartholomew of Exeter   27
Bartholomew of Farne   29–30, 57
bears, apparitions as   62
beauty of apparitions   5, 12, 26, 32, 54,
      59, 64, 103
Bedford   41, 55
beguines   12
bells   42
      protect against spirits   76
Bemerton, Wilts.   26
Bercilak   20, 65–6
Berkeley, Glos.   64
Beverley, Yorks. ER   4, 8
Bielby, Yorks. ER   68
Biggleswade, Beds.   55
birds, apparitions as   54. *See also* crows;
      doves; ravens
bishops   27, 113
black, apparitions in   13, 16–17, 33, 38,
      51, 55, 56, 58, 61, 63–4, 69, 85.
      See also Aethiopians
Blangy   60
blindness, follows encounters   10, 84,
      93, 97
bodies consigned to water   97–8
bridges   91
Bridlington, Yorks. ER   121
Brihtric the steward   54
Bromyard, John   15, 19, 37, 66–7, 98

brownies   99
bugge as place-name element   75 *and
        passim* 78–124
bulls, apparitions as   69
burgesses   9
Byland, Yorks. NR   42, 97

Callaly, Northumb.   102
Cambridge   48–9
cangun as place-name element   76,
        110–12
Canterbury   28
Cantilupe, Thomas   59
caves   42, 108–10
changelings   11, 40, 76, 110–12
charms   10, 34–7, 52, 53, 61, 118
cheese   26
childbirth   109
children, apparitions as   4, 40, 41, 58,
        66–7, 68
Christchurch, Hants.   27
Christina of Dunfermline   4–5, 12, 25
Christmas, encounters at   84
chronicles   37–43
churches   20, 33, 59, 81–2, 110
churns   102
circles protect against spirits   33
Cirencester, Glos.   8
Cistercians   42
Cleeve, Som.   73
clefts   113–14
clergy. *See* bishops; friars; hermits;
        monks; nuns; priests; Templars
clergy, apparitions as   56, 58, 59
clergy, celibacy of   10–11, 68. *See also*
        concubines
Clerk, Agnes   16
Clerk, Marion   16, 57
cliffs   112
Clun, Shropshire   84
Coggeshall, Essex   38, 43
Colchester, Essex   100
Cold Kirby, Yorks. NR   97
Coldingham, Berwks.   54, 58, 64
colour of apparitions. *See* black; green;
        red; white
concubines   33, 61, 67–8, 97
Corstophine, Midlothian   66
cries, apparitions make   93

cross protects against spirits   29, 33,
        35, 59
crosses, wayside   93, 106, 111
crossroads   73, 93
crows, apparitions as   64–5
Croydon, Surrey   38
Cumberland   3
cups, stolen from Otherworld   44, 50
Curridge, Berks   13
Cutteslowe, Oxon.   91
Cwœnthryth   98

Dalton, Yorks. NR   58
Danby, Yorks. NR   73
dawn, encounters at   92
dead bodies, apparitions as   11, 55,
        59–60, 69
death, follows encounters   39, 68
Demon Servant tale-type   67
demons   13–14, 17, 21–2, 27–8, 29,
        33–4, 44, 47–8, 56–7, 58, 59, 62,
        65–8, 91, 97, 107
demons, possession by   21, 34. *See also*
        madness
dēofol as place-name element   76, 82–3,
        86, 91, 98, 106, 113
Derbyshire   77
Dinnington, Northumb.   115
dismemberment, in encounters   3, 85
ditches   101
divination   118
dogs   63, 94
    apparitions as   13, 16–17, 27, 31–2,
        33, 38, 61, 62, 69, 78–9
donkeys, apparitions as   69
doves, apparitions as   64
dragons, apparitions as   27, 69
Drakelow, Derbs.   61–2, 69
dreams   5, 6, 13, 18, 61. *See also* altered
        states; visions
drunkenness   53, 59, 62
Dublin   62
Dudley Castle   38
Duggleby Howe   50, 121
dumbness, follows encounters   25, 51,
        53–4, 83–4
Dunfermline, Fife   4–5, 8, 25, 27, 56,
        61, 64, 84, 102
Dunsford, Devon   102

Dunsmore Heath   39, 60
Dunwich, Suffolk   11
Durham   16
dwarfs   17, 36, 52, 58, 108
dweorg as place-name element   76, 82,
      92, 98, 107, 108, 110

Eadsige of Winchester   24
echoes   107
Edenham, Lincs.   32
Edric Wilde   48, 59, 103
Elidyr of St David's   45–6, 57, 112
Ellingham, Northumb.   30, 56
elves   16, 18, 20, 35, 36–7, 82, 103.
      See also *ælf* as place-name element
Ely   23–4, 52
Essex   28
Eudo   47
Eustace of Stackpole   67
exempla   31–4
exorcism   98–9
eyes, apparitions have fiery   59, 63

fairies   10, 15–16, 40, 57, 60, 68, 73,
      74, 78, 97
Fairy Bride tale-type   86–7
fairy rings   103–4
Farne, Northumb.   29–30, 84, 109
Farnham, Yorks. WR   46
Fates   51
fēond as place-name element   76, 82, 92,
      106
fields   83–6, 103, 113
fifel as place-name element   76
Fifeshire   54, 84
Finchale, Durham   22, 57, 59, 65
fire, apparitions as   69
fire, reactions to after encounters   11
fires, take place after encounters   61, 63
flagð as place-name element   76
flying, encounters involve   32, 58, 60
folktales. *See* Demon Servant; Fairy Bride;
      Friend among the Fairies; Lemman
      Mine; New Suit of Clothes; Stolen
      Cup
Folkton, Yorks. ER   123
food, danger of Otherworldly   30, 32,
      43
footprints, left by apparitions   38, 62

fords   91
Forest of Dean   120
Fraunceys, John   58, 82
friars   31, 37
Friend Among The Fairies tale-type   30
Furies   24, 51

gates   92
Gerald of Wales   14–15, 43–6, 67, 109
Gerard (spirit)   99
Gerbert   47
Gervase of Tilbury   43, 46, 47, 48–50,
      57, 63, 97, 112–13, 120
ghosts   4, 15, 37–8, 60, 63, 69, 93.
      See also walking dead
Gibb, Katharine   66
Glastonbury, Somerset   119
goat-riders, apparitions as   29, 38, 57
goats, apparitions as   69
gobelin as place-name element   75, 77
      and passim 78–124
goblins   89
Gormire   97
gram as place-name element   76, 91
grants   63
Great Ashfield, Suffolk   16
green, apparitions in   35, 42–3, 65–6
Green Children   41–3, 66, 112
Grendel   20, 53, 76, 91, 95–7
grim as place-name element   76–7
Guibert of Nogent   27
Guinehochet   34
Gwestin Gwestiniog   48, 86, 103
Gwyn ap Nudd   119

Haddington, East Lothian   9, 12, 100,
      110
hagiography   20–2
Hancock, Agnes   10
hares, apparitions as   32, 62–3
haycocks, apparitions as   69
Haydock, Lancs.   93
headless apparitions   39, 60
Headley, Hants.   40
healers   10, 16, 28–9
Hell, ride to   33, 64
Henno cum dentibus   48
Henry VI   13
Henry of Poitou   38

herbs protect against spirits   28
Hereford   56
Herefordshire   62
Hereward the Wake   117
Herla   57, 66, 113
Herlething   56
Hermann of Laon   27
hermits   21–2, 29–30, 47, 59, 62, 65
Heslington, Yorks. ER   94
hills   118–24
hindlegs, apparitions on   62–3, 69
hob as place-name element   76–7, 101
holes   108–9, 112
holly   16, 60
Holmesfield, Derbs.   115
Holy Land   26
holy name protects against spirits   31–2,
    60, 94
holy water protects against spirits
    16–17, 63
honesty valued in Otherworld   45
horns, apparitions blow   56
horns, drinking   30, 65, 120
horse's feet, apparitions have   9, 110
horses, apparitions as   22, 38, 49, 63,
    64, 69, 94
household spirits   40, 46, 98–9
Hugh of Lincoln   27
hunters, apparitions as   15, 38, 56
hunting   41, 62

Ieuan ap Gwilym   14
illness, follows encounters   9–10, 20,
    35, 52, 55
incubus. *See* lover
Ingleby Arncliffe, Yorks. NR   35
Inglethorpe, Norfolk   7
Inglewood Forest   61
Inverkeithing, Fife   69
Ireland   56
iron protects against spirits   93
islands   29, 78, 109
Isle of Man   60
Isle of Wight   97

Joan of Kingsley   39–40, 67
John the clerk   31–2, 89
John of Dunfermline   35
John of Powderham   13–14

John de Tregoz   59
Julian of Norwich   67
justice enforced after death   37–8, 98

Ketell of Knaresborough   46–7, 62
Kilpeck, Herefs.   14
King's Lynn, Norfolk   100
kings of Otherworld   17, 45, 119
Kirkby Stephen, Westm.   102
knights   7–8, 40, 48–9, 61, 103
knights, apparitions as   8, 48–9, 55–6
Kormák   123

ladies, apparitions as   3–4, 5, 26, 51–4,
    64–5
lakes   86, 97
lamias   110
Lanercost Chronicle   37–8, 102
Langley Park   38
Lantfred of Fleury   24, 53, 64
laughter   89
Lavenham, Suffolk   40
Leduart, Maiot   14
Lemman Mine tale-type   28
Leofstan of Suffolk   97–8
Lewisham, Kent   38
light, apparitions as   68
Lincoln   100
Lindisfarne, Northumb.   109
literacy   7–8
Llangollen, Denb.   119
Llyn Syfaddon   86
London   11, 90
lover, encounters as a   7, 11, 39, 62–3,
    67–8
Lucian of Chester   91, 107
Luton, Beds   8, 51
Lyon   111

madness   21, 64
    follows encounters   3–4, 14, 16–18,
        59, 62, 69, 90, 114
Maisemore, Glos.   115
Malekin   40–1, 58
Malmesbury, Wilts.   97
Map, Walter   43, 47–8, 57, 66, 113
mares (animals). *See* horses
mares (spirits). *See* nightmares
Markby Priory   37

marks on body, left by encounters   26, 54
Markyate, Herts.   38
marshes   94–7
Matilda of Lindsey   93
Meilyr of Caerleon   14–15, 44–5, 56, 58, 68
Meridiana   47
mermaids   100
Mersington, Berwks.   85
Midsummer, encounters at   84, 85
Mildenhall, Wilts.   100
mills   67, 99, 102
Minster-in-Thanet   54
miracles   22–7, 30–1
misers   66–7
missiles in body, encounters leave   36, 49, 52
mistress, encounters as a   14, 68, 118–19
monks   8, 10, 14–15, 37, 42, 56, 64
mounds   120–4
music, apparitions make   13
Mutinus of Dunfermline   25, 51, 53, 84
Myddle, Shropshire   110

Nailbourne   38
Nevenon, Christiana   7–8, 11
New Suit of Clothes tale-type   99
Newstead, Yorks. NR   93–4
nicor as place-name element   75, 78, 82, 99–100
nightmares   13, 17, 35–6, 52, 58–9
niht-mare as place-name element   76, 87, 92
nine, number of apparitions   52–3
Noke, Margaret   14
noon, encounters at   85, 92
Norway   53, 123
number in apparitions. *See* nine; three
nuns   5

Old Norse   75–7, 79–80, 86, 91, 104–7, 116, 118
Old Sarum   5
Olga   47
Oliver the clerk   68
Osbert of Dagworth   40
Osbert Fitz Hugh   48–9

Oxford   14

Pan   66
Peak Cavern   46, 113
Pembrokeshire   44
Penrith, Cumb.   61
Peterborough   38, 56
Philip of Hereford   62
pilgrimage   26, 28, 54
Pitminster, Somerset   90–1
pits   41, 114–16
Pittington, Durham   84
pixies   78
pixyleading   89
place-names   73–4
   deliberate   101
   fabulative   81
   fanciful   102
   incident   83
   shift-names   80
Pointon, Lincs.   55
pokere as place-name element   75, 85, 91
poltergeists   20, 41, 44
pools   97–100, 115
portuni   46, 47, 57, 89
poukes   46
preaching   31–3
prediction   15, 38, 59, 60
priests   4, 9, 10–11, 14, 16, 40, 41, 90–1, 97
privacy, required after encounters   7
procession, apparitions in   14, 17, 55
protection against spirits. *See* axes; bells; charms; circles; cross; herbs; holy name; holy water; iron; straw
pūca as place-name element   74–5 *and passim* 78–124
pūcel as place-name element   74, 78, 81–2, 85, 90, 91, 98, 104, 116, 119
pygmies   45, 57

queens of Otherworld   5, 103

Ralph of Coggeshall   40–4, 112
Ranulf Le Gros   8–9
ravens, apparitions as   65, 69
red, apparitions in   3–4, 58, 61, 66–7
Reginald of Durham   22, 53, 57

Reinburgis of Wallingford   8–9, 12, 23–5, 51–2
repentance   31, 33, 40, 41, 56, 63, 64, 93, 113
Repton, Derbs.   116
Richard de Calne   41
Richard of Sarum   5–6, 23, 51
Richard of Sunderland   17, 30, 65, 84, 102
Richard of Wombridge   84
riders, apparitions as   8, 36, 38, 49, 56
riding on people, apparitions   33, 36
Rievaulx, Yorks. NR   63, 69
Ripon, Yorks. WR   121, 123
rivers   9, 85, 100–2, 104–5
roads   79, 89–94
Robert of Edenham   32, 62
Robert of Kenilworth   113
Robin Goodfellow   89
Rochester, Kent   56
ruins   110
Ryal, Northumb.   67–8
Rypon, Master   99

St Ives   13, 62–3
St John's-wort   28, 52
Saints
    Æbbe of Coldingham   23, 54, 64, 86
    Æthelthryth of Ely   9, 20, 23–4, 54
    Aldhelm of Malmesbury   97
    Bartholomew the Apostle   11
    Collen of Llangollen   119
    Cuthbert of Durham   16–17, 29–30, 84, 109–10
    Cynehelm of Clent   98
    George of Cappadocia   52
    Godric of Finchale   21–2, 23, 54, 57, 59, 62, 69–70
    Ivo of St. Ives   13
    John of Beverley   4, 8, 10
    Margaret of Dunfermline   5, 23, 25, 27, 35, 64
    Mildthryth of Thanet   54
    Modwenna of Burton   61–2
    Osmund of Sarum   26
    Samson of Dol   52–3, 67
    Swithun of Winchester   23, 24, 30
    Thomas of Canterbury   6, 13, 17, 23, 35

Wulfstan of Worcester   23, 83, 114
    See also Henry VI
Salford, Warks.   108
Salisbury Plain   6, 55, 59
Sandford, Henry   113
Satan   67
Scarborough, Yorks. NR   38
scinna as place-name element   76, 112, 120, 122–3
screawa as place-name element   76, 119, 120
scucca as place-name element   75, 78, 88, 91, 92, 98, 101, 105–6, 119, 122–3
seasons for apparitions. See Christmas; Midsummer
seasons reversed in Otherworld   46, 113
seers   14–15, 16, 18, 29, 34, 44–5, 60. See also divination; prediction
Sempringham, Lincs.   55
sex. See lover; mistress
shapelessness of apparitions   22, 69
sheets, apparitions as   63
shrines. See Beverley; Canterbury; Coldingham; Dunfermline; Durham; Ely; Finchale; London; Malmesbury; Minster-in-Thanet; St Ives; Winchester; Worcester
Sicily   113
Simon (spirit)   67
Simon de Montfort   62
skratti as place-name element   75, 86, 88, 91, 92, 121
skyrsi as place-name element   76, 105
small size of apparitions   14–15, 40, 46, 57–9. See also dwarfs; pygmies
Snowball of Ampleforth   9, 15, 35, 56, 59, 61, 65, 69, 102
Somerset   10
sound, apparitions make   13, 56, 93, 102
spiders, apparitions as   58–9
spoons   113
Staffordshire   31
Stephen of Hoyland   17
stiles   92
Stolen Cup tale-type   44, 50, 123
stones   92–3
storms   6, 38, 61, 106
straw protects against spirits   29
stroke, follows encounters   9, 23

Strubby, Lincs.   37
succubus. *See* mistress
Sunday observance   32, 58, 62
surgery, performed in encounters   52,
     59
surnames   78
Sussex   78

tall size of apparitions   59
Tankerlay, James   97
Taunton   9, 51, 90–1
Templars   43
Terrington, Norfolk   101
theomacha   52–3, 67
thieves, apparitions as   91
Thornton Abbey   10, 53
Thorpe Bassett, Yorks. ER   4
three, number of apparitions   51, 93
thurses   98–9
thyrs (þyrs) as place-name element   75, 77
     and passim 78–124
times for apparitions. *See* dawn; noon;
     twilight
toads, apparitions as   69
transportation, in encounters   26
treasure   16, 22, 45, 62
trickster spirits   46–7
troll as place-name element   76, 88, 90,
     113
tunnels   45, 113. *See also* caves
Turvey, Dublin   32, 89
twilight, encounters at   92
twisting, encounters inflict   10, 53, 84
tylwyth teg   15

ugliness of apparitions   51, 53, 68

valleys   104–7
vampires. *See* walking dead
visions   13, 26, 55, 64. *See also* altered
     states

wælcyrige as place-name element   76, 85
walking dead   44, 61–2, 97
Wallingford, Berks.   8

Walsall, Staffs.   115, 120
Walsingham, Thomas   3–4, 39–40
Walter of Kelloe   16–18
Wandlebury   48–9
Warwickshire   90
Watling Street   91
Watson, Agnes   90
Wayneman, Roger   97
wells   86, 116–18
Welsh   15
West Rainton, Durham   59
Westmorland   55
Wetton, Staffs.   109
whirlwinds   93
white, apparitions in   6, 35, 40, 51, 55
Wild Hunt   56
William of Aberdeen   69
William of Birdforth   93–4
William of Newburgh   40, 42–3, 50,
     112, 120
William Paternoster   8, 68
Willy Howe   50, 121
Winchester   9, 24, 51, 59, 64, 85, 91, 120
windows, encounters through   16, 60
Winsford, Cheshire   100
Wiriet, Stephen   44
witches   36, 52–3, 61, 64, 117
wodewoses   76
woe waters   38
Wombridge, Shropshire   84
woods   39–40, 52–3, 56, 61, 68, 91,
     111, 120
Wool, Dorset   115
Woolmer Forest   39–40, 67
Woolpit, Suffolk   41–2
Worcester   83
Wulfstan the Cantor   24
Wye, Kent   69
Wykes, Suffolk   41
Wymond of London   11, 12–13
Wynfeld, William   3–4, 8, 12, 38, 66,
     86

York   62, 79, 94
Yorkshire   38, 77

www.ingramcontent.com/pod-product-compliance
Ingram Content Group UK Ltd.
Pitfield, Milton Keynes, MK11 3LW, UK
UKHW010841190626
472399UK00002B/55